Japanese Machizukuri and Community Engagement

Over the past few decades, Japan has faced severe earthquake disasters, an increasing aging population, declining birth rates, and widening social disparities. These issues have served to highlight gaps left by top-down governance approaches and the urgent need to create resilient societies using more traditional models.

Japanese "machizukuri" has developed to become an exceptional example of bottom-up creative approaches based on collective action and use of local resources. Since its evolution in the 1960s, machizukuri has come to define diverse and creative community-driven management models, by which local communities are enabled to actively tackle problem-solving.

Including contributions from experts directly engaged in the process, this book explores the original development of machizukuri in Japan, its diffusion through East Asia and the positive outcomes of this transfer. Combining theoretical explanations with practical case studies, from pre-disaster planning in Tokyo, to the revitalization of historic towns and rural areas around Japan, the book looks at specific solutions, tools, and links between academics, communities, organizations, governmental bodies, and the private sector. It will appeal to researchers in planning, community engagement, architecture, urban design, and sustainable development.

Shigeru Satoh (PhD) is Professor Emeritus of Waseda University, former Director of Research Institute of Urban and Regional Study and former President of Architectural Institute of Japan. He has spearheaded the Japanese machizukuri movement (a community-based comprehensive approach to improving built environmental practices) both in theory and actual practice.

Planning, Heritage and Sustainability
Series Editors: Paolo Ceccarelli and Giulio Verdini

The speed of growth of Global South's emerging countries has quickly imposed, in recent years, new priorities in the urban agenda of this part of the world. In particular, the controversial relationship between the loss of local/regional identity and the modernisation is increasingly becoming a matter of great concern especially in Asia, Africa and Latin America. In these contexts the modernisation implies an unprecedented wave of urbanisation that is seriously threatening, in some cases, the survival as such of the traces of the past, especially the urban or rural heritage, or broadly speaking, the tangible and intangible dimensions of local cultures. Notwithstanding that western countries are facing similar disruptive forces the Global South requires different analytical frameworks and approaches to sustainability.

Titles in the Series

Heritage Sites in Contemporary China
Cultural Policies and Management Practices
Luca Zan, Bing Yu, Haiming Yan, Janli Yu

Japanese Machizukuri and Community Engagement
History, Method and Practice
Shigeru Satoh

Japanese Machizukuri and Community Engagement
History, Method and Practice

Shigeru Satoh

LONDON AND NEW YORK

First published 2020
by Routledge
2 Park Square, Milton Park, Abingdon, Oxon OX14 4RN

and by Routledge
605 Third Avenue, New York, NY 10017

First issued in paperback 2021

Routledge is an imprint of the Taylor & Francis Group, an informa business

© 2020 Shigeru Satoh

The right of Shigeru Satoh to be identified as author of this work has been asserted by him in accordance with sections 77 and 78 of the Copyright, Designs and Patents Act 1988.

All rights reserved. No part of this book may be reprinted or reproduced or utilized in any form or by any electronic, mechanical, or other means, now known or hereafter invented, including photocopying and recording, or in any information storage or retrieval system, without permission in writing from the publishers.

Trademark notice: Product or corporate names may be trademarks or registered trademarks, and are used only for identification and explanation without intent to infringe.

Publisher's Note
The publisher has gone to great lengths to ensure the quality of this reprint but points out that some imperfections in the original copies may be apparent.

British Library Cataloguing-in-Publication Data
A catalogue record for this book is available from the British Library

Library of Congress Cataloging-in-Publication Data
Names: Satoh, Shigeru, author.
Title: Japanese machizukuri and community engagement/
Shigeru Satoh.
Description: New York : Routledge, 2020. | Series: Planning, heritage and sustainability | Includes bibliographical references and index. |
Identifiers: LCCN 2019040040 (print) | LCCN 2019040041 (ebook) |
ISBN 9780367193522 (hardback) | ISBN 9780429201851 (ebook)
Subjects: LCSH: Community development–Japan–Citizen participation. | City planning–Japan–Citizen participation. | Urban policy–Japan–Citizen participation.
Classification: LCC HN730.Z9 S28 2020 (print) |
LCC HN730.Z9 (ebook) | DDC 307.1/40952–dc23
LC record available at https://lccn.loc.gov/2019040040
LC ebook record available at https://lccn.loc.gov/2019040041

ISBN 13: 978-1-03-223889-0 (pbk)
ISBN 13: 978-0-367-19352-2 (hbk)

Typeset in Sabon
by Wearset Ltd, Boldon, Tyne and Wear

Contents

List of figures	viii
Preface	x
Acknowledgments	xii
Notes on contributors	xiv

PART I
History and Method of Machizukuri — 1

1 Introduction to machizukuri — 3
SHIGERU SATOH

2 Brief history of machizukuri in three regions in East Asia — 12
SHIN AIBA

3 The first generation: the emergence of machizukuri — 17
SHIGERU SATOH

4 The second generation: participation, collaboration and co-creation — 48
SHIGERU SATOH

5 The third generation: aiming at open area management — 60
SHIGERU SATOH

PART II
Method and Tools — 71

6 Machizukuri methodology and tools — 73
SHIGERU SATOH

vi *Contents*

7 Machizukuri and planning   91
SHIN AIBA

PART III
Experiments and Case Studies   99

8 Regenerating the urban structure in historic districts: an approach through projects representing traditional culture and crafts, created by entrepreneurs and craftsmen in Takaoka City   101
YOSUKE MANO

9 Discovering the authenticity of the historical landscape and the original urban context through small collaborative design projects in a local castle-town city, Tsuruoka City   112
KEISUKE SUGANO

10 Revitalization of the central urban area by local residents in Nabari City, Mie Prefecture   122
KENJIRO MATSUURA

11 The rebirth of mixed-use blocks in the decayed historic centre of Takefu in Echizen City, Fukui Prefecture   133
SHINJI NOJIMA

12 Reorganization of the local housing production system for maintaining and improving the historic landscape   143
KOSUKE MASUO

13 The urban renewal method based on the community principle: the case of the Yuyuan area of the Shanghai Historical Scene Conservation District   153
CHENGQI ZHAO

14 Development of the Furano Machizukuri Company connecting rural areas and urban core revitalization in Furano city   163
KATSUHIRO KUBO

15 Post-disaster reconstruction of central Ishinomaki through the formation of local initiatives   174
YOSUKE MANO AND AKIHIRO NODA

Contents vii

16 Regeneration of the cultural landscape of the fisheries city of Kesennuma through collaboration in machizukuri by multiple project-implementing bodies   185

TOSHIHIKO ABE

17 Community empowerment recovery after the Chichi Earthquake: the case of Taomi Ecovillage, Puli   195

LIANG-CHUN CHEN, CHIA-CHAN LIAO AND JIE-YING WU

18 "SOHO City Mitaka": machizukuri as creative urban governance   210

HIROSHI SAITO

19 Machizukuri as glocalization: progress in highly dense "shitamachi" lower-town areas in collaboration with Tsukishima community school, Tokyo   220

HIDEAKI SHIMURA

20 Machizukuri in the future   229

SHIGERU SATOH

Glossary of technical terms particular to Japanese   238
Index   240

Figures

1.1	Chronological table of Japanese machizukuri	8
2.1	Three periods, social change and legal systems changes	13
3.1	Mano machizukuri plan and projects	24
3.2	Kyojima machizukuri plan and projects	37
4.1	Ichitera-Kototoi machizukuri projects	52
4.2	Taishido machizukuri projects	55
5.1	Kurokabe machizukuri projects	65
5.2	Genbei-gawa river projects and trail map	67
6.1	*Ma*: blurred boundaries and intermediate shared areas	75
6.2	Design simulation game workshop using landscape simulation system	79
7.1	Design game in Tsuruoka	94
8.1	Historical assets, and places operated by local initiatives in the Old Town of Takaoka	104
9.1	Spiral diagram showing the process of machizukuri in Tsuruoka City	114
9.2	Project map of each phase corresponding to spiral diagram	115
10.1	Approach of revitalization by the community management committee in Nabari area	125
10.2	Project map of the revitalization plan for the central urban area in Nabari City	127
11.1	Situation and development method of block area before and after project	135
11.2	Promotion system of town planning during development and later	139
12.1	Approach and effect of self-reconstruction housing support by the regional style housing	147
13.1	Horizontally expanded collective housing model	157
13.2	Diversified methods of district renewal	159
14.1	Plan of business development in Furano central city	168
14.2	Possibility of large-scale cooperation linking agriculture and tourism	170

15.1	Projects of post-disaster reconstruction in central Ishinomaki	178
15.2	Features and systems of COMICHI Ishinomaki	180
16.1	Projects realized by post-earthquake machizukuri	189
16.2	Collaborative framework for post-earthquake machizukuri	190
17.1	Taomi Ecovillage's post-disaster recovery promotion stages	199
18.1	Development process of the *kosodate conbini*	216
19.1	Tsukishima and Nagaya School in Tokyo Bay area	221
19.2	Glocal activities and interaction	223
20.1	Identification and expansion of machizukuri in sense of value structure	230

Preface

What is machizukuri?

This book presents the evolution of machizukuri practice in the past 50 years, reviewing its history, theory, methods, and some of the latest case study examples. One by one, starting from a historical background, this volume presents the different challenges machizukuri has been confronted with, the formation of its strong theoretical base, and the accumulation of different methods and techniques during this lengthy process. Then, a wide range of recent case studies, with which the authors of this book have been directly involved, complement the picture to further portray and detail the previous theoretical ideas and help the reader build up a comprehensive idea of what machizukuri is. Finally, the discussion looks into the future of this unique approach.

Japanese machizukuri, which could simply be translated into English as community design and development or building, has already been introduced by some books written in English (Sorensen and Funck, 2007). Besides, in addition to this book, machizukuri has also been introduced by Japanese academics in publications and journals.

The written documentation on Japanese machizukuri is vast. One of the most comprehensive pieces of literature is a series of ten thematic books published by the Architectural Institute of Japan (Satoh, 2004) to which Shigeru Satoh, the editor of this book, was a chief editor, and which has become a classic reference work. In each of them, researchers simultaneously involved in on-site practice in each related field were responsible for the editing and also introduced relevant case studies. Additionally, there are numerous research papers, books, and other materials focused on specific machizukuri actions related to the Mano district machizukuri (Hilly, 2010), which will be introduced later. The book presented to the international community in English by Sorensen and Funck (2007) is also very representative. In it, eight of the 13 chapters introduce diverse topics presented by Japanese authors. Based on their different results, this book reconstructs the notion of machizukuri, which has developed rapidly in recent years, from a historical perspective, and reviews its methodology and specific tools.

Preface xi

The editor of this volume has been directly involved with machizukuri practice since the late 1970s, when machizukuri activities began to become formalized. Since the 1990s, he has been in touch and worked together with all the peers who have authored this book. Through the years, these professionals have positioned themselves at the forefront of machizukuri development, including theory, practice, and, especially, the development of new methods. All of them have a background in architecture and have worked on the improvement of physical environments, but they have also integrated the social atmosphere of the communities who inhabit them, which is the foundation of the keyword "machizukuri" (Satoh, 2019).

This book provides English-speaking readers with a systematic compilation of such practical experiences and the knowledge acquired through them during this half century of machizukuri history, which have helped coined the term "machizukuri" and provide a clear idea of what is.[1]

Even though the book has been structured in a formal way, following the traditional notion–history–method–techniques–case studies format, the editor has paid special attention to creating a comprehensive dynamic volume, in which the different dimensions presented are easy to find, connect, and mix, helping readers approach machizukuri from whichever aspects interest them the most. Thus, each reader is encouraged to follow the order that better suits him/her and to jump from one section to another, looking for complementary answers expanding on specific topics. Some readers might find it more interesting to approach the case study examples first, understand their specific circumstances and methods, then return to machizukuri theory with a clearer image of what the concept represents, and being able to fully grasp more intangible ideas. There is also the possibility of understanding the theory and evolution of machizukuri first, and then read about cutting-edge case studies with a historical perspective, understanding machizukuri s place and relevance in modern society.

Note

1 So far, Shigeru Sato has edited six book on machizukuri in Japanese. In addition, in 2015, he was awarded the Jusoken-Shimizu Yasuo Award for the practice and theory of machizukuri.

References

Hilly, P. (2010). *Making Better Place: The Planning Project in the Twenty-First Century*. Palgrave Macmillan

Satoh, S. and Architectural Institute of Japan (ed.). (2004). *Machizukuri no Houhou* (Method of Machizukuri). Tokyo: Maruzen (in Japanese).

Satoh, S. (2019). Evolution and methodology of Japanese machizukuri for the improvement of living environments, *Japan Architectural Review*, vol. 2. no. 2. pp. 127–142, doi:10.1002/2475-8876.12084; https://rdcu.be/bIe4b.

Sorensen, A. and Funck, C. (eds.). (2007). *Living Cities in Japan*. Routledge Japanese Studies Series. Nissan Institute.

Acknowledgments

The contents of this book are based on different practical experiences. The results were created together with the local government officials, the leaders of community organizations, and experts, who worked together on machizukuri practice. Each author has contributed to create the results described in this book. I cannot mention all of them personally here, but I would like to express my gratitude to all the people who have contributed to machizukuri practice. In addition, many students and researchers at my laboratory at Waseda University have been involved in various projects and have played an extremely important role in pushing forward both research and development, and machizukuri practice. Especially, acting as mediators of machizukuri processes developed together with local residents, all these persons have opened up the door to new machizukuri ideas and power to act. This does not only concern my own research group, but in recent years, many other academics have also involved with machizukuri. My gratitude goes also to these students.

Moreover, concerning the description of the history of machizukuri in this book, and the feelings and motivations in the initial years of machizukuri, which I did not experience personally, I interviewed key persons to be able to present a realistic picture. I am grateful to all of them.

Paolo Ceccarelli, Professor Emeritus at Ferrara University in Italy and editor of these series, gave us the opportunity to publish this book. Since 1995, he has initiated a series of workshops around the world together with UC Berkeley School of Environmental Design, and Waseda University. For about two weeks every year different students and faculty members collaborate to hold these urban design experiences from which we were all able to learn a lot. In this context, students from Waseda University made proposals based on machizukuri, sometimes creating a fierce confrontation with the group from Berkeley, who promote traditional and legitimate urban design. Since my own research stay at Berkeley in 1991, Emeritus Professors Alan Jacobs, Richard Bender, and Peter Bosselman have joined various discussions on machizukuri and made critical suggestions. I would like to sincerely thank them here.

Acknowledgments xiii

Besides, this book is the result of a long research process in which numerous colleagues and students from my research laboratory in Waseda University have taken part. At the same time, communities and Public Administration representatives have contributed greatly to the project. Additionally, various research foundations have supported this work. I am deeply indebted to all of them for their support.

Contributors

Toshihiko Abe (PhD) is Community planner, Architect, and Research fellow of Institute of Urban and Regional Study of Waseda University. He has practiced action research on disaster restoration from the Great East Japan Earthquake and tsunami, 2011.

Shin Aiba (PhD) is Professor of Tokyo Metropolitan University. He is an expert in civil society changes and government changes that began in the 1990s. He is also a leading theorist in city planning and machizukuri in population decline in society that has become a problem since the 2010s.

Liang-Chun Chen (PhD) is retired professor of National Taiwan University, and former director of the National Science and Technology Center for Disaster Reduction Taiwan. He has been committed to both research and actual practice in community empowerment, community design, and community-based disaster reduction in Taiwan.

Katsuhiro Kubo (PhD) is Professor of Hokkaido University of Science. He has continued his research on the linkage between urban improvement and redevelopment projects. This research analyzes the result of the linkage socially and spatially, and has presented the development of the machizukuri movement for the next generation.

Chia-Chan Liao is currently the president of New Homeland Foundation. He is a famous cultural worker, especially in the field of community comprehensive empowerment in Taiwan. Mr. Liao has assisted in post-disaster recovery work at Taomi village for more than 20 years.

Yosuke Mano (PhD) is Associate Professor, Tokyo Institute of Technology. He is an expert in residential and culture-led urban revitalization in Japanese provincial cities. He has also collaborated with NPOs, inhabitants, architects, and local creators in many urban revitalization projects and local activities in historical cities in Japan, especially after the Tohoku earthquake disaster.

Kosuke Masuo (PhD) is an architect. He specializes in practicing the machizukuri movement through architectural design, urban planning, and research. His practical research introduced in this book received a doctoral dissertation award from the general incorporated foundation Jusoken.

Kenjiro Matsuura (PhD) is Associate Professor of Chiba University. He promotes practical research activities related to community design, urban design, and architectural design utilizing regional resources in local cities.

Akihiro Noda (MA.Eng) is CEO of LLC SMDW, and Invited researcher of the Research Institute of Urban and Regional Study of Waseda University. He is an architect and city planning consultant. He is also an expert who assembles both architectural plans and business plans to embody projects from the machizukuri movement.

Shinji Nojima (PhD) is Professor of University of Fukui. He has researched the method of urban revitalization based on the autonomy of the city, mainly in local cities, and practiced town development including designing Mikuni Station in Sakai City and Eco Village in Wakasa Town. He was visiting scholar at the School of the Built environment at Oxford Brookes University in 2008.

Hiroshi Saito (PhD) is Associate Professor of Toyo University. He studied both theory and practice of collaborative planning through his PhD research at the School of Architecture, Planning and Landscape, Newcastle University, UK. His main academic interest is how community-based planning and machizukuri can apply civic creativity to improve places.

Shigeru Satoh (PhD) is Professor Emeritus of Waseda University, and former Director of the Research Institute of Urban and Regional Study, and former President of the Architectural Institute of Japan. He has spearheaded the Japanese machizukuri movement (a community-based comprehensive approach to improving built environmental practices) both in theory and actual practice.

Hideaki Shimura (PhD) is Professor of the School of Architecture at Shibaura Institute of Technology. He has developed many community participation design methods including community design workshops. He was visiting scholar at the Institute of Urban and Regional Development at University of California, Berkeley in 2009.

Keisuke Sugano (BArch, MA.Arch, Dr.Eng.) is Assistant Professor of Kanazawa Institute of Technology, and former researcher at Delft University of Technology. His main research theme is ecological urban design by reevaluating the traditional blue-green infrastructure in the historical urban area, from the perspective of ecology, landscape, and public image.

xvi *Contributors*

Jie-Ying Wu (PhD) is currently Associate Professor at University of Taipei and former secretary general of the Disaster Management Society of Taiwan. His research interests include disaster management policies, post-disaster recovery, and urban planning.

Alba Victoria Zamarbide Urdaniz (Doctor of Architecture) was the recipient of the 2018 ENCATC Research Award on Cultural Policy and Cultural Management, and is currently working at the UNESCO World Heritage Centre under the Cities Programme. Her research addresses new tools and models for community engagement and regional management, with a special focus on historical territories. She has extensively contributed to this book as translator and assistant editor for Chapters 1, 3–6, and 20.

Chengqi Zhao (PhD) is the head of EIH, a researcher at the Urban Regional Institute of Waseda University, and a former head of Isozaki Arata China Office. In the field of urban renewal in China, he first proposed the methodology of urban renewal based on "property rights change" for the goal of the protection of indigenous people and the inheritance of regional culture.

Part I

History and Method of Machizukuri

1 Introduction to machizukuri

Shigeru Satoh

What does machizukuri mean?

Compared to papers and books published in English so far, machizukuri seems close to community design and community development. However, the word "machizukuri," which is a direct alphabetization of the Japanese pronunciation, cannot be replaced by these English terms. That is because this word contains various concepts and a special nuance that cannot be reflected by the English terminology.

Searching for proper ways in English to translate the term "machizukuri," academics find it very difficult to compose a suitable expression equivalent in meaning (Watanabe, 2007). There are in English, for sure, keywords like "community development," "community building," "place making," or even "community improvement," but the perspective of each is narrow and their meanings limited. It is not uncommon though, for the Japanese language to refer to a whole sophisticated idea by creating an inexplicit and vague expression.

In Japanese the term "machizukuri" is also new. It started to be more frequently used from the 1970s as the combination of two different concepts, "machi" and "zukuri." The word "machi" was originally represented by the Chinese character "*chou*,"[1] which refers to a square unit of arable land with a length of about 110 meters/side that could be cultivated by a single adult man. Later, the "chou" was used to established the urban grid divisions in ancient capitals such as Kyoto. Units of a similar extension were used to define city blocks, which were usually named according to the activities developed inside them (e.g., different trade groups), adding the suffix "-machi."[2] Around the fifteenth century in Kyoto, the meaning of "machi" changed. Both sides of a street started to be given similar "machi" names.[3] The assembly of these linear "machi" represented a mixture of activities and human links. Then, in the late fifteenth century, the late Middle Ages in Japan, trades and social classes, such as merchants, artisans, and even low-rank noble families, gathered in similar urban areas and constituted autonomous urban management systems. Wealthy merchants in the region also established and started businesses in town and all

4 Shigeru Satoh

this reflected on a unique urban culture of the "machi shuu" (machi people), represented by the tea ceremony, Nou-gaku theater, Ren-gaku shared poetry, etc; these activities represent a culture of giving and creating human links. This became an important foundation to modern Japanese culture (Hayashiya, 1990).

In other words, "machi" is a term that not only represents a specific delimited area inside a city, but also a "place," including its social organization as a basis for people to interact and create urban culture.

So, the word "machi," which could be translated as "community and its shared place," has a distinctive vivid nuance. The machi portrays the physical environment in which social activities take place and, in this way, the concept defines not only the material structure of the town, but the place where intangible aspects of local communities and the built environment combine.

The other half of machi-zukuri, the tri-syllable "-zukuri," means "to make." It does not simply mean to make inanimate things; it rather means to cultivate things with full effort, heart, and soul, while participating in the lengthy process of making and animating them. Accordingly, the full term "machizukuri" signifies the making and management of machi with care and respect. Apart from giving heed to the town's physical environment, machizukuri genuinely takes the social context into account in its roots and origins. Tradition, cultural elements, industrial structures and education, or breeding, are considered. Thus, machizukuri embraces a process at the pace of life of the local community in which it strengthens and self rebuilds. As explained above, "zukuri" does not mean to create new things, but to enhance them without sacrificing their original essence. Accordingly, machizukuri also embodies such a process. It means to upgrade a place, little by little, applying a set of schemes for local cultivation.

So, the word machizukuri has a complex meaning with no easy translation. Nowadays, machizukuri represents at the same time a philosophy, an approach, a vision, a series of methods and tools, etc. Besides, the concept has grown to involve a wide range of topics, scales, stakeholders, etc. In this way, machizukuri not only portrays the participation of local residents in government-led urban planning and design, but also the facilitation of voluntary community activities for the improvement of the social and physical environment along with their collective management.

The space and place created through machizukuri are full of human diversity, similar to the rich quality ecosystems created through natural processes, which do not depend on a conscious plan.

This "machi" is created collaboratively based on the results and experiences of machizukuri, and it is different from the "modern urban space," occupied by high-rise buildings and cars.

The birth of the term "machizukuri" dates to the 1960s.[4] The term was born from the residents' activities that faced the deterioration of the living

Introduction to machizukuri 5

environment following a period of rapid economic growth. At that time, the administration began to promote decentralization and participation in decisions relating to urban management. These activities involved experts and local governments in bottom-up processes that aimed at solving the problems of the local communities. We can say thus that it was born as a bottom-up planning concept, which aimed especially at the improvement of living environments.

Initially, machizukuri appeared as a theoretical concept, a social ideal that later had to go through an experimental phase of trial and error in order to evolve into effective on-site practice. These trial-and-error attempts to work with local communities led to the definition of clearer action strategies that concerned local citizens and required their special participation. As a result, machizukuri was coined as a generic term referring to community participation and district activities. In the 1970s, machizukuri achieved great popularity and was the object of numerous discussions and studies. With it, the outline of machizukuri gradually shaped up.

The term "machizukuri" encompasses the ensemble of approaches and activities based on the resources existing in each local society, carried out by diverse actors in order to improve the quality of life and surrounding living environments. Therefore, we should first acknowledge that machizukuri is an inclusive general concept that portrays an attitude towards community planning and empowerment.

However, by the early 1970s, apart from "machizukuri," words like "community design," "community development," and "community revitalization" were utilized to refer to similar processes. The use of the Japanese term "machizukuri" written in the Japanese hiragana phonetic alphabet was gradually extended and consolidated. This was motivated by the milder and friendlier image of the word compared to either adopted English words written phonetically in the katakana alphabet (used for loanwords from foreign languages), or the rigid kanji characters for "machi." Besides, the term facilitated the engagement of common people in machizukuri campaigns because it bore a nuance that was easily perceived by residents. In any case, the term "machizukuri" has now come to bear an extremely broad meaning.

In this way, machizukuri practice took up the objective of realizing ideal visions for the machi. The machi represented both a shared place and a community model that was to be realized by locals. The experts involved in the process had to continuously look for the new meanings and shapes adopted by machizukuri, and the kinds of methods and theories that were necessary to make the most of it. Not only were trans-disciplinary discussions between experts promoted, but also real on-site experiments that involved local communities and specific public policies were developed.

A popular magazine, *Toshi-Jutaku* (*Urban Housing*), addressed this cutting-edge theme at the time, and made it the annual focus of the series in 1975, which was called "Methods of machizukuri." The following

6   Shigeru Satoh

words by its editor, Makoto Ueda, enables us to understand what machizukuri meant at the time:

> Physical plans alone do not solve the whole (urban) problem. Programs are necessary. These cannot not be isolated from physical plans, and should serve to challenge the existence of easily made boxes (with respect to bigger buildings without context), facilities, roads and squares. This goes beyond "box making," giving the physical plan a clear direction towards the community living in the area, which can be considered "machi-making." Nowadays, the social nuance that the term "machizukuri" bears is being used as a slogan by planners, companies and government bodies, and is experiencing a kind of boom. Our task is to make sure that machizukuri (is used as) more than just a slogan, but also involving contents that go beyond the planning of modern architecture and cities, bringing contents that can be opposed to it.
>
> In response to these issues, architectural experts and the administrative planners mainly, together with resident leaders, have taken up a mission to promote machizukuri activities.
>
> (Ueda, 1975, p. 1, lines 15–20)

The last volume of the year of *Toshi-Jutaku* was a "Primer of Machizukuri" (No. 12, published in December 1975 and edited by *Shutoken Sougou keikaku kennkyujo* (Capital Region Comprehensive Planning Institute (CRCPI)[5]). The volume called itself a "machizukuri catalog" and presented different forms of residents' participation, collaborative systems that had just taken off, and related legal systems. Through it, it was possible to understand what the machizukuri processes that had emerged at the time were trying to look for and unveil.

At the time, the idea of machizukuri was still not completely clear, and discussions took place led by Professor Takamasa Yoshisaka at the head. It is interesting to understand the personal thoughts on machizukuri of the individuals who led the efforts to find an appropriate definition for machizukuri during this period. Among them, not only great expectations and enthusiasm for machizukuri were mentioned, there was also great confusion about the absence of a clear system. For example, Kichiemon Kawana, Professor of Urban Planning in Tokyo Metropolitan University, mentioned that "after the war, while talking a lot about democratization (of Japan), and the high level of growth that has been achieved so far, now, machizukuri is being regarded as a critical issue."

In addition, he discussed the still unclear condition of machizukuri and the many contemporary thoughts on social issues and new models adopted. He pointed out that "during this time, large families were broken, replaced by mono-nuclear families, and with them, losing the traditional family care-system, and now there is no alternative system or institution

Introduction to machizukuri   7

that can help recover it and maintain our society," and "inside this, being told to do machizukuri developing strong ties with local neighbors that can supply this care, is very chaotic, and it is difficult to understand what the clues are and what to create."

Takamasa Yoshisaka did also mentioned that

> if you do not break it at once, you cannot get away from the shell of the family, the shell of the village, the shell of the hometown, etc. It took 100 years to do so. So, I think it would be better to restructure in a larger new organizational system again in [even if it takes] the following 100 years (referring to new systems, such as machizukuri),

stating thus the importance of evolving in ways similar to the community is underlined.

Such a complex evolutionary and interdisciplinary process is what we call now "the discovery of machizukuri."

The discovery of machizukuri

Chapter 4 of this book describes the history of machizukuri and how the term has evolved to acquire its current meaning. From the 1960s to the 1970s, machizukuri rose as a force in opposition to traditional urban planning. The chapter describes the gradual accumulation of experiences, which have become the foundation for contemporary machizukuri through three different generations of practice. The evolutionary process of machizukuri can be divided into three periods as follows.

The first generation corresponds to the origins of the philosophy of machizukuri from the late 1960s to the early 1980s. At the time, formal participatory methods and systems were developed to face diverse problems.

The second generation worked supporting autonomous community initiatives, which involved collaboration and co-creation in designing local urban spaces. From the mid 1980s, many experimental cases tackling very diverse topics appeared, creating a broad reference framework for machizukuri processes.

Finally, since the late 1990s, the third generation of machizukuri corresponded to the design of comprehensive management systems at different scales as a way to integrate all these different efforts.

The accumulation of experiences throughout the previous three generations gave shape to actual machizukuri practice. To provide the reader with a clear idea of how machizukuri has been implemented, Chapter 4 describes the different methods and tools that have been specifically developed or adapted through machizukuri experiences. Additionally, Chapter 5 explores how machizukuri has influenced traditional urban planning through diverse interactive exchanges between both.

BASIC RELATED INFORMATION		MACHIZUKURI DEVELOPMENT
FIRST GENERATION		
Promulgation of Basic Law for Environmental Pollution Control.	1967	
	1967	Reformist mayors elected in major cities.
Model community policy of the Ministry of Home Affairs designated forty model districts	1971	
	1972	Residents' movement against the destruction of local landscape and environment in Karasuyama-Temple-town, Setagaya Ward.
	1974	Establishment of the Japanese Association for Historical Townscape Conservation.
Tokyo Metropolitan Government released the results of comprehensive risk assessment on each area (Chou-Chou-Moku) in 5 levels.	1975	
Amendment of the Law for the Protection of Cultural Properties to include the "Conservation Districts for Groups of Traditional Buildings".	1975	
	1977	Implementation of playground as a result of machizukuri movement with resident and expert in Setagaya Ward, Tokyo.
SECOND GEN.		
	1981	Enactment of local government's machizukuri ordinance in Kobe City.
	1984	Establishment of Nara Machizukuri Center taking the lead in machizukuri activities.
Amendment of the City Planning Act cause being obliged to create a masterplan through residents' participation.	1992	
	1994	Development of practical methods for public participation such as Waku-Waku workshop.
Great Hanshin-Awaji Earthquake.	1997	
THIRD GENERATION		
NPO law passed in parliamentary decision motivated by citizen groups.	1997	
"Machizukuri Three Law" enacted to revitalize the central shopping areas.	1998	
	2000	Mukou-jima Events attract attention toward community development activities.
Long-term care insurance system launched to support daily life of aged person.	2000	
"Machizukuri for walkable Life" plan openly solicited from National Government.	2000	
	2001	10 volumes of the "Machizukuri Textbook" published by the Architectural Institute of Japan.
Niigataken Chuetsu Earthquake.	2004	
Promulgation of Landscape Law taking advantage of local government's efforts to preserve landscape.	2004	
	2011	"Machizukuri Citizens' Operation" published.
Great East Japan Earthquake.	2011	
Promotion of the compact city planned by the location optimization plan.	2014	

Figure 1.1 Chronological table of Japanese machizukuri.

Contemporary machizukuri practice

Throughout the process of discovery of machizukuri mentioned above, various efforts were carried out, not only challenging traditional planning methods, but also promoting the definition of social systems, planning techniques and technological development. Nowadays, machizukuri has come to define the very diverse and creative community actions and management models by which local communities are enabled to actively engage in problem-solving, and which have been gradually systematized through years of practice.

In this way, machizukuri, entered a period of original adaptation and evolution, and started being used more widely.

In this book, Chapters 8 to 19 present different examples of successful machizukuri practice in diverse contexts. These cases explore, among others, the new possibilities and side effects of tourism that emerge from the regeneration of commercial and residential mixed-use districts, the lives of residents in historical city centers, and the possibilities for protection of cultural landscapes. Furthermore, reconstruction projects from frequent earthquake disasters constitute an opportunity for development of new machizukuri activities. In times of crisis, rehabilitation processes required the cooperation of experts and local administration in order to support and assist local communities. Therefore, in such situations, machizukuri activities developed rapidly, having to face a reality that had not been considered up to that time, and thus, these cases became a new proving ground for machizukuri practice. As one of the main examples, the efforts that followed the Great East Japan Earthquake in 2011 portray the evolution of machizukuri applied to reconstruction processes.

Definition and redefinition of machizukuri

It is necessary to clarify the definition of the term "machizukuri" whenever dealing with it as an object of academic research. However, as mentioned above, "machizukuri" has come to be used without a clear meaning and is widely utilized as a general term.

Some experts have defended the use of a wide definition. For example, as Watanabe (2011) points out, for a definition, there should be a necessary and sufficient proof to establish that A is B. This means that an objective definition should not discuss what machizukuri should be like, wants to be like, seems to be, etc., but should simply refer to a series of activities that serve to improve the physical and social environment of a community through the cooperation and collaboration of diverse actors.

However, as explained before, the evolutionary process of machizukuri has been promoted by sharing its positive meaning and ideals for its development, thus by narrowing down its meaning according to practical experiences. Experts involved in actual machizukuri practice have thought

10 Shigeru Satoh

widely about what machizukuri should be and this has become the object of intense debate. In such a context, in the early 2000s, when the third machizukuri generation appeared, the author of this chapter, together with the Architectural Institute of Japan, was the Chief Editor of ten town development textbooks that tried to redefine machizukuri (Satoh, 2004). In the first volume of the series, Shigeru Satoh presented it as follows: Machizukuri speaks for a series of persistent activities planned to improve the quality of the machi, its space and its communities. Based upon the resources of a local community and integrating the manifold subjectivities in cooperation, machizukuri activities seek to enliven urban areas by energizing its communities, revealing the spirit of the locality (Satoh, 2004).

This definition narrows down machizukuri as a way to better understand its issues and to embrace the desires and hopes on what it should be and what it could develop into. All the cases presented in this book fit into this definition and present cutting-edge context-specific experiences. Nevertheless, at the end of the book, and based on the results obtained by these cases, the future expansion of the term will be explored.

Notes

1 The character "machi" has two different readings in modern Japanese. "Chou" according to the Chinese pronunciation, or "machi" in the Japanese pronunciation. Both of them represent the same idea.
2 For example, "gofuku-machi" was used to refer to Japanese dress trader areas.
3 In Japanese the expression "both-sides-machi" appeared referring to these streets. This is especially clear in urban areas such as "Tera-machi" or "Kawara-machi" in Kyoto, which correspond to zones along main streets. This new type of "machi" was more difficult to delimit than the block "machi," and at the same time both types of ideas were superimposed.
4 Before the 1960s, Watanabe (1997) had already discussed the term "machizukuri." Nakajima (2003) pointed out that "machizukuri" was used for the first time in 1947 by the urban planner Kan Hideshima.
5 CRCPI was established in 1973 in order to promote specific machizukuri to define basic plans with Professor Takamasa Yoshisaka, from Waseda University, as the president of the group.

As a member of the above-mentioned, Kichiemon Kawana, Michihiro Okuda, an urban sociologist who specialized in contemporary community theory, and three other members of the Yoshisaka laboratory conducted theoretical research and planned work on specific machizukuri projects.

References

Hayashiya, T. (1990). *Machishu – Kyoto ni okeru Shimin Keiseishi (Machi-People – History of the Emergence of Citizens in Kyoto)*. Tokyo: Chuuou Kouron Shuppansha.
Satoh, S. (2004). *Machizukuri no houhou* (Method of Machizukuri). Tokyo: Maruzen.

Ueda, M. (1975). Machizukuri no shuhou – nenkante-ma (Techniques of Machizukuri – Annual issue). *Toshi Jutaku 7501*, p. 2. Tokyo: Kashima Shuppan.

Watanabe, S. (2007). Toshi Keikaku vs Machizukuri: Emerging Paradigm of Civil Society in Japan. 1950–1980, in Sorensen, A. and Funck, C. (eds.), *Living Cities in Japan: Citizens' Movements. Machizukuri and Local Environments*. London: Nissan Institute; Routledge Japanese Studies Series.

Watanabe, S. (2011). The Logical Structure of the Definition of Machizukuri. *Journal of the City Planning Institute of Japan*, 46(3): 673–678.

2 Brief history of machizukuri in three regions in East Asia

Shin Aiba

Introduction

There are many countries in Asia, but when considering terms such as "citizen participation" and "machizukuri," three regions in East Asia come to mind: Japan, Taiwan, and South Korea. In the late 1960s, the term "machizukuri" began to be used in Japan, and in the late 1980s, the term *she chu ying tsao* appeared in Taiwan, and similarly, the term *maeul mandeulgi* (town development) appeared in South Korea. These movements developed in the three regions that realized democratization and economic growth after World War II.

All these – *machizukuri, she chu ying tsao,* and *maeul mandeulgi* – have three common characteristics. The first characteristic is "spontaneity," or being a self-motivated action by citizens and residents, rather than a government-initiated action. The second is "publicity," or being recognized as an action that has the agreement and consent of various people living in the area, rather than a radical action of particular person or group. The third is "universality" inside each region, rather than specific phenomena in a certain case. In other words, spontaneous actions that have public recognition and have developed nationwide with universality are *machizukuri, she chu ying tsao,* or *maeul mandeulgi.*

This section aims to give an outline of how these three movements developed in each region. Social situation, democratization, and economic growth are necessary to develop each movement in each region. And also it is necessary for spontaneous actions to act legally, and to build legal systems to certify these actions as public actions, and to establish a legal system to support and promote them nationwide.

I will clarify the history of these three movements in the following three periods, along with clarifying social change and legal systems changes (Figure 2.1):

1   The pioneering period: Pioneering spontaneous actions are taken in response to changing social circumstances.

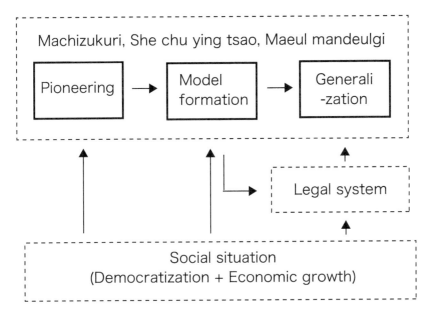

Figure 2.1 Three periods, social change, and legal systems changes.

2 The model formation period: Pioneering actions are accepted by local governments and local residents as a model, and the government builds legal systems to place them.
3 The generalization period: Spontaneous actions spread out in every area of the region boosted by legal systems.

The pioneering period

After economic growth, Taiwan and South Korea democratized in 1987, and *she chu ying tsao* and *maeul mandeulgi* were born triggered by this democratic change of situation.

Until then, martial law had been imposed in Taiwan, and there were rights restrictions such as on freedom of speech. In 1968, the government launched a "Community Development Policy" to promote the development of public facilities, such as waterways and nurseries, and to carry out the development of the physical environment in order to ensure a minimum standard of living in each community. After democratization, policies to cultivate non-physical systems were added to it. From the side of the citizens, citizens' campaigns to preserve historic townscapes began in the late 1970s. At the same time, NGOs working on various topics were established, as for example, the "Snail without a shell campaign," which tackled urban housing problems, the "OURs (Organization of Urban Re...)," and so on. These became pioneering activities that led into the model formation period in the mid-1990s.

14   *Shin Aiba*

In South Korea before democratization, neighborhood movements increased: the "peasant movement" from the 1960s, "the urban poor movement" from the late 1960s, and the "democratic movement" from the 1970s. The government began the Saemaul Undong (New Community Movement) in the 1970s. This comprised the improvement of physical and non-physical conditions for rural communities, and although as part of that it inherited the peasant movement, it was mostly carried out through a top-down process. After democratization, spontaneous actions had increased, such as the space improvement movement in Insa-Dong in Seoul, in the 1990s, and the "Break down the wall" campaign in Busan. These became pioneering actions and led into the model formation period in the mid-1990s, as in the case of Taiwan.

Similar actions had occurred in Japan in the end of 1960s, but the social situation was different. Economic growth had settled down, although lifestyles were affluent at the end of 1960s. Neighborhood protest movements against the ill effects of economic growth also became active in 1960s. However, democratization had already occured in 1945 after World War II. When neighborhood protest movements became active, the political system known as the "1955 System" was established based on a democratized society, and subsequently, the "Reformist local government (RLG)" was formed. The 1955 System was a political system that continued from 1955 to 1993. This was a stable political system wherein the ruling Liberal Democratic Party occupied two-thirds of parliamentary seats. RLG was composed of cities run by reformist mayors who belonged to the Socialist Party of Japan or the Japanese Communist Party. Their power was magnified from the 1960s to the 1970s, encouraged by neighborhood protest movements that formed the basis for this increased RLG, and the pioneering machizukuri movement was subsumed within RLG policy. That is to say, more than ten years after democratization, machizukuri was born, amid the immobilization of the political system by political parties. Within that system, the model formation period began.

The model formation period

The model formation period began in both Taiwan and South Korea in the mid-1990s. In Taiwan in 1994, the central government's "Council for Cultural Affairs" formulated a "*She chu ying tsao* Policy," and at the same time, Taipei City government formulated an "Environmental Improvement District Plan." These two policies suggested a model of activity based on the "community (*she chu*)" as a social unit.

In South Korea, local elections for the mayor of the local government began in 1995, and the model formation period began with the promotion of citizen participation or *maeul mandeulgi* in local government. Aside from changes in government, citizens' groups' distinctive *maeul mandeulgi*

Machizukuri in three East Asian countries 15

was also being carried out, and their participation in local governments took the general name of *maeul mandeulgi*.

In Japan, the model formation period began with the Ministry of Home Affairs starting up community policies in the 1970s and with the establishment of the municipal comprehensive plan system. Then, within ten years of these policies being attempted, the district plan system was established by the 1980 City Planning Law. Therefore the period until 1980 is regarded as the model formation period.

In South Korea and Taiwan the generalization period immediately followed the model formation period; however, in the case of Japan, the generalization period began in the 1990s. Taking as an example the systematization of "district plans," the only local governments that set up systems for tackling machizukuri were Kobe City and Setagaya Ward. As mentioned above, a model of machizukuri was formed in limited RLGs amid an immobilized political system.

I will now examine the differences between the models created in each region. All models have at their center the term "*she chu*" (community) in Taiwan, "*maeul*" (town) in Korea, and "*machi (community)*" in Japan.

"*She chu*" is defined as a social and autonomous unit. In Taiwan, the "Community Development Policy (*she chu fa zhan*)" was adopted in 1968, and *she chu ying tsao* was an extension of this policy. South Korea's "*maeul*" originally meant "town," but the word "*dong*" is now used for town as an administrative unit. The word "*maeul*" has taken on the meaning of campaigns or actions that cannot be undertaken by social or autonomous units. In Japan, there have been traditional, regional, autonomous organizations called "*choukai*" (district councils). The reason for introducing the new term "community" was because these autonomous organizations were not able to assimilate the influx of new residents in the post-war population increase. In other words, "community" was proposed as a new structure that would surpass the traditional "*choukai*." In this way, *she chu* is used as a term that recognizes the continuity from prior policies, *maeul* is used as a term that is differentiated from prior policies, and *community* is used as a conceptual term.

The generalization period

The generalization period in the case of Taiwan began in 2000. This was a time of political change in which the Democratic Progressive Party formed the new government. *She chu ying tsao* was given a central position in the reconstruction after the 1999 Chichi earthquake. Subsequently, its generalization accelerated, with the government's publication of the "New Historic Town *she chu ying tsao* Plan" in 2002 and the creation of the Community Planner system in all prefectures in 2001.

In the case of South Korea, the generalization period began in the mid-2000s, when establishing concrete support systems for *maeul mandeulgi* became a trend. In 2006 "livable city" policies were established by the

16 Shin Aiba

Balanced Development Committee. This became nationwide, which led to the establishment, in 2014, of nationwide organizations for *maeul mandeulgi*, and the creation of *maeul mandeulgi* regulations in 87 local governments by 2015, with *maeul mandeulgi* centers in 19 places.

In Japan, the turning point that marks the entry to the "generalization period" was the 1992 revision of the City Planning Law, which proposed citizen participation in the planning process of "city planning master plans," to local government. Later on, triggered by the Great Kobe Earthquake (1995), the NPO (non-profit organization) law was established in 1998, and in 2000, various laws were amended based on the Omnibus Decentralization Law. In the 2000s, machizukuri spread nationwide.

Conclusion

Following a long model formation period in Japan, generalization began in the 1990s, and over ten years, a system to support machizukuri was developed. In Taiwan and South Korea, following a short model formation period, generalization rapidly progressed by setting up of new systems in rapid succession. This difference in speed may have allowed *she chu ying tsao*, *maeul mandeulgi*, and *machizukuri* to develop differently, even though they currently seem to be similar.

In recent years, an expansion of citizens' initiatives based on spontaneity, publicity, and universality has been observed in other Asian countries, namely China and Singapore. In these countries, where democratization has developed divergently (or has not developed), it is possible that citizens' initiatives will also develop differently.

Initiatives in Taiwan, South Korea, and Japan have affected each other's development. There have been continuous information sharing and exchanges between three regions; for example, the reconstruction machizukuri experience after the Kobe earthquake in Japan in 1995 was shared for reconstruction *she chu ying tsao* after the Chichi earthquake in Taiwan in 1999. Besides there have been several regular international conferences, including the Pacific Rim Community Design Network, and many actions involving China and Singapore may develop in the future.

These initiatives could be described as great democratization experiments, and continuous observation is needed to determine how they will develop in the future.

References

Aiba, S. (2005a). The development history of the machizukuri method in Japan after the 1960s, *Proceedings of International Symposium on Urban Planning 2005*, Korea Planners Association.

Aiba, S. (2005b). Comparative history of community design in Korea, Taiwan and Japan (in Japanese, Korea and Chinese), Proceedings of ASCOM 2008 Fall Worksop in Seoul, pp. 3–100, ASCOM.

3 The first generation
The emergence of machizukuri

Shigeru Satoh

Introduction

In the midst of many anti-establishment protest movements and riots that emerged simultaneously all around the world in the 1960s, machizukuri was born as an ideal philosophy grounded on local discussions about the improvement of the built environment, lifestyles, and the local community.

Influenced by the general critical mood and supported by a time of high economic growth in Japan, this social movement asked for more participation, independence in the decision-making process, and for the establishment of a real democracy that could give voice to the whole scope of the Japanese population. This meant including the opinions of regular citizens, which had not been listened to by governments before.

This was a time of many difficulties, but also a time of hope for enterprising people, who saw in it new opportunities. During this first generation of machizukuri, as different activities rallied, it was extremely important to establish principles and theories, along with clear visions. First of all, the local community leaders who strongly stood up against the negative effects of urban planning, environmental policies and administrative measures, became the leading figures during this period. Second, academics and experts were also awakened by these community movements. Then, architects, who were aware of the limitations of the existing top-down urban planning methods, sociologists, who aimed at achieving a decentralized society, and experts from the public administration observed the different problems on-site and joined active practice. The people at the heart of this movement belonged to a generation that had been involved in university student revolts during the late 1960s, and who enriched city planning practice and the public administration bringing in a social mission. Third, enthusiastic ambitious local government officials and planners belonging to national institutions also responded to the quest.

Struggles from these three different standpoints helped give shape to the concept of "machizukuri." In this way, this first machizukuri generation worked through trial and error processes to find adequate principles and

18 *Shigeru Satoh*

ideas to build up a new philosophy of public participation and engagement. The diverse initiatives that ran in parallel learned from each other and developed particular methods. This chapter will take a look at the birth of these first machizukuri actions and present their specific outcomes through detailed examples.

From protest movements to machizukuri: Mano district as a touchstone for machizukuri practice

The starting point of machizukuri practice can be found in the case of the Mano district of Kobe city, which is the longest example of continuous machizukuri efforts led by locals and has become a touchstone for machizukuri practice.

The community-led activities in Mano, a southern area of the Nagata ward, to the West of Kobe city, can be traced back to anti-pollution campaigns and grew to become one of the main references for general machizukuri practice during the first generation in the 1960s. In this context, it is true that local residents played the leading role in the practical development of the machizukuri process for the maintenance of the living environment in Mano. However, linked to this, it would not be just to ignore the important role of the local government in developing unique cutting-edge urban planning policies and systems. Kobe city was at the forefront of cutting-edge policies developed by the local administration in Japan between the 1970s and 1990s. In response to the community movements, the municipality faced up to social and urban issues, and developed a special administrative model centered on the linkage of urban planning and machizukuri, connecting the latter to various kinds of administrative systems and public works (e.g., connecting machizukuri local plans, developed by each community, to city Master Plans).

In this way, the Mano machizukuri process focused on the communication, cooperation, and exchanges between diverse stakeholders (public and local), and on the creation of multiple materials, which greatly influenced successive machizukuri practice. For this reason, this chapter presents the case in detail.[1]

The start of machizukuri in Mano (1965–70): protests against pollution

As just mentioned, the origins of machizukuri can be traced back to the resistance movements that appeared against the public nuisance caused by public environmental pollution. The misuse and neglect brought about by a period of high economic growth in the 1960s caused serious pollution problems in several areas. The Japanese term "*kougai*" can be translated as "public nuisance and environmental pollution." However, the concept also involves the mental, physical, and economic damage caused to local residents

The first generation 19

and the general public by the destruction of nature and the living environments that accompany harmful business and human activities. Officially, under the Japanese "Basic Environment Law" (1993),[2] the term refers to air pollution, water pollution, soil pollution, noise, vibration, ground subsidence, odor, and so forth. However, there are other possible implications such as food pollution, the destruction of living environments, or the scarcity of sunlight caused by high-rise buildings. These issues can equally be considered as *kougai*.

Under diverse circumstances, resistance campaigns against pollution in residential areas made the turn toward creative machizukuri, actively working on environmental improvements based on their own community initiatives; these streams of community movements were in fact directly linked with the residents' movements and campaigns against *kougai*. In this context, the specific activities that were born in Kobe City, Hyogo Prefecture, are especially significant. The community movement in Japan first broke out in the Maruyama district of Kobe city. In the Rokkou Mountain area, land reclamation activities caused an unceasing downhill flow of trucks carrying excavated soil to the foothills of Maruyama, resulting in unbearable traffic and pollution for the local residents. In response, locals took action. They started publishing and distributing their own local newspaper, and the establishment of their own community councils soon followed. With this, the former protest movements started materializing into creative, positive, and significant local resident machizukuri movements, which were also in charge of the running and maintenance of public facilities such as playgrounds, kindergartens, and nurseries for youngsters.

In 1967, the Maruyama district was designated a "Model District for neighboring living unit planning" by the municipality of Kobe. Then, in 1971, it became also a "Model District for Community Development" promoted by the Ministry of Home Affairs.[3]

After the resistance movements, these tools were to promote machizukuri activities. Nevertheless, the movement started to die out by the 1980s due to the feuds between old and new residents (Hirohara, 2013). Yet the Maruyama movement somewhat influenced the Mano district[4] to develop similar activities.

The lower Mano district presented a traditional lower-town "*shitamachi*" structure, in which wooden terraced houses were mixed with small-scale factories creating a very dense urban fabric; this was sarcastically called a "pollution department store."

This context pushed forward the uprising of residents' movements under the outstanding figure of a leader, normally the chairperson of a community association, which appealed for environmental protection from air pollution by nearby factories affecting the residential conditions.

Then the administration of Kobe City became involved. In 1970, the local government, residents, and the companies that had caused the pollution problem reached a tripartite agreement for its prevention. In July 1971,

20 *Shigeru Satoh*

the Mayor of Kobe city, Tatsuo Miyazaki, who had attended the opening ceremony of a park nearby (also a result of these activities), visited the district and at a meeting with local residents offered the following suggestions:

> I would like to discuss together on how to plan the district, to integrate the ideas with the vision at the governmental level, to create the best local plan for the area and implement it. To do so, I would like to ask people in the district for serious research, without compromising each others' interests. The city has the intention to acquire the necessary land in the meantime.

Prior to this, in 1970, Yoshizou Mohri, an outstanding leader of the community movement (who continued leading the movement later), had also said "we need to cherish a grassroots democracy [...] raising new citizens' awareness of community development by themselves." This led to the creation of a "Machizukuri School," which was held as a series of eight small-scale lectures[5] inviting experts and city officials to raise local residents' awareness (Mano Machizukuri Promotion Council, 2005).

In this way, the same movement that had pursued and achieved the creation of pollution bans reached a stage where the residents themselves were finally able to draw up a Machizukuri Plan.[6]

The second period of machizukuri in Mano (1971–78): transition towards a machizukuri plan and design, policy, and exploration

The activities for the improvement of the living environment of the Mano district had already begun in 1965, gradually leading to the establishment of a "grassroots democracy," implemented by local autonomous management groups and systems. However, even in areas that had united under protest movements, at this stage, when they faced the definition of a Machizukuri Plan, it was difficult to reach agreements on the kind of process at which they would aim. While the groups that had taken the initiative in previous movements thought "let's define the plan by our own means," more conservative groups disagreed, arguing that "planning should be left to the administration." As a consequence, the definition of a specific action plan had to wait until 1977.

On the other hand, Kobe City officials continued developing diverse studies to proceed in more systematic ways. In 1965, Kobe City formulated the first City General Plan. At that time, inside the plan the idea of a "neighborhood unit" was used in the design and development of newtowns.[7]

There is no doubt that the fierce residents' movement that had taken place in 1963 in the Maruyama area had had an impact on Master Plans, emphasizing the importance of nearby communities. For example, at the time, Deputy Mayor Miyazaki formed a study group under the topic

The first generation 21

"Considerations on a livable Kobe"; the considerations discussed here would later come to life. In 1969, when Miyazaki became Mayor, the City Planning Department of Kobe City commissioned the urban planner Eisuke Mizutani to research the concept of the "machi unit." This referred to a built-up area with a population of about 10,000 to 50,000 inhabitants, which gathered houses, and community and recreation places, and which represented an average size of living space of close communities. This was a way to theoretically define the traditional "machi" on the basis of a modern physical space.

Then the whole municipality was divided in 34 machi units and specific measures were discussed for each one of them (Kobe City "Machi Unit" Outline, 1974). This approach was incorporated into the new Kobe City General Plan in 1976.

On the other hand, linked to this, in the first years of the 1970s, the City Planning Department also tried to find ways to categorize priority action areas and necessary interventions according to the quality of their living environments. To do so, scientific data to support their own implication in existing initiatives in downgraded areas, such as the Mano district were needed. In order to gather strong evidence to support such kinds of public investment, the department adopted the so-called Community Renewal Program methodology, which was being experimented in New York City at the time. To facilitate the urban analysis, this method divided the municipal residential areas into small units of roughly 1 ha, called "*chou-chou-moku*,"[8] similar in size to a superblock. Detailed data were collected for each unit according to five overlaying topics: "dwelling dense areas" (old wooden house density), "dwelling-industrial mixed areas," "road maintenance" (undeveloped neighborhood roads), "maintenance of community-related facilities" (e.g., parks), and "core" strategic development districts. Then, the layers were overlapped to create synthetic maps and identify priority action areas. With this, a new public action zoning system was considered. It defined residential environment conservation, rehabilitation and improvement, and redevelopment areas[9] (Tarumi, 2012). The results of the analysis were presented in September 1977 in the shape of "environment *karte*"[10] and distributed to the residents to encourage discussion of the definition of necessary measures (Kobayashi, 2014, 2018). Of course, the results presented by these *karte* pointed at the Mano district as one the areas that most required the application of countermeasures. In this way, based on the objective results provided by the analysis indicators, the actions argued for by machizukuri movements in the Mano district were acknowledged and embraced by the public administration. From this, public efforts were put into the development of a specific action model.

Mr Tarumi, who was responsible for these tasks at the Kobe Municipal Government, was also in charge of machizukuri in the Mano district. The Mano district, in response to a suggestion made by Mayor Miyazaki in 1971, had organized periodic round-table informal discussions hosted by

22 *Shigeru Satoh*

the head of the Nagata Ward. Through them, the main objective was to spread awareness among community leaders and to discuss "machizukuri," of which no one had yet a clear image.

During this time, even though fundamental rules to develop general machizukuri were envisioned, the formulation of a clear machizukuri concept was not achieved, and discussions continued without a clear plan. Under these circumstances, at the call of Mr Tarumi, machizukuri round-table talk-in discussions "with the help of experts, and representatives of diverse groups, started in 1977" (Tarumi, 2012).

These talk-in sessions were regarded as preparatory meetings for the design and development of machizukuri plans, but now based on the already existing data of the various analysis *karte*. From the following year, in 1978, a total of five small intensive meetings were conducted. In the final round, 22 people gathered for the preparation of a "machizukuri discussion meeting." In December of the same year, the group was finally established in order to define a Machizukuri Plan for the following two years. Thus, while the environmental *karte* studies allowed spotting and addressing specific problems, machizukuri aimed at collective evaluation and co-creation, and of a future image for the areas. This would be essential in changing people's motivation.

One of the key figures of this process was Yuji Miyanishi, familiar with the activities in the Mano area. At the time, he was a fellow student at Professor Kichiemon Kawana's[11] group in Tokyo Metropolitan University, under which direction he developed community *karte* for Kochi City and Kobe City. In this context, the group started to focus on the Mano district. "Yuji Miyanishi played a key role in organizing the machizukuri plan while gathering the residents opinions and adjusting the plan based on the city s institutional system and organizational structure" (Tarumi, 2012). Miyanishi has since then been involved in the machizukuri process of the Mano district.

The third period of machizukuri in Mano (1978–85): machizukuri plans and legal assessment

The "Mano district machizukuri discussion meeting," established in 1978, gathered community group leaders from 15 *jichi-kai* community associations and 12 keypersons inside the district (such as shop owners, factory owners, and women's associations) in cooperation with four academics, experts, and four city government officials. This unified under one single platform the various working groups that existed in the area. From this, in 1980, the group created a Machizukuri Plan to envision the "future of the district in 20 years" (see Figure 3.1). The plan worked as an official proposal and was presented to the Mano District residents and the City Government. Thereafter, in 1980, the group expanded and formalized into the "Mano Machizukuri Promotion Council." However, at the time, no preestablished procedure existed to allow the government to formalize and implement these kinds of plans. Consequently, bottom-up ideas were not directly linked to governmental plans.

In 1981, following the ongoing actions, and facing these new legal needs, Kobe city created the so-called "Machizukuri Ordinance," which became a certification tool for the proposed plans.

In 1980, the District Planning system had been introduced in the City Planning Law. This meant that within the framework of this law the definition of some planning aspects is delegated to the local government, which was obliged to define clear ordinances. However, Kobe city established an independent Machizukuri Ordinance, separated from the City Planning Law, in order to promote comprehensive machizukuri through autonomous community initiatives. Besides, in response to the movements in the Mano district, Kobe city decided to support and officially adopt the Machizukuri Plans that had been defined by the Machizukuri Council as part of the planning strategy of the municipal administration. These Machizukuri Plans covered a broader area than ordinary district planning ordinances.

In this context, Machizukuri Ordinances were institutionalized in the form of autonomous ordinances. Through the official "Kobe city planning and machizukuri agreement ordinance," the Mayor of Kobe city finally accredited the Mano Machizukuri Promotion Council to develop the Machizukuri Plan that had been presented in 1980. Added to this, Kobe City adopted also a special "Mano District Plan" as part of the agreement, which was legally binding inside the city planning law. This helped to promote the development of actions proposed in the Machizukuri Plan, such as small parks, small-scale redevelopment initiatives, construction of daycare-leisure centres, and so forth.

The agreement between Kobe city together with the Mano Machizukuri Promotion Council on the Machizukuri Plan was based on two main pillars, defining rules and designing the physical environment. This implied that both bodies played essential roles in its realization, and also meant that in order to make participation of local residents happen, the activities of the Council had to reflect the needs and hopes of the general population. On the other hand, the role of the Council was also to help these requests be reflected in the public works promoted by the Public Administration in the area. We can say thus that the intermediate stakeholders, machizukuri "producers," played a key role bridging, coordinating, and leading local residents and the Administration.

The fourth period of machizukuri in Mano (1985–): the gradual progress of machizukuri projects

The Mano district was later designated "Model Project for the improvement of living environments" by the Ministry of Construction. Based on

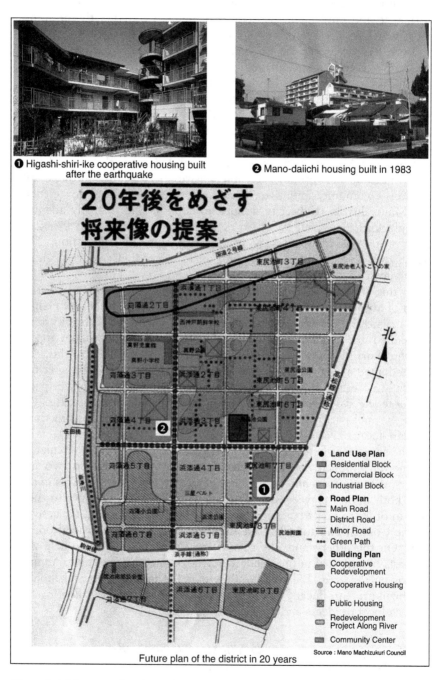

Figure 3.1 Mano machizukuri plan and projects.

The first generation 25

this new status, in 1984, Kobe city presented a "support menu" to the local community, which including possible projects to define the implementation of the 1980 Plan.

This included, for example, a proposal to improve the street pattern in the neighborhood through a north–south road axis that crossed the centre of the district. Along this road, a program called "Coexistence of Public Housing with Cooperative Redevelopment of *Nagaya*[12] areas" was implemented (e.g., after reconstruction of detached houses and traditional *nagaya* townhouses into apartment blocks, the original property owners were granted the property of extra floors and the use of store space and commercial locals, 107 public housing units were created in the upper floors). Besides, road improvement, cooperative redevelopment, improvement of local parks and public assembly rooms, etc. were carried out while being mutually connected. Such neighborhood maintenance and improvement actions progressed slowly, as they required carefully seeking the agreement of landowners involved in the different projects through gradual machizukuri practice.

Then, in 1990, the "Model Project for the improvement of living environments" was replaced by the "Community Living Environment Improvement Project." It provided a more specific second phase plan to assist the continuation of the machizukuri project. Then, in 1995, the Hanshin-Awaji Earthquake caused great damage to the area, although thanks to the collaboration of local residents in extinguishing the first outbreaks of fire, the damage was limited. Besides, based on the area improvement plan that had been prepared, reconstruction projects were accelerated. Thus, ten years after the disaster, the different projects of various scales that had been encouraged since the 1980s were embedded in the neighborhood.

The three principles established by the Mano machizukuri process

The circumstances described above made of Mano a reference case representative of the first machizukuri generation. Taking it as an example, three principles can be identified.

First, the limits of the area in which residents would develop machizukuri activities in an autonomous way were identified. The Machizukuri Council was then formed with representatives of the *jichi-kai* and other groups in the area. This council represents the residents and takes on the responsibility of promoting and managing machizukuri activities.

Second, under a clear institutionalized cooperation between the local government and Machizukuri Council, joint efforts must focus on the realization of certain public objectives based on a plan agreed by both parties. To that end, the Administration provides support to the district in the form of human and financial assistance, or public investment.

26 *Shigeru Satoh*

Third, both the Machizukuri Council and the administration must authorize professional experts to provide support to the activity of the council, and the conditions under which the experts can carry out these continuous support activities.

Evaluations of the Mano machizukuri process

The Mano machizukuri process is a typical example of the first generation. The project goes from problem-solving to co-creation and thus presents a contradiction: its organizational structure is very formal but at the same time, it supports co-creation. First, whole action districts in which problems could be tackled in an autonomous way were delimited, and taken as a "machi." Visions for the "machi" were created, and then machizukuri activities were developed in such areas. Through this, the project explored the different theoretical roles that machizukuri could have.

In addition, the project presents two main features: on the one hand, the energetic activities developed by local residents; and in parallel, the use of special Machizukuri Ordinances to promote actions in areas that required improvements according to official living environment *karte*. This well-regulated system characterized the first generation of machizukuri and became one of the basic principles of machizukuri later on. However, such a solid and rigid organization (requiring the creation of specific action groups, plan, etc.) was sometimes ponderous, and subsequent machizukuri developed into a multilayered, more open system that was not necessarily bound by this principle.

At this point, it is important to understand how the very special case of Mano has been perceived. According to the academic expert Toru Inui,[13] "the Mano machizukuri experience spread throughout the country as a beautiful story that put the focus on local residents"[14] (Mano Machizukuri Promotion Council, 2005). The case was idealized and became a touchstone for machizukuri practice among experts. However, Inui, who first joined activities in the Mano district after the Hanshin-Awaji earthquake, had the chance to get involved in the process, interact with local residents, and experience first-hand the situation in the areas. Thus, he was able to understand that in reality the machizukuri process had in fact gotten into murky waters, and most of the local people were indifferent to it and did not take action. Yet, he recognized that the "machizukuri centered on local residents" described in books and reference articles was rather different from reality.

Within the action areas there were also local groups that focused on "soft" aspects, such as welfare for the elderly, and not only on the improvement of the built environment. But as mentioned above, the success of the project did not only rely on community participation. In parallel, the development of measures by the local administration contributed significantly to a smooth development of the machizukuri process.

The first generation   27

It is possible to recognize here the importance of establishing subtle relationships between powerful local leaders and the people who can support them, and even more, the people that are indifferent to them. However, the idea of a "beautiful story" that made local residents the main focus of the project spread fast and became widely known. In response to this, Inui defended the importance of local people in the Mano area presenting their own personal experience.

To better understand the generalized ideas in the case of Mano inherited by subsequent machizukuri practice, the following four points summarize the assessment of the project given by academic experts at the time.

First, in general, the case was regarded as an outstanding endeavor but at the same time, it was considered exceptional and rare in the Japanese context, and thus, not fit for replication. In other words, this became an important reason not to attempt similar machizukuri actions.

Second, some government officials assumed that local residents alone were able to propel machizukuri practice in the Mano area. Thus, if taking this as a reference, the administration should provide support to communities only after such reactive movements emerged. This was the reason why machizukuri practice was not actively encouraged by public bodies.

Third, understanding the reality of the Mano machizukuri process, experts also underlined that centering decision-making and implementation of actions on local residents might entail serious difficulties. Thus, it was assumed that government officials and experts should take the lead and try to promote machizukuri.

Fourth, another posture praised the spirit and soul of the "if you try, you can do it" defended by the experience in Mano. But at the same time, experts showed a deep understanding of its complexities. Taking Mano as an objective reference case, actors involved in other machizukuri processes argued that the careful study and understanding of the local circumstances could help stakeholders "wake up" and design unique actions. The final objective would be to devise original suitable ways to tackle local problems adapted to each particular local context.

Thus, the "beautiful story," even if having emerged to some extent from a misunderstanding, became the basis of the third and fourth postures above, which, in turn, became the basis of machizukuri development. Furthermore, we can say that the first machizukuri generation provided successful prototypes for subsequent machizukuri practice. These cases became examples of cooperation between ambitious residents' leaders, the public administration, and experts, from their own different standing points, to overcome the various conflicts that normally appear throughout these processes. This underlines the importance of presenting the case of Mano in its full complexity; it neither needs to be "softened," transforming the different issues encountered into a "beautiful story," nor isolated,

28 *Shigeru Satoh*

considering it a once-in-a-lifetime singular case. On the contrary, the approach adopted here was not such a good practice example to the point where it could not be taken as a down-to-earth reference. Thus, the case was taken as a basis for subsequent machizukuri and overcome by them.

Subsequent machizukuri in Kobe city

Machizukuri activities in the Mano area have continued ever since. The establishment of Machizukuri Councils by means of Machizukuri Ordinances was consolidated locally. However, in 1982, the Nakasone Cabinet, of neoliberal tendency, was formed.[15] Under the new policies, the national system and budget allocation for urban development did not expand to include projects for the improvement of dense built-up areas as had been previously expected (Tarumi, 2012).

Later, in 1990, regulations were established to create "community welfare centers" for each elementary school ward in the whole city[16] through what were called *"Fureai*[17] Machizukuri Projects." The purpose of this was to develop machizukuri dedicated to making everyday life comfortable, in close communication with the local civil society, aiming at promoting self-support and cooperation of all citizens, including senior citizens, disabled people, children, and other civil groups. Thus, in this case, machizukuri promotion related to welfare and soft assets, rather than focusing on the built environment. To do so, following the above-mentioned zoning in elementary school wards, *"Fureai* Machizukuri Councils" were established combining various local organizations, such as residents associations, women s associations, local children's welfare committee councils, volunteer groups, etc. While the Councils operated the centers in an independent way, Kobe city subsidized part of the expenses to support various activities in fields such as welfare, environment, disaster prevention, and education. Thus a double management system was established. Machizukuri ordinances granted specific rights to carry out machizukuri activities related to improving the built living environments (hard assets), and supported the establishment of "Machizukuri Councils" in particular districts. In addition to this, "Fureai Machizukuri Councils" were created to deal with comprehensive issues related to public welfare leverage for the whole city (soft assets).

In parallel, in 1993, just before the Great Hanshin-Awaji Earthquake, Machizukuri Councils had been established in 12 districts in Kobe city, which required proper measures for the improvement of the physical environment (e.g., "Mano District Machizukuri Council"). The action areas of these Councils occupied 880 ha, 14 percent of the total built-up area (Yasuda and Miwa, 1993). In addition, many of them had already started their activity.

Under these circumstances, the Great Hanshin-Awaji Earthquake occurred in 1995. Kobe city, based on the past results, called upon

The first generation   29

Machizukuri Councils to carry out urban redevelopment and land readjustment projects inside their areas of influence.[18] Besides, a system to authorize them as official planning subjects was also introduced. During the reconstruction process, the local administration and the machizukuri councils for reconstruction, urban planners and machizukuri practitioners, cooperated and the recovery proceeded smoothly apart from occasional disagreements.

With this, the value of reconstruction efforts thanks to the "power of machizukuri" was once again recognized, continuing up until today. As a result, the Mano district has become a benchmark for community-led machizukuri, and has been featured in numerous papers, books, and publications. Among them, the publication in 2005 of "The Longest Machizukuri in Japan: Commemoration of Ten Years of Post-Earthquake Reconstructions" (by the Mano Machizukuri Promotion Council) requires a special mention. So far, the case of Mano had been presented from the point of view of academics and experts, but this time the publication was written, edited, and published by those who had been involved in the process, the local residents. This was not just a mere compilation of facts, but it also allowed reading between the lines, giving voice to the different people involved in the machizukuri process.

The case has been highly valued among academics and has been treated as an exceptional and very unique example of machizukuri development. Yet, on the other hand, sometimes these can be one-sided interpretations that greatly emphasize its exceptional character. This has discouraged practitioners from replicating it or taking it as a reference. Nevertheless, as the publication proves, the Mano machizukuri process emerged from a very universal endeavor, from the will to take care and think about one's living environment.

This spirit became the basis of subsequent machizukuri movements, and the systems developed through it will become an important foundation for the second and third machizukuri generations.

Improvements in neglected high-density built-up wooden areas as an anti-disaster solution: examples in Tokyo

Another situation that required the development of related machizukuri activities was that of the traditional built-up density in Japanese cities. The majority of urban areas in Japan consisted of wooden buildings, especially in poor urban contexts where old houses were concentrated along narrow labyrinthine alleys.

In such places, the quality of the living environment was generally low. In addition, due to the high concentration of wooden houses, these areas are vulnerable to disaster. The risk of collapse of structures in the event of a large earthquake, and consequent fire propagation, is considerable. On the other hand, in these areas, from a social point of view, it is possible to

30 *Shigeru Satoh*

find strong human bonds that shape the local communities. As a consequence, aware of these dangers, implementing disaster prevention actions that address the improvement of such a complex urban tissue was an urgent priority for the local residents as well.

The "Kawazumi sixty-nine period theory" contends that there is a specific period of time in which the probability that the cyclic Kanto Earthquake will strike Tokyo again is higher. Taking this into account (according to calculations), in the latter half of the 1960s, the improvement of the disaster prevention performance of the lower-city high-density built-up wooden areas that spread in the eastern part of Tokyo seemed to be an urgent task.

At the beginning of the 1970s, the Koto Disaster Prevention Plan was put into practice by means of vast redevelopment plans (which included the embankment of riversides and the creation of new evacuation spaces serving wide urban areas). On the other hand, in 1975, the Tokyo Metropolitan Government assumed the potential high risk of the region in case of repetition of the Great Kanto Earthquake. This was an urgent measure for both the city of Tokyo and for the different district administrations, which conducted a risk assessment in which five risk levels were identified for each *chou-chou-moku* analysis sector (see the Mano case). However, it seemed difficult to completely reconstruct densely built-up wooden urban areas through urban redevelopment and land readjustment projects. Moreover, local residents did not want their familiar environment (social and physical) to be replaced by large-scale public urban development projects, and instead wished to improve the areas while maintaining the existing community. In other words, here, disaster prevention measures had to be tackled through novel forms of machizukuri. These kinds of projects required that residents took action on their own initiative to develop such ideas. Thus, the administration and the local community had to work together, with the assistance of experts, and seek suitable methods to gradually improve the living environment.

Efforts towards machizukuri by Minobe's reformist Tokyo Metropolitan Government

By the end of the 1960s and the beginning of the 1970s, left-wing parties won the elections in major cities like Yokohama, Tokyo, and Kyoto. Initially, these new governments attempted to establish community or machizukuri councils for promoting participatory systems. These new types of community councils were partially inspired by foreign models. The idea came from a will to create more democratic and heterogeneous community organizations that could give voice to a wider range of people, beyond the social groups represented in traditional community associations. However, these traditional groups still had a strong presence inside Japanese communities and ultimately, the new boards never overthrew their power.

Since then, both types of group have coexisted, sharing and even overlapping topics, tasks, functions, and people. Nevertheless, their coexistence has somehow helped improve the social environment.

In 1971, Minobe's[19] reformist Metropolitan Goverment (1967–79), through the Tokyo Planning and Coordination Bureau, published in the form of a proposal the idea of "a Tokyo of public squares and blue skies," and presented it to the Tokyo citizens as a political pledge for his two-term consecutive mandate. Inside it, the idea of a "civil minimum" was the main pillar of the proposal. In it, six "Model Plans for Local Community Units" were presented along with color plans according to the features of area. The proposal aimed at being implemented through "autonomous machizukuri conducted by local citizens" (Tokyo Metropolitan Government, 1971).[20] In order to achieve this, the Tokyo Metropolitan Bureau of Development collaborated with external research institutes to conduct a series of research studies for the improvement of the local community environment. As part of it, in 1995, the laboratory of Takamasa Yoshisaka, in the Urban Planning Department of Waseda University, was commissioned with defining a specific vision for the improvement of livable districts ("Tokyo-Proposal for a City Vision," March 1976 (Tokyo Metropolitan Government, 1976)). This report defined three Tokyo Model Districts, for which human-scale visions of the areas respecting the local resources were designed.

In 1975, for the 23 wards of Tokyo, a new system was established by which ward-mayors were elected by the direct decision of local residents. This meant that mayors did not directly depend anymore on the Metropolitan Government,[21] and that they had the authority to define their own urban strategies. Even though it did not become a general trend, some of the new mayors attempted locally the implementation of particular urban visions and new policy making was promoted. In this context, residents' participatory machizukuri in each district became an important subject for reformist local mayors, who shared the same political views as Minobe, and were eager to deliver his vision for "a Tokyo of public squares and blue skies."

Various efforts to realize such a vision were developed. Above all, districts that most needed disaster prevention measures were chosen, and designated "model districts," which embarked on participatory machizukuri processes.

Groping for ways toward machizukuri: the case of the Setagaya ward

In the middle of the 1970s, after the reform of the management structure for the Tokyo wards, the administration of the Setawaya ward was one of the first to aim at developing a new system and to work on machizukuri with clear goals. Besides, the transfer of authority over urban planning

32 Shigeru Satoh

matters from Tokyo Metropolitan Government to the ward facilitated the initiative. During the mandate of reformist Mayor Ohba, activities focused on improving the living environment of local residents as a means of disaster prevention.

The Setagaya ward already had a population of about 750,000 inhabitants at the time, and presented a strong public awareness. Then, with the involvement of various experts, Setagaya was consolidated as a sort of machizukuri mecca. The Setagaya Ward is generally considered a high-end residential area. However, several parts of the district were re-urbanized without a clear improvement of old spontaneous road patterns.[22] Besides, the open land lots of single-family detached homes were fragmented (e.g., relinquishing parts of their gardens), new constructions appeared in them, and the urban density increased. Thus, in 1975, the comprehensive risk assessment study developed by the Tokyo Metropolitan Government spotted many high-risk areas.

At the time, by request of the Setagaya ward, the CRCPI,[23] directed by Professor Yoshisaka, started research in the areas. With the contents of the "Tokyo-Proposal for a City Vision" report (see previous section) in mind, the group worked on how to implement this vision. The results were presented in the "Notes on the Setagaya Ward Machizukuri" (Setakaya Ward, 1977, 1978).[24] The first publication focusing on dense urban areas inside N7 beltway in Tokyo, and the second on areas outside the ring where farmlands still remained, they both presented possible measures at neighborhood level. Here, as in the case of Kobe city, the data were analyzed according to different *chou-chou-moku* zones.

At the time, the recently graduated Takashi Inoue, who was responsible for the research, mentioned:

> I have walked through every street and corner of the neighborhood. The "method of discovery" (see Chapter 6) was in the back of my head, but first of all, I needed to start looking and feeling it with my own body.

Thus, even without a clear method, this was the first sign of a war against the rigid concept of the city by a young planner with a traditional background in architecture. In this way, the academic research team and the officials from the public sector decided to understand first the problems of the whole ward, to set targets among them, and to promote dedicated machizukuri actions for each district.

First, in 1979, local residents of the Kitazawa district were invited to hold a roundtable discussion and to present three alternative approaches. Then, based on these ideas, the creation of a plan for urban improvement was proposed. Residents agreed and a tentative Machizukuri Council was established. Similar to the Mano district in Kobe city, this was a council that operated in the area targeted by the plan for its specific development

The first generation   33

and through a community agreement. The first three alternative approaches presented to local residents were: widening streets narrower than four meters, eliminating street corners, and improving neighborhood playparks built by the community. These were all measures for the improvement of the living environment, and thus, for the rehabilitation of the "machi." Through them, residents, cooperating with the administration and providing small pieces of land, would be able to improve the living environment of the whole district. As a resident, this was also an opportunity to ease the anxiety about the possible consequences of disaster in the neighborhood and to take preventive actions.

At the time, the word "workshop" had never been used by the Machizukuri Council. In any case, similar tools, such as writing different opinions and ideas around a map, were used during participatory discussions to ensure that everyone's ideas were sufficiently reflected. Twenty-five council meetings were held, and "machizukuri proposals for action" were put together. This proposal was submitted to the ward's Mayor and shared among local residents through the Machizukuri Council s information bulletin.

In June 1982, the Setagaya ward established the "Setagaya Machizukuri Ordinance." Based on it, the Kitazawa district was voted by the ward assembly as the first "Machizukuri Promotion District," and a specific project budget was also secured. In addition, the ward presented the locals with a "machizukuri basic plan" to develop specific projects of physical character. Locals discussed the plan and later, in 1994, a special ordinance authorized the creation of a formal "Kitazawa Machizukuri Council"[25] to start working on the plan (according to CRCPI, 1985, and interview with Kakuro Inoue in May 2019). Thus, the machizukuri process in the Kitazawa district, in which both local government and experts were involved, became an important model for participatory planning supported by public funds.

On the other hand, inside the Setagaya ward, the Taishido district was one of the areas that presented the biggest challenges facing disaster prevention. In 1980 a briefing meeting to present this situation to locals was held, but unexpectedly it triggered a wave of strong criticism. Local residents, who had opposed the development of high-rise buildings in the area before, did not feel comfortable with the idea of a machizukuri project led by experts and the government, as the Setagaya ward suggested. On top of that, there was a general atmosphere of distrust toward the ward administration, which did not provide sufficient support to these opposition movements. In this way, machizukuri in the Taishido district became an opportunity for local residents, the administration, and experts to seriously consider the meaning and implications of residents' participation.

Going through various conflicts, the Taishido district opened up the way for machizukuri transition from the first to the second generation (see Chapter 4).

34 *Shigeru Satoh*

Machizukuri for the improvemnt of living environments in high-density built-up wooden areas: the case of Kyojima district in the Sumida Ward, Tokyo

The Kyojima district, in the Sumida ward of Tokyo, scored the highest possible rank (rank 5) in the Risk Survey conducted by the Tokyo Metropolitan Government. The area had formed immediately after the 1923 Kanto earthquake outside the urban areas affected by the disaster. At the time, poor and small wooden *nagaya* townhouses were built for the victims and workers who engaged in reconstruction projects. With no proper urban plans in place, wetlands and rivers were reclaimed, and houses were built closely along winding farm roads. Later, the area escaped American air raids during World War II, and the dense urban pattern, packed with simple wooden dwellings, remained. In the 1960s, some of the constructions were rebuilt into two-storey houses, and the urban density increased even more. This made of it one of the highest risk areas in case of earthquake in Tokyo.

In 1971, the Metropolitan Government announced the intention to develop a conventional slum-clearance plan for the whole Kyojima district, which faced strong opposition from local residents. In this area, despite the old constructions and the dense urban pattern, relations between locals were cordial and community bonds were strong. While aware and concerned about the disaster threat, local residents appreciated their living environment. The *chou-nai-kai* for example, which represented a conservative standpoint and had a strong autonomy, had promoted the placement of fire extinguisher boxes on the corners of the main streets in the neighborhood. With it, whenever there was a fire, the residents cooperated in putting it out, avoiding great fires from spreading, and taking great pride in it.

Based on this context, research to define a plan and action method for machizukuri aiming at the improvement of this living environment was conducted by a group led by Professor Yukio Ohtani from the University of Tokyo. The results were summarized in the "Research Report for the Kyojima District in Sumida Ward: Essays on District Planning" (Tokyo Metropolitan Planning and Coordination Bureau, 1974). Building types were extracted, reconstruction methods examined, and the establishment of a residents' council for consensus building was proposed. Furthermore, the Metropolitan Government Tokyo conducted a complementary questionnaire research with local residents. Its results clarified that the majority of the local population considered that measures were necessary, and from this, discussions with local associations followed.

Later, the Ministry of Construction legislated the "Model Project for the Improvement of Living Environments" to provide these projects with an effective official support system. The Kyojima District was one of the first cases approved by the Ministry in 1979 to benefit from this system

The "Model Project" functioned as a test case that partially and gradually adapted the method of the slum-clearance project for the whole area to the real needs of the district. That is, in a part of the district, low-rent public housing (called community housing in Japan) are built for residents involved in the project; in addition, the roads within the district are partially widened to reduce disaster risk. These partial projects did not require involving the whole district population, instead, they allowed focusing only on the necessary parts, leaving general road and park planning, among others, to the administration. However, to encourage the development of small-scale cooperative redevelopment projects for other old *nagaya* townhouse areas the government still needed to coordinate private landowners and residents. This type of public intervention in the development of partial private housing projects is called "living environment improvement type," a machizukuri type that aims at improving local housing and urban spaces through the promotion and linkage of cooperative mixed-use block projects.

In 1980, a first briefing session was held in the Kyojima district to encourage local project implementation through participatory machizukuri. Local residents presented diverse standpoints with respect to machizukuri. As local associations (neighborhood, merchant, etc.) were well established in the area, the administration addressed these groups first. The leaders were in fact concerned about the whole district, and not only their main work areas, so conversations proceeded smoothly and an agreement was reached at this point. These leaders were in a position to explain machizukuri to the rest of the population. However, residents did not normally show interest in such initiatives unless the projects directly affected their own lands or dwellings.

Thus, in 1982, the "Outline for a Machizukuri Plan" was agreed. It defined strategic uses zones inside the district and measures for the improvement of each zone. "Community Housing"[26] was also proposed following the "rolling method"[27] (see Figure 3.2). The plan presented a neighborhood where homes, factories, and shops could coexist, and where the existing community life can continue.

These public projects did not plan new street patterns and each intervention followed the existing winding roads. Nevertheless, these partial interventions incorporated general ideas and objectives for gradual regeneration of the urban pattern of the neighborhood; among others, developing different small-scale private three- to four-storey cooperative housing blocks, or relocating and concentrating together factories, shops, and dwellings within the area.

A strategy for the improvement of road connections to facilitate transit, evacuation, and access of rescue services in case of disaster was also defined. This strategy did not involve imposing completely new street

36 Shigeru Satoh

patterns, but using existing roads and connecting to them to new small axes. This meant that these new roads would be achieved by encouraging landowners to develop small cooperative housing projects, which would save space for the future road, and once linked, would achieve the desired street layout. Based on this idea, the gradual implementation of small projects was promoted (Yamamoto, 1999).

After that, in 1982, the Tokyo Metropolitan Government established the "Kyojima Machizukuri Public Corporation" to support activity in the area, and worked on the implementation of the project.

In this way, disaster prevention machizukuri in the Kyojima district was developed in the form of "improvement type" machizukuri through three main methods: (1) the establishment of a Machizukuri Council through direct participation of local residents; (2) a strategic action zoning and gradual widening of roads within the district; and (3) a stage-by-stage housing renovation strategy through various methods, including "community housing" and cooperative redevelopment. However, one of the main weaknesses of this approach was that, to achieve the desired urban regeneration, it was necessary to implement a series of strategically located projects that required the coordination of individual rights agreements. Thus, relying on the success of local consensus to develop private initiatives and at the same time achieve the desired general vision for the neighborhood was troublesome.

As mentioned above, the case of machizukuri development in the Kyojima district represents the local opposition to the complete razing and redevelopment of public projects. In this case, in the middle of an attempt to preserve the local community, the administration and experts conducted machizukuri activities in line with local desires. In response to the will of local residents, ambitious young public workers who had experienced the turbulent social context before 1970, architects and planners who wanted to explore new directions for city planning, and university academics tried to develop cutting-edge ways for machizukuri practice oriented toward the preservation of local society. However, despite having such an ordered approach, it was difficult to gain the understanding of residents and landowners when it came to individual projects, which did not proceed as originally planned.

In comparison, the neighboring Mukoujima area, in the Ichitera-Kototoi district, presented alternatives to overcome such problems. Here, more autonomous initiatives were developed; this chapter will address them later. Kyojima stayed in touch with and was inspired by the parallel approaches that were emerging already during the second machizukuri generation.

Later, the Kyojima Machizukuri Public Corporation was transferred from the Metropolitan Government to the ward administration, establishing a system closer to the area, and promoting "improvement type" machizukuri. After the Great Hanshin-Awaji Earthquake, disaster prevention

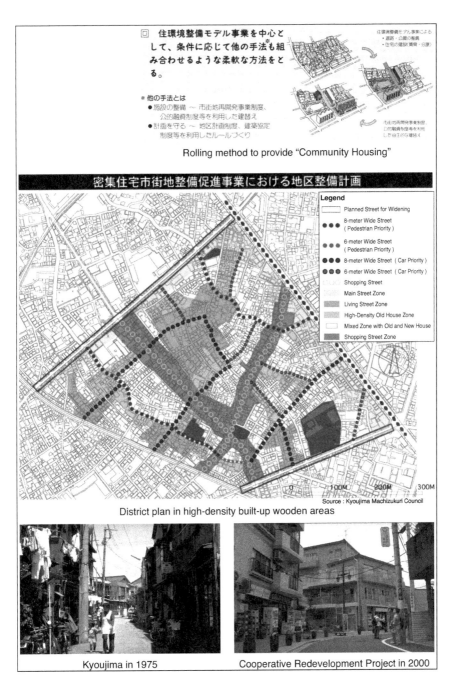

Figure 3.2 Kyojima machizukuri plan and projects.

38 Shigeru Satoh

became an even bigger issue in policy development; even the traditional Urban Renaissance Agency[28] participated in such projects, which were implemented intensively. For example, the sites occupied by factories around the private railway station adjacent to the district were the object of large-scale redevelopment projects, which brought satisfactory results from the point of view of disaster prevention. The convenience of living next to the city center attracted the younger generation and brought a popularity boom to *shitamachi* downtown areas, changing drastically the appearance of the areas. Under these circumstances, influenced by new machizukuri activities, movements appeared even in the Kyojima district.

However, how to rebuild the community integrating the new and the old residents remains a pending issue to this day.

Machizukuri aiming at the protection of living environments

"Right to sunlight" campaigns against "building kougai"

In the early 1970s, the disputes caused by the so-called "building *kougai*" turned out to become serious social issues between the residents, developers, and the administration. Before 1969, urban density was controlled by absolute height limit control measures. However, building codes were reset and adopted the Floor Area Ratio (FAR) to favor certain high-rise projects. After 1969, when the "Absolute Height Limit" of the allowed constructions inside a block was eliminated, high-rise buildings developed in great contrast to the existing environment in various places throughout Japan. This became a serious nuisance to the living environment to the extent that the term "*kougai*" was retaken, and "building *kougai*" was coined, putting high-rise buildings on the same level with other types of *kougai*-pollution. This made it clear that urban planning and building regulations were ineffective, and residents, with the support of experts, had to stand up for conservation of living and historical environments.[29] In this context, the machizukuri movement appeared as a complementary strategy that rapidly achieved great importance.

Among the many opposition movements to new developments, the movement of Karasuyama Teramachi district, in the Setagaya ward of Tokyo, represents a case of machizukuri practice born from opposition movements (Itoh, 1978). As a result of the process, the existing rich greenery in the area and the local living environment were almost completely preserved.

In the early 1970s, a religious organization had come up with a sudden plan for rebuilding a large temple complex in the district. In this case, if only urban planning regulations had been applied, the local environment would have been destroyed by the project. Regulations were ineffective against the proposed construction plans, which would have blocked solar access in neighboring residential areas. Added to this, residents and support groups became conscious that this project would have a critical impact on the ecosystem of the area (e.g., the underground water system).

As a reaction, tenacious negotiations took place between residents' organizations, supported by theoretical claims by experts, and project supporters. The opposition groups succeeded in obtaining a reduction in the height and scale of the construction project, and taking advantage of this momentum, the movement proceeded to develop other activities aiming at the conservation of the living environment in general. This led to the creation of a "machizukuri charter."

In the Taishido district of the Setagaya ward in Tokyo, in the first half of the 1970s, a construction plan for a 15-storey high-rise condominium was presented to the local community. The residents carried out a fierce resistance movement, which would later transform into machizukuri practice.

The theoretical leader of this movement, the lawyer Yoshitaka Igarashi, had experience as a lawyer in trials, and was key to establishing new regulations such as the "right to sunlight."[30]

Movement towards the conservation of traditional culture

Another reference example is that of the Fushimi district in Kyoto, in the early 1980s. Here, the traditional *machiya* town houses had been maintained up to modern times. Unexpectedly, a proposal to build a high-rise block of apartments was made, triggering an intense local opposition campaign in reaction.

This movement not only underlined the importance of the traditional townscape, but also the activities, knowledge, and human links that supported it. This included the various traditional building techniques and craftsmen, and the so-called "culture of the *machi*-people," which is the basis of these cultural practices. Thus, these lifestyles that take place is a particular space and make use of its resources are linked to environmental culture in its broad meaning. However, in this case, loose regulations did not limit such harmful projects, which could be accepted by law. And so, the opposition group lost the claim in court. Nevertheless, as a consequence, a machizukuri movement supporting the conservation of the traditional evolving townscape was born.

Before, in the 1970s, Otaru city in Hokkaido witnessed a movement to preserve "canals and stone warehouses as cultural assets." Local people were familiar with canals, which were a symbol of this port city. As landfill plans for the construction of a wide road advanced, locals stood up to protect a group of traditional jagged roof warehouses in the Arihoro area. This event triggered in 1973 the creation of the "meeting to protect the Otaru canal" movement, which developed various activities with the support of experts, and achieved the reduction of landfills by half. When news spread, the "canals and townscape of Otaru" became known

40 *Shigeru Satoh*

nationwide, and the machizukuri activities that followed succeeded in regenerating the town as a touristic spot. However, this movement addressed the whole urban structure, creating conflicts between political and residents' groups, and presenting difficulties different from other machizukuri projects (Horikawa, 2018).

In any case, from the 1970s to the beginning of the 1980s, there was a major paradigm shift. During this period, which has been called the "first generation" of machizukuri practice, resistance movements against the destruction of historical and traditional assets took place all over Japan. This created a momentum that fostered the transformation of such movements and the birth of creative machizukuri. Whenever urban planning systems could not assist the improvement and conservation of calm living environments, the cooperation of residents, experts, and municipalities produced alternative methods to address these delicate dimensions of the urban environment. This is what we now call machizukuri.

Protection of historical townscapes

In historical quarters composed of traditional *machiya*-style wooden buildings, the fast pace of rapid economic growth was gradually replacing historical constructions and features, and thus depriving local business districts of their cultural attractiveness. In this context, movements for the preservation of these declining old streets started.

Parallel to this, in the European context, added to the destruction of a considerable number of historical city centers during World War II, cities had to confront a prevailing modern urbanism that imposed over traditional patterns. To face such a trend, France, for instance, passed the *Law on the Safeguarding and Valorisation of Historic Centres* in 1962, which introduced the concept of historic conservation areas. In the UK as well, the *Civic Amenity Act*, issued in 1967, recognized the collective value as a reason for preservation of urban areas of artistic or historical interest. Both instruments sought to legislate policies and create plans to preserve the attractive character of historical city centers.

In Japan, the Law for the Preservation of Ancient Capitals, such as Kyoto, Kamakura, and Asuka, was enacted in 1966. Later, in 1975, motivated by a growing national interest to protect cultural assets, the (Important) Conservation Districts for Groups of Traditional Buildings[31] was introduced, extending the national protection to "historical townscapes" (including scenic townscapes, blocks, and groups of buildings in both urban and rural areas). In order to bring this law into effect, experts had to work hand-in-hand with local residents, and this made machizukuri proceed.

The movement for the preservation of historical districts in Japan was initiated in Nagizo-Tsumago. These two post towns were set next to each other along the mountain trail that connected Edo (Tokyo) and Nagoya,

The first generation   41

called the Nakasendo, which prospered as a commercial route during the Edo period. The towns took action for the preservation of their historical post-town environment and studied its regeneration. In 1974 the "Japanese Association for Historical Townscape Conservation" was created, and the movement extended nationwide, and continues to be active until today. As a consequence, architecture experts all over the country felt attracted by such preservation movements, and started to become personally involved.

Similar activities took place in other small post towns, etc., and the information exchange and cooperation progressed through experts and local activists. Although a series of surveys for the reevaluation of such areas was launched, the academic groups in architecture schools (professors and students) would be the ones who, taking the local character as their base, would work together to design a new methodology for machizukuri application in historical areas.

The term "historical townscape" (*machi-nami*) emerged from these preservation movements. Here, the "*machi*" refers to the place where the daily activities of artisans and tradesman take place, and by extension, it also refers to the culture of the community inhabiting the historical town. On the other hand, the term "preservation" (*hozon*) was also coined, meaning to protect daily activities, livelihoods, and the physical scenario in which they are formed. This also implied ultimately taking a new look at tradition, reevaluating it, and cultivating its context in its full integrity.

Such steady historical preservation activities were promoted during the first machizukuri generation, until the 1980s. From the second generation onwards, these towns will be examples of great transformation successfully integrating tourism as well. In this context, the tourism industry was also expected to appreciate the historical townscapes in the broader context, and to learn from their environmental and traditional know-how.

Chapter conclusion

Based on diverse experiences, clear principles and new methods for machizukuri practice slowly consolidated. In this first phase of machizukuri development, the ideas for the improvement of the living environment were typically implemented by means of five different strategies: (1) establishing a "Machizukuri Council" with direct participation of residents; (2) processing of district "Machizukuri Plans"; (3) making use of "Machizukuri Ordinance"; (4) developing methods for the improvement of poorly prepared residential districts and assistance to housing redevelopments, stage by stage, with the help of a district Machizukuri Plan; and (5) the amendment of the country's legal system by the Ministry of Construction to officially integrate the innovative methods listed above.

First, Machizukuri Councils had to be formed. The name "Machizukuri Council"[32] was normally used when a community group gathered with the purpose of developing a specific machizukuri project. In order to carry on with the machizukuri process democratically, a legitimate representative organization was needed. With the support of this organization, the district Machizukuri Plan was drawn up and recognized as a legitimate vision by the community.

On the other hand, for cases targeting for example, the general environmental improvement of a whole district, other names were used instead (for example "*Chiku* Council"). In these cases, the action areas of the groups practically matched the districts served by elementary schools or junior high schools.

The second tool is the Machizukuri Plan. Once the basis for machizukuri was consolidated, a future vision for the area or district, including physical space and related lifestyles, had to be established as a target image with the consensus of the local community. Then, a plan and strategy to carry out this ideal vision were needed accordingly.

From here, the third tool is the creation of a special "Machizukuri Ordinance" (Takamizawa, 1999) independently established by municipalities through council votes. This implied the official recognition of the Machizukuri Council as a municipal group and, hence, of all the decisions taken by it. In parallel, a legal basis was created, which included among others a support system for councils by representatives of the administration and experts, the introduction of tax subsidies, and the preferential adoption of various projects. This kind of machizukuri ordinance was adopted in 1980 in Kobe City and in the Setagaya Ward of Tokyo, two of the most cutting-edge community activity areas where the practice of machizukuri was already well developed.

When a district Machizukuri Council is certified by the Local Administration Council based on this ordinance, an agreement is set up between the two parties. On the one hand, the administration promises to cooperate and support the realization of the plan designed by the Machizukuri Council. On the other hand, the Machizukuri Council has to make the efforts required to carry out the plan by itself. Under such a structure, the costs for expert advisors and activities to support the activities of the Machizukuri Council are provided.[33,34]

Based on a shared vision, by means of consultation, machizukuri gradually helped realize different projects that met common targets as a way to materialize participated visions for the built environment and the local community. These projects came to be defined in the Machizukuri Plans. District Machizukuri Plan agreements were easy to obtain since they bore no legal enforceability. However, even though these plans could be informally agreed upon as a whole district plan; when proposing, for example, the widening of narrow streets or joint reconstruction projects, the necessary direct consent of the land owners could not be obtained, and thus the progress of these kinds of machizukuri projects was often difficult.

The first generation 43

By 1980, Machizukuri Plans had the support of the Machizukuri Ordinance, and yet the plans were still not legally binding (Satoh, 1999). Even at national level, an exhaustive revision of the Japanese legal system had to be prepared to address machizukuri practice. Thus, at this point, the first objective was to revise the city planning legislation in order to allow more detailed planning control. Here, in contrast to the Machizukuri Plan, "District Planning" was introduced in City Planning Law in 1980 as a system that enabled the establishment of detailed planning conditions on the architectural form and the location and composition of streets and parks within a district, with the consent of the relevant rights holders in the area. Although the agreement of the rights holders was a prerequisite, through District Planning it became possible to decide aspects as precise as the height of the buildings and the position of vertical built surfaces, helping the Machizukuri Plan become more realistic.

In addition, the "Model Project" was created. The Ministry of Construction legislated "the Model Project for improvement of the community living environment" to be an advanced reference system. Since creating a new law is always difficult, the Japanese Government dedicated a special line item in the budget to these kinds of projects and set up a system in the style of an open-call to select specific machizukuri projects.[35] The Mano and Kyojima districts were the first cases approved by the Ministry in 1979 to benefit from this system and to carry out the construction of their own community housing blocks. Projects for the improvement of community living environments could carry on from this point.

Until the early 1980s, Japanese machizukuri experienced an exponential growth, being promoted through coordination of residents, local governments, and experts. The first generation consolidated the principles of participation and decentralization, based on the initiatives of local community groups. Consequently, the development of principles, justified goals and methods, democratic systems, and procedures was of utmost importance for this first machizukuri generation.

However, although some cutting-edge practical examples were born during this period, emphasis was specially placed on theoretical ideas and on the defense of the principle of legitimacy by inclusive participation. Thus, despite the great advances in discussion and planning, the implementation of the projects agreed through machizukuri practice did not advance easily.

In this way, at the time of the full development of the machizukuri support system, Nakasone reached the national government (1982–86) and adopted a different posture. The administration, in line with with the policies of Reagan in the United States and Thatcher in the United Kingdom, aimed at establishing the neoliberal economy, without attention to social policies. Not surprisingly, urban policies nationwide also turned their focus to large-scale urban development, encouraged by the vitality of the private sector and significant deregulations. Such policies were adopted

44 *Shigeru Satoh*

all across the country, even in places like Kobe city, which had been at the forefront of machizukuri activities for the improvement of living environments.

Notes

1 Many reports and research papers exist in relation to this subject. Many authors in English have also introduced the subject to foreign readers; for example Sorensen and Funck, 2007, or Healey, 2010.

   In this case, this chapter is based mainly on the example of Mano as presented by the Mano Machizukuri Promotion Council (2005). Besides, papers by experts directly involved in the process for its early stages, such as Hirohara, 2013, and Miyanishi, 1993, 2003, have been reviewed. Last but not least, papers by Tarumi, 2012, a public administration planner in charge of the city-planning department in Kobe city at the time, and Kobayashi, 2014, a city-planning consultant who was conducting joint research with the government, since the 1970s, have been considered for this text. The author of this chapter also interviewed both experts individually and examined these records.

2 www.env.go.jp/en/laws/policy/basic_lp.html.

3 This meant creating community centers to develop experimental ways of local community governance.

4 Downtown area near the port also inside the Nagata ward.

5 The topics were: *kougai* and citizens, health and machizukuri. These meetings brought experts and academics together to talk about these issues.

6 A future vision for the area, including physical space and related lifestyles, had to be established as a target image with the consensus of the local community. Then, a plan and strategy to carry out this ideal vision were needed accordingly.

7 Newtowns referred here to large-scale residential areas newly planned by Land Readjustment projects.

8 In this case, between two and five *chou-chou-moku* analysis units correspond with action areas. At the same time, the Mano area was composed of three *jichi-kai* areas, and in parallel, five to six *chou-chou-moku*.

9 For example, in cases where the residential environmental quality was damaged, bottom-up initiatives, like the Mano machizukuri, were encouraged by these objective numerical data. In areas defined as strategic development districts by the analysis, if the results were negative, the option was however to improve through top-down models or to redevelop.

10 The *"karte"* (a word used for personal medical records in Japanese) are information sheets or charts that presented analysis data according to the different topics both separately, and integrated in result maps.

11 Kichiemon Kawana (1915–98) was an architect and urban planning expert who worked also as a professor at Osaka City University (at the time). He led the development of the first Urban Master Plan in Kobe City. He also became interested in the activities of the Maruyama area and the Mano area thereafter. Afterwards he became a professor at Tokyo Metropolitan University, and developed important work that supports machizukuri from the academic field.

12 Substitution of traditional *nagaya* low-rise wooden townhouses.

13 Toru Inui was a Professor at Ritsumeikan University specializing in community participation. His mentor, Endo Yasuhiro, had been involved in the Mano project since the beginning and was one of the first members of the Mano Discussion Group. Inui also joined the Mano project and continued supporting local initiatives and producing academic papers on these topics.

The first generation   45

14 Discussion minutes.

15 Japan's cabinet with Yasuhiro Nakasone as Prime Minister.

16 Areas that did not maybe require urgent physical interventions according to previous analysis deserved, however, to prepare welfare support systems. Thus, these initiatives applied to the whole city area.

17 The term "*fureai*" refers to the power of sharing ideas, good contacts, sharing, chatting, friendship, and other forms of "passive" bonds.

18 Even outside the areas where the so-called "improvement-type machizukuri" projects had been implemented.

19 Ryoukichi Minobe (1904–84), a Marxist economist, was elected by civil society as the governor of Tokyo representing the Socialist Party and the Communist Party. His reformist government energetically promoted welfare and citizen participation initiatives. He became popular even before becoming governor, when he used to lecture on TV on economic issues in an easy-to-understand manner.

20 This idea marked an era of urban policies and plans based on citizen's participation and community. The political academic Keii Matsushita, who advocated for the "civil minimum," and Takashi Asada, who was the lead planner of six major urban projects in Yokohama, participated as external advisors.

21 Until 1975, ward mayors were public officers subordinated to the Tokyo Metropolitan Government, and thus, implemented the policies introduced by it. With the administrative change, ward mayors won more independence on urban matters, and would be able to define their own local policies.

22 Narrow roads of difficult access are common in Japanese unplanned living environments.

23 Capital Region Comprehensive Planning Institute (see Chapter 1).

24 No. 1, March 1977 and No. 2, March 1978.

25 The Machizukuri Council already existed, but here, through the special ordinance, the group was established officially and with a legal character.

26 Public housing blocks for residents of the land lots targeted by the reconstruction projects.

27 This refers to relocation of residents of project areas within the same neighborhood.

28 National agency established in 1955, which has supplied much affordable housing and has been involved in many urban development projects; www.ur-net.go.jp/overseas/index.html.

29 Lawyer Takayoshi Igarashi and his group played an important role in developing the theory and starting the movement defending the rights of residents to sunlight access against building *kougai* (Igarashi, 1980). As a result of these activities, the revision of the Building Standards Act of 1976 introduced regulations that limited the amount of shadow that can be cast by buildings. However, zoning according to this Act tends to be defined loosely, and especially after that, disputes over rights to sunlight continued in areas other than residential use.

30 In 1974, he won a trial for reduction of the number of floors to ten (even seven in some cases).

31 *Dentoteki-Kenzoubutsugun-Hozonchiku* in Japanese (Conservation Districts of Traditional Buildings (CDTB))

32 The "Machizukuri Council" ("*Kyogi-kai*") originates from previous forms of community associations, such as "Chounai-kai" and "Jichi-kai," which had maintained their significant traditional roles within Japanese communities. Moreover, youth associations, PTAs (parent–teacher associations), and the boards of small industries that were the cause of nuisance in the area are also involved.

46 *Shigeru Satoh*

33 The official groups and tools were not adopted by all city councils because establishing new ordinances was complicated.

34 Numerous studies exist on machizukuri ordinances. Takamizawa (1999) is worth a special mention.

35 Local governments in partnership with the Machizukuri Councils would send schematic project proposals for common spaces or facilities to the central government. If selected, the central and local governments would partially fund these projects. When a proposal was selected it would be approved as a public "model project," becoming of "public nature" without the need of a Machizukuri Ordinance. These processes always involved local governments, but at the same time they allowed communities to work without the added difficulty of the creation of the Machizukuri Ordinance.

References

CRCPI (1985). *Machizukuri Genba Houkoku (On-site Report of Machizukuri). Machizukuri Kenkyu 25*. Tokyo: Doujidai-sha.

Gregory, J., Lewis, D., and Chang, C. (eds.). (1977). Community Design: By the People. *Process: Architecture*, 3. Tokyo: Process Architecture Publishing.

Healey, P. (2010). *Making Better Places: The Planning Project in the Twenty-First Century*. London: Palgrave Macmillan

Hirohara, M. (2013). Senshinteki Machizukuri Undo to Chounaikai – koubeshi Maruyama, Mano, Fujisawashi Tujidou Nanbu no Hikaku kenkyu (Advanced Machizukuri Activity and Neighborhood Association), in Iwasaki, Nobuhiko (ed.), *Zouhoban Chounaikai no kenkyu (Revised and Enlarged Version, Research on Neighborhood Associations)*. Tokyo: Ochanomizu shobou.

Horikawa, S. (2018). *Machinami Hozon Undou no Riron to Kiketu (Theory and Conclusion of Townscape Conservation Activity)*. Tokyo: Tokyo Daigaku Shupan-kai (Tokyo University Press).

Igarasi, T. (1980). *Nisshouken no Riron to Saiban (Theory and Trial of the Right to Sunshine)*. Tokyo: Sanseido.

Itoh, T. (1978). *Toshi oyobi Chiiki Keikan Hozen Seido no Tenkaikatei to Keikanshichou ni kansuru Kenkyu (Research on Development Process of Urban and Regional Landscape Conservation System)*. Doctoral dissertation. Tokyo University.

Kawasumi, H. (1971). Proofs of 69 Years Periodicity and Imminence of Destructive Earthquake in Southern Kwanto District and Problems in the Countermeasures Thereof. *Journal of Geography (Chigaku Zasshi)*, 79(3): 115–138. https://doi.org/10.5026/jgeography.79.3_115.

Kinoshita, I. (2007). *Wa-kushoppu (Workshop)*. Kyoto: Gakugei Shuppan.

Kobayashi, I. (2014). Kobe no Machizukuri Zenshi to Machizukuri Center (Pre-History of Machizukuri in Kobe and Machizukuri Center). *Sora*, 9: 9–15. Kobe: Kobe Machizukuri Center.

Kobayashi, I. (2018). Tosikeikakuka Mizutani Eisuke no Machizukuri wo Hurikaeru (Machizukuri of Urban Planner Eisuke Mizutani). *Ie to Machinami*, 11: 14–22

Kobe City. (1974). *Machi-Juku Sobyou ("Machi Unit" Outline)*.

Mano Machizukuri Suisin Kai. Mano Chiku Fukkou Kinenshi (ed.). (2005). *Nihon Saichou Mano Machizukuri (The Longest Machizukuri in Japan. Mano Machizukuri Suishin Kai)*. Kobe.

Miyanishi, Y. (1993). Kobe-shi Mano Chiku – Jumin Shudou Gyousei Sanka no Machizukuri (Machizukuri Led by Residents and Administrative Participation), in *Sankagata Machizukuri no Tenbou (Outlook of Participetory Machizukuri)*, pp. 57–60. Urban Planning Committee of AIJ. Tokyo: AIJ

Miyanishi, Y. (2003). Mano Chiku – Jumin Shudou no Machizukuri (Machizukuri Led by Residents at Mano District). *Handbook of Environmental Design – Toshi Ciiki 1 Project Hen (Urban and Region 1, Project Volume)*, pp. 134–137. AIJ. Tokyo: Maruzen

Satoh, S. (ed.). (1999). *Machizukuri no Kagaku (Science of Machizukuri)*. Tokyo: Kashima Shuppannkai.

Satoh, S. (2004). Sustainable Community Improvement in Japan: Infill Redevelopment Where Everyone Can Continue to Live, in Sorensen, A., Marcotullio, P.J., and Grant, J. (eds.). *Towards Sustainable Cities: East Asian. North American and European Perspectives on Managing Urban Regions*. London: Routledge. 2017. (First published by Ashgate Publishing Company in 2004.)

Satoh, S. (2019). Evolution and Methodology of Japanese Machizukuri for the Improvement of Living Environments. *Japan Architectural Review*, 2(2): 127–142. doi:10.1002/2475–8876.12084 https://rdcu.be/bIe4b.

Satoh, S. and Architectural Institute of Japan (ed.). (2004). *Machizukuri no Houhou (Method of Machizukuri)*. Tokyo: Maruzen.

Setagaya Ward (1977, 1978). *Setagayamachizukuri Note (Notes on the Setagaya Ward Machizukuri)*, Tokyo: Setagaya Ward.

Shutoken Sougou Keikaku Kenkyujo (ed.). (1975). *Machi Tsukuri Nyumon (Introduction to Machizukuri)*. Toshi-Jutaku, no. 12. Kajima Shuppan Kai.

Sorensen, A. and Funck, C. (eds.). (2007). *Living Cities in Japan*. Nissan Institute. London: Routledge Japanese Studies Series.

Takamizawa, M. (1999). Machizukuri Jourei (Machizukuri Ordinance), in Satoh S. (ed.). *Machizukuri no Kagaku (Science of Machizukuri)*, pp. 284–289. Tokyo: Kashima Shuppannkai.

Tarumi, E. (2012). Kobe no Machizukuri – Souseiki no Omoi to Ima (Machizukuri in Kobe – Thoughts at the Beginning and Now). *Sora*, 7, pp. 21–29. Kobe: Kobe Machizukuri Center.

Tokyo Metropolitan Government. (1971). *Hiroba to Aozora no Tokyo Kouso (Tokyo Plan of Public Squares and Blue Skies)*. Tokyo: Tokyo Metropolitan Government.

Tokyo Metropolitan Government. (1976). *Tokyo – Machi no Sugata no Teian (Tokyo: Proposal for City Vision)*. Tokyo: Tokyo Metropolitan Government

Watanabe, S. (2006). Machizukuri in Japan: A Historical Perspective in Participatory Community-Building Initiatives, in Hein, C. and Pelletier, P. (eds.). *Cities. Autonomy. and Decentralization in Japan*. London: Routledge, pp. 101–114.

Watanabe, S. (2007). Toshi Keikaku vs Machizukuri: Emerging Paradigm of Civil Society in Japan. 1950–1980, in Sorensen, A. and Funck, C. (eds.). *Living Cities in Japan: Citizens' Movements, Machizukuri and Local Environments*. London: Nissan Institute and Routledge Japanese Studies Series.

Yamamoto, T. (1999). Bunmyaku no Kaidoku to Machizukuri (Decoding Urban Context and Nachizukuri), in Satoh, S. (ed.). *Machizukuri no Kagaku (Science of Machizukuri)*. Tokyo: Kashima Shuppannkai, pp. 67–82.

Yasuda, C. and Miwa, K. (1993). Kobe-Ikiiki Shitamachi Suishin Kyougikai no Machizukuri Shien (Machizukuri Support by Kobe-Ikiiki Lower Town Promotion Meeting), in *Sankagata Machizukuri no Tenbou (Outlook for Participatory Machizukuri)*, pp. 65–68. Urban Planning Committee of AIJ. Tokyo: AIJ

4 The second generation
Participation, collaboration, and co-creation

Shigeru Satoh

Introduction

By the early 1980s, institutions and methods for promoting machizukuri were already arranged. However, the established model was rigid and did not leave much space for creativity. Thus, complementing the visions and plans for the improvement of the living environment defined through machizukuri practice with specific projects (cooperative redevelopment, etc.) would still face several difficulties. In order to overcome such problems, in parallel to a continuing first generation, the second machizukuri generation arose, aiming at the communities directly working on site, narrowing down the work topics, and targeting more specific places close to the community. Accordingly, during this period, the main efforts were put into developing creative methods linked to specific machizukuri projects.

Looking for a more touching form of participation

For local residents, cooperating in joint reconstructions and street improvement according to a district Machizukuri Plan agreed by the Machizukuri Council entailed putting their own property at the service of a common objective. In order to accomplish such plans, in addition to incentives (such as subsidies), the personal motivation and initiative of the participants were indispensable. Besides, it was necessary that the residents became interested and involved in the management of public space. Thus, it was essential to raise motivation to effectively involve locals throughout the whole machizukuri process, from analysis to management. In this context, trying to break through such a situation, a second generation of machizukuri appeared.

Further on, from the mid 1980s, trying to encourage spontaneous participation and initiatives, machizukuri practice focused on supporting the legitimacy of autonomous community groups. In order to do so, projects started to link diverse work topics (such as park design, improvements for disabled people, etc.) with the different groups and organizations existing inside the local community. With this, the aim was to produce some first

The second generation 49

experimental specific outcomes, and thus, promote theme-specific autonomous machizukuri. That is to say, the second generation of machizukuri practice corresponds with the development of specific work topics, practical experimentation, and dissemination of the appeals of machizukuri practice among the general public.

According to these new objectives, during this period, the main efforts were put into the design of the participatory processes and the development of tools for consensus building (such as workshops) applied to specific projects; in other words, the invigoration of participants' collaboration, creativity, and subjectivity. To achieve this goal, clear particular issues that concerned residents were raised, workshops that facilitated active participation were held, and participatory design experiences were attempted. In 1978, when the special magazine issue "Community Design: By The People" was published (Gregory *et al.*, 1977), participatory design methods developed in the United States were introduced to Japanese professionals. Based on these ideas, various unique methods were attempted. Using the experiences of the first machizukuri generation, creativity was boosted by the cooperation of residents and the value of committing to machizukuri was shared. For example, in densely built-up "*shotengai*" shopping areas and residential districts, residents and shop owners would pursue common goals, such as creating machizukuri guidelines and legal district planning for maintaining their living and business environment, or developing cooperative redevelopment projects. Also, through various workshops, it was possible to increase the motivation and commitment of the participants to managing and operating a variety of public facilities. The various groups engaged in this second generation of machizukuri not only discussed and debated, but also, by means of citizen participation tools, established consistent schemes to help local residents engage in machizukuri in different ways.

New wave for disaster machizukuri: accumulation of small local actions in Ichitera-Kototoi

In the Ichitera-Kototoi district, the Mukoujima area in the Sumida ward of Tokyo, machizukuri focused on disaster prevention activities created locally by the residents.

Disaster prevention efforts in living districts – "there's no need to escape" machizukuri

By the early 1980s, six disaster prevention centers, which also served as wide evacuation sites, were built through large-scale redevelopment projects along the Koto delta. However, the sites were located three kilometers away from some of the households to which they gave shelter. Evacuating to such areas in the event of an earthquake presented a great difficulty for elderly, children, disabled people, etc. Therefore, the need

50 *Shigeru Satoh*

to improve the safety of densely populated built-up wooden areas from the inside was raised. In a first attempt, planners, public workers, and community leaders in cooperation launched a machizukuri project under the motto, "As safety can be secured there is no need escape," targeting the Sumida ward. In 1985, the Tokyo Metropolitan Government started a Model Project that aimed at improving inner neighborhood areas as a way to create what were called Disaster Prevention Living Areas.

In the Sumida ward, machizukuri initiatives typical of the first generation had started already in the Kyojima district, but apart from public projects (such as community housing) the projects that were supposed to be developed by collaboration of inhabitants in an autonomous way did not progress smoothly (e.g., cooperative housing). However, in the neighboring Ichitera-Kototoi district and the old Mokoujima area,[1] alongside Disaster Prevention Living Areas Model Projects, new methods were attempted. The Ichitera-Kototoi district employed the Model Project method proposed by the Tokyo Metropolitan Government. The ward, in order to further develop the project, selected a proposal made by a planning office, which presented a method completely different from that of Kyojima. First, the district called upon local volunteers. More than a dozen of them responded to the call and were encouraged to organize "*wai-wai*[2] meetings" by themselves. *Wai-wai* is a term that implies the freedom to talk about various things in a festive and happy manner. This character is completely opposed to the Machizukuri Council of the first generation, composed by representatives of the different organizations in the area.

In this context, the work of professionals like Toshiya Yamamoto, Professor of Meiji University, who joined the movement as a machizukuri consultant, was especially relevant. In Yamamoto's words, "staff and consultants of the ward jumped into the local area and argued that they should all together push machizukuri forward, and thus, machizukuri activities adopted the character of citizen activities" (Yamamoto, 1999). Through workshops, surrounding large-scale maps, residents were able to check the neighborhood areas, discover the resources that machizukuri provided them, and present and complement various ideas. Such methods created a thrilling chance for locals as they matched the "*shitamachi* downtown temperament" of residents, which was reflected in a will to do things by one's own means. On top of that, the local "Hitokoto (One Word) Festival" was used as a way to publicly announce and create expectations about the different activities that would take place during the year.

In 1986, a new organization for disaster prevention, named the Hitokoto Society, was set up gathering six neighborhood associations and *wai-wai* meeting members in the Mukoujima area. Machizukuri proposals presented to the Ward Mayor from the Hitokoto Society were accepted, and several good results were obtained from machizukuri practice. The machizukuri plans for the Ichitera-Kototoi district were later set up, small plazas were prepared as neighborhood anti-disaster bases, streets were redesigned, and an Ichitera-Kototoi Machizukuri Center and other facilities were created. Besides, other innitiatives appeared everywhere in the district: the "Kawaraban Bulletin," or flyer handout, was published and distributed in the area; special symbols to mark, give importance to, and pay respect to "*roji*" alleys, linked to the historical "*Rojison*" (God of the roji – the alleys). Taking the existing historical context as a basis, all these initiatives acted as keypoints for disaster prevention and had a clear direction on the horizon, the so-called "soft machizukuri." This was characterized by mild starts based on various kinds of human activities in a social context.

Thereafter, a group of young artists came to the area and took part in machizukuri organizing the Mukoujima Exposition in 2000 and the Art-Roji in 2001. Abandoned factories in the area were renovated as galleries. In addition, a number of dilapidated wooden houses and tenements were also refurbished by artists coming from Japan and from all over the world. These dwellings were turned into exhibition and service spaces, and some of the participant artists even stayed to live in the area. A "machizukuri design game," presented in Chapter 5, was also held as an art event. This was featured in the news by four different television stations, and NHK, Japan's National Public Broadcasting Corporation, created a one-hour documentary that received a great public response.

Through these activities, new attractions and fresh energies were born in the district. The Mukojima Institut was created as a platform for the multiple activities that followed. Thus, machizukuri, presented as a wide-range of local activities, gained wide public attention, which created an image quite different from the first generation.

At this point, the local community came to understand that the entire energy of the area should be used as the basis for disaster prevention. While having this as the main objective, both the administration and external specialists should also back up the region's own capability to fight against disaster.

Shigemoto Sahara, who had been trained as an architect, was the leader of the movement and at the center of activities inside this type of machizukuri. He conceived the "Mukojima 100 Flower Garden," an open space inside a traditional wooden *machiya*, which inherited a tradition from the local people of the Edo period. Some of the neighbors in the area still embodied the special sensibility and culture of Edo "*chou*" people (see Introduction), and getting involved with machizukuri was a way to promote the development of the area while enjoying their special local pride and using it as a form of social energy.

The limits of machizukuri in the Ichitera-Kototoi district

Even if the machizukuri activities had been propelled by a proposal from the administration, the projects evolved from small activities to later address problems in the whole area.

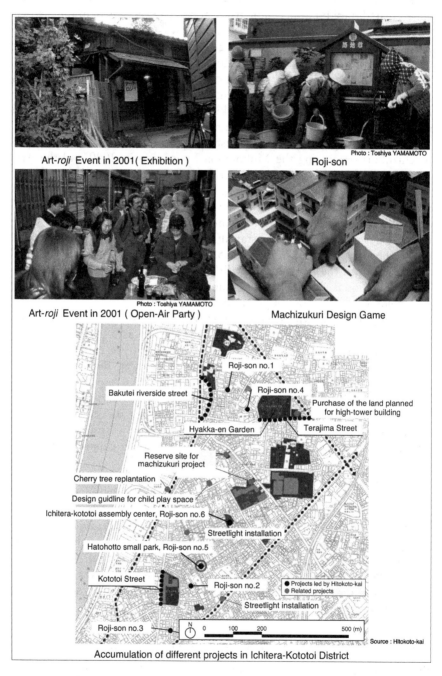

Figure 4.1 Ichitera-Kototoi machizukuri projects.

The second generation 53

However, despite some positive results, the Hitokoto Society had no ability to coordinate and control private development projects, which were far from the machizukuri concept. It also lacked the skills to advocate for modifications of development plans. We can say thus that the Ichitera-Kototoi machizukuri lacked a formally authorized power body, such as the Machizukuri Council. This underlined the need for machizukuri plans and sound coordination among each of the local groups and interested parties to progress together for the improvement of the living environment.

Machizukuri conducted by residents for the improvement of local lifestyles: measures taken in Taishido

Participatory machizukuri and participatory machizukuri design were trends in the late 1980s and early 1990s. Local governments and experts who specialized in participatory approaches led the movement to include participation of residents in the design of parks and public facilities in various ways. Since the establishment of the Machizukuri Ordinance in 1982, the administration of the Setagaya ward, in Tokyo, promoted machizukuri in local communities. Machizukuri in the Taishido district began in the 1980s as part of the machizukuri initiatives for the Setagaya ward. Various workshops were held for residents to discuss their way of life, solve conflicts with other communities and form a consensus on machizukuri. With it, machizukuri for the improvement of the area was implemented. Since then, this "participatory machizukuri" has been implemented continuously for more than 30 years. The case of Taishido is a leading example of machizukuri practice through which the local residents themselves established a Machizukuri Council and the measures for the improvement of their own way of life, while the self-governance mechanism in the area was maintained. Taishido will remain in the history of machizukuri as a series of activities that channelled the evolution of machizukuri practice from the first to the second generation.

In 1980, when the government of Setagaya-ku organized a residents' meeting in preparation for machizukuri practice in this area, the participants strongly criticized the way the government had taken on the matter. This criticism was based on the climate of mistrust towards the government that had arisen from the way it had handled the conflict surrounding the right to sunshine mentioned in previous chapters. Residents' criticism never ceased during the seven meetings that followed. In the end, Masanosuke Umezu,[3] who led the machizukuri movement in the Taishido district, appealed to the local residents and proposed: "Let's study and act for our community by ourselves" (Umezu, 2015). Many residents supported his appeal and voluntarily established a Machizukuri Council in 1982 composed of members publicly selected mainly among his supporters.

At the time, participatory design methods had been applied to the Kitazawa District of Tokyo (see Chapter 3). Now, in this case, methods developed from the experience of a *machiaruki* (street walking) survey, conducted in 1983, and discussions inside the council, which allowed all the people concerned with and interested in machizukuri to participate directly and casually in the process.

> It was decided that the council should not make decisions on matters such as community issues and planning of machizukuri projects by itself, but it should rather create venues where the people concerned with machizukuri could participate in these discussions. Accordingly, the matters concerning *machikado hiroba* (street corner plazas) were discussed in the *Hiroba Kaigi* (conference on plazas), roads issues were discussed in the street conferences, and construction of large buildings were discussed in the conferences held by four stakeholders (the council, community residents, business operators and the administration of the Setagaya ward), respectively.
>
> (K. Inoue[4] in an interview held in May 2019)

In this way, residents studied and designed machizukuri as a way of creating the places they lived comprehensively through various methods. As a result, nearly 20 *machikado hiroba* (street corner plazas), unique small parks adapted to the local environment, were developed using lots, such as parts of land that had been saved for street construction but remained unused.

In addition to the activities mentioned above, in 1985, residents prepared the "10 Interim Proposals for Machizukuri" based on the results of council discussions. The "*Seseragi* (small stream) Restoration Plan" along the Karasuyama green path, which crosses the center of the district, which was included in these proposals, faced strong opposition from residents along the path, despite the fact that it had been deliberately designed through participatory methods. The stream had been previously channelled and buried, and a green path had been constructed on the top of the conduit. As the path had deteriorated, the Machizukuri Council proposed a plan to restore the original stream. However, as the stream had caused flooding in the past, the residents along the stream strongly opposed the plan for fear of new floods. The plan was then revised with the participation of the residents who had opposed it and the "*Seseragi* Restoration Plan" was redesigned and constructed by Atelier Zoo in 1990. The Seseragi Green Path is now a popular spot frequented by many people.

Since 1986, the Machizukuri Council has been divided into three working groups and has focused on more specialized matters, including the drafting of a Machizukuri District Plan required by law. In accordance with the district plan adopted in the city planning in 1990, narrow streets were widened one after another, and old and dilapidated wooden-house

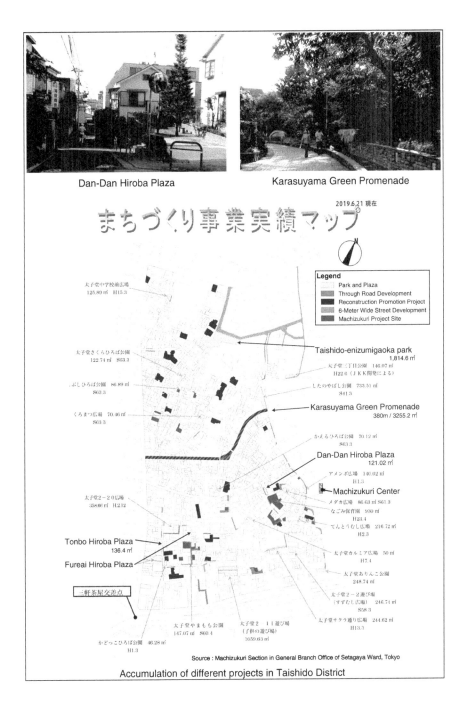

Figure 4.2 Taishido machizukuri projects.

56   *Shigeru Satoh*

areas were redeveloped with the support of subsidies from the central government. By 1992, 18 new apartment buildings (180 apartments) had been constructed.

While the physical environment was being improved, there was also a need to link machizukuri activities closed to the lives of many ordinary residents. In 1990, the machizukuri specialist Kakuro Inoue coordinated a series of self-organized workshops on "Machizukuri for Development of Communities where People can Live until an Old Age" and "Machizukuri for Creation of a Zero Waste Society" in 1991. Both workshops counted on the participation of residents of all ages and experts from outside the community. The *Rakuro* (Work with Ease) Club was established later in accordance with a proposal put forward during the workshops. Besides, since the mid 1990s, activities (including those of the club) were implemented for comprehensive machizukuri practice involving the entire community. These included measures for the aging population and community greening.

Not only Taishido residents, but also the experts and local public workers, learned, understood, and discovered what machizukuri is through the above-mentioned process. The different conflicts of actions and trial-and-error experiences helped improve both the organizational systems and the physical environment of the community. Although no one can predict it accurately, the active involvement of people concerned with machizukuri, even in the form of strong resistance, led to the above-mentioned processes. In this way, community residents accumulate experience, refine its methods, and come to share the same spirit through machizukuri. It is not too much to say therefore that machizukuri in Taishido began based on the well-organized system and methodology of the first generation. Residents who felt that the original system or methodology were not appropriate questioned them and produced their own results through trial-and-error experiences; this is what is called the second generation of machizukuri. Finally, the residents tried to use these results for the development of a third generation.

Later, at the end of the 1990s, after the 1995 Great Hanshin-Awaji Earthquake, various conflicts emerged between the local government and residents. The Plan to Promote Development of Disaster-Resistant Cities, prepared by the Tokyo Metropolitan Government after the earthquake, made of the Santa Street, on the boundary between the Taishido district and the adjacent Mishuku district, its focal point and proposed a rapid intervention to widen it up to six meters. As a consequence, various problems emerged during discussions with the resident organizations in the areas. Despite this first opposition, through a series of events, the residents agreed to the widening of the street and the works were completed. However, this project contradicted the will of the residents who wanted to rehabilitate the community more slowly, by themselves, and based on the consensus of the community (Umezu, 2015).

The second generation   57

Accumulation of experiences in anti-disaster machizukuri

In the 1980s, after some twists and turns, anti-disaster machizukuri was implemented in various ways in Tokyo, which is expected to be hit by a large earthquake in the coming years. The Ichitera Kototoi Council of the Sumida ward organized a meeting for information exchange, "The Anti-Disaster Machizukuri People's Conference in Sumida" in March 1990. Representatives of 13 communities in Tokyo engaged in anti-disaster machizukuri processes participated in the conference. The participants recognized the significant diversity in anti-disaster machizukuri actions implemented by the different communities, and exchanges on better methods between the communities took place in an enthusiastic atmosphere (*Machizukuri* Study (CRCPI, 1990)).

"*Machinami*" townscape machizukuri

The first condition for machizukuri could be to define the planning object-ives in mutual understanding and make the projects advance towards this goal through consensus building. However, it is nearly impossible to put this mutual consent explicitly into practice, for the tasks to achieve the revitalization of the "*machi*" and the maintenance of livings environments are far from clear. In other words, the value of the so-called "landscape," understood as physical scenery we can have in front of our eyes, is easier to reach by mutual consent than the value of the so-called "*machinami* historical townscape," a ghostly picture in our minds.

Of course, special district plans must be approved in order to preserve historical landscapes. But at the same time, citizens must be educated to promote lifestyles in coexistence with history and the revival of traditional techniques.

Nara-machi is the oldest merchant community in Nara. It has existed since Nara was the capital of Japan in the eighth century, called Heijo-kyo at the time. One main street lined with traditional merchant houses remained until the 1970s, but the houses were left unrepaired and dilapidated because of a decrease in commercial activities. Volunteers in the community and experts from outside the community established the Nara Community Research Society to preserve and restore this historical street. In 1984, the Nara Machizukuri Center was established to lead not only the preservation of the street, but also the reactivation of traditional industries. The center opened its activity base in 1995, the Naramachi Monogatarikan, which placed traditional culture and stories at the core of machizukuri practice.

Once the activities to restore the pride of the community began to take off, the implementation of various community activities followed. Many merchant houses have been repaired in the traditional style since then and various types of new business have emerged in the community. The street has now become a bustling historic tourism area.

58   Shigeru Satoh

Another important example is the group of activities, known as restoration machizukuri, developed at the *Ichiban-gai* (First Street) in Kawagoe City, near Tokyo. Activities started with the intention of preserving the "*kura*" historical warehouses (complex of shop and living space) in Kawagoe's "*machinami*" historical streetscape. The process, which started in the 1970s, tried to simultaneously protect the local culture by revitalizing the activity in the historical shopping street and recovering the local industries. Now, *Ichiban-gai* has also become popular tourist destination attracting about 700,000 visitors a year.

All these are successful examples of how machizukuri activities that began with *machinami-zukuri* (townscape improvement) have created numerous famous tourist destinations. Nevertheless, beyond that, comprehensive machizukuri for entire areas is required to prevent over-reliance on tourism and its harmful effects on the survival of the local community.

Machizukuri through workshops

During the 1990s, residents studied their own living areas through their own senses and experience in workshops held all over the country. It was also a time when people who had previously profited from the bubble economy now tried to face the problems resulting from its collapse.

One of the major references for such workshops was the experience of Taishido district in the Setagaya ward. The Setagaya Machizukuri Center was established in 1992 as an organization affiliated with the government of the Setagaya ward. The center published a book in four volumes entitled "*Sanka no Dezain Dogu Bako* (Toolbox for Designing Participation)" in which the methods used in the different workshops were explained (Setagaya Machizukuri Center, 1993, 1996, 1998, and 2002). During this period, the First National *Waku-waku* (a Japanese adjective describing a state of happiness and excitement) Workshop was held in Kochi city in 1994. In the same year, the people that engaged in machizukuri activities in the Setagaya ward of Tokyo also coordinated a series of workshops on park design in Kobe city, a city known for its cutting-edge machizukuri practice. The workshops were also used to train local public workers and experts in machizukuri. Before concluding the workshop sessions, the 1995 Great Hanshin-Awaji Earthquake hit the area. Ikuo Kobayashi, who organized the workshops, mentioned that what the participants had learned in the workshops contributed significantly to the subsequent machizukuri restoration projects for the city. These workshops were neither necessarily designed for a specific community nor meant to be linked to a specific context. This meant they were flexible enough to be used to define and develop different projects with different specific purposes (such as the creation of adventure playparks). Thus, through the implementation of such diverse workshops, the second generation of machizukuri spread throughout the country.

Chapter conclusion

The issues tackled in these cases corresponded to particular circumstances and produced particular results. In such a way, even though relevant, these first practical experiences did not reach the original aim of fostering generalized comprehensive community development movements based on local lifestyles. Yet, through participation and collaboration on various topics, emphasizing the promotion and control of the initiatives by the local residents, the awareness on comprehensive area management by local stakeholders and communities grew, and led to the third generation of machizukuri.

Notes

1 Mokuojima represents the area occupied by this old town, but it has no legal or administrative implications nowadays. After the administrative reform in the 1950s, Mokujima was divided into different districts, such as Ichitera-Kototoi, which refers to a smaller and well-delimited administrative area inside what was the previous territory of Mukoujima.
2 The word "*wai-wai*" in Japanese means clamorous or noisy, and has a festive character.
3 From the book *Kurashi ga aru kara machi nanoda – Taishido jumin sanka no machizukuri* (*A Community Exists because People Live There – Participatory Machizukuri in Taishido*) (Umezu, 2015).
4 Kakuro Inoue of CRCPI (Inoue, 1993), who studied machizukuri in the Setagaya ward in the publication of "Setagaya *Machizukuri* Note," was dispatched to Taishido by the government of the Setagaya ward as a machizukuri consultant.

References

Gregory, J., Lewis, D., and Chang, C. (eds.). (1977). Community Design: By The People. *Process: Architecture*: 3. Tokyo: Process Architecture Publishing.
Kinoshita, I. (2007). *Wa-kushoppu* (*Workshop*). Kyoto: Gakugei Shuppan.
Umezu, M. (2015). *Kurashi ga aru kara machi nanoda – Taishido jumin sanka no machizukuri* (*A Community Exists because People Live There – Participatory Machizukuri in Taishido*). Kyoto: Gakugei Shuppanshan-sha.
Yamamoto (1999). Chiiki Shutai no komyunithi – Bousai Seikastuken Zukuri (Local Active Community – Making Anti-Disaster Neighborhood District. In Satoh, S. (ed.). *Machizukuri no Kagaku* (*Science of Machizukuri*). Tokyo: Kashima Shuppannkai, pp. 114–124.

5 The third generation
Aiming at open area management

Shigeru Satoh

Introduction

The third generation began to appear at the beginning of the twenty-first century as a new form of machizukuri in which various stakeholders cooperated, managed, and governed an open area through a continuous layering and integration of their activities inside a global strategy agreed by all of them. That is to say, it corresponds with multi-stakeholder partnerships for comprehensive area[1] management.

Of course, the autonomous initiatives that had emerged during the first generation, and the topic-linked activities and networks of the second continued. In other words, during the third generation, these previous methods were assembled, encompassing various topics, in order to cooperate in the management of more comprehensive and open areas. Furthermore, the machizukuri that covered such areas had to adapt and evolve to integrate ecological and topographical dimensions in territorial management systems. This included both mayoral cities and their surrounding agricultural and coastal rural areas.

In consequence, work was not limited to punctual interventions like the local parks of the second generation. There was an effort to expand machizukuri activities based on broad themes such as the ecological environment. In this way, the third generation appeared gradually to coordinate more open and holistic communities.

The Great Hanshin-Awaji Earthquake

In 1995 the Great Hanshin-Awaji Earthquake occurred. This was a city-type earthquake that particularly affected built-up areas of Osaka Bay, being especially severe in Kobe City. At that time, machizukuri initiatives addressed reconstruction efforts giving way to a third generation of machizukuri practice.

Even before the earthquake struck developed areas of Kobe City, various collaboration efforts between experts, the local administration, and community organizations were already taking place in the area. After the disaster, volunteers from various cities throughout Japan joined the existing networks for local cooperation and, under the accumulation of efforts, new machizukuri methods were developed and adapted.

After the earthquake, in all the areas where reconstruction projects of any sort were carried out, regardless of their public or private nature, Reconstruction Machizukuri Councils[2] were unquestionably established. In the aftermath of this massive disaster that had affected a great number of residents, reaching agreements and approving the contents of the reconstruction projects through discussion within these councils were necessary, even for public plans. In the case of Kobe City, such processes progressed according to existing Kobe Machizukuri Ordinances and served as a reference for other areas. Thus, at the critical time of reconstruction from the great earthquake, the various organizations born during the second generation of machizukuri gathered under the Machizukuri Council umbrella group, and thanks to this, area management systems, essential for an integrated reconstruction, were easily created. Gradually, many different stakeholders joined the machizukuri process at some point. Once again, they organized themselves in new platforms and organizations for area management similar to the Machizukuri Council, but grouped around diverse themes, making clear that such a comprehensive scheme was needed.

Lessons from the Great Hanshin-Awaji Earthquake reconstruction process: pre-disaster reconstruction machizukuri

Reconstruction machizukuri afer the Great Hanshin-Awaji Earthquake was promoted through Machizukuri Councils that focused their action on well-delimited districts. However, the areas were not completely closed, and activities did often go beyond the limits of such districts. Thus in reality, reconstruction machizukuri progressed through the cooperation of actors working on wider areas. Both experts and local leaders formed networks, and through them, developed diverse comprehensive and open machizukuri activities linked by a clear transversal topic: reconstruction.

From April 1995, the author of this chapter with his group of students joined reconstruction machizukuri activities in the Noda-hokubu area in the Nagata ward, in Kobe. The local Machizukuri Council lent a room for meetings, and hosted the students there. In turn, they recorded the state of the discussions during meetings, and presented diverse machizukuri proposals to the Council. The so-called "retirement home for the elderly," based at the Council, became a hub for information exchange during reconstruction machizukuri. It also became the place where various experts, people involved in activity groups, and administrative staff gathered for discussions.[3]

In this district, reconstruction was partially carried out through land readjustment projects, but also the Noda-hokubu Machizukuri Council led and defined a district plan and various other new support systems were introduced.

62 *Shigeru Satoh*

The reconstruction advanced smoothly through "improvement type" machizukuri (see Chapter 2). Among other projects, several small and mid-size cooperative reconstruction projects chained to restore the quality of living space, upgrading traditional *roji* alleys as community spaces. These efforts positioned activities in the Nagata ward at the front line of successful machizukuri practice.

Another important example in the same area is the community road that extended on a North–South axis from the Daikoku Park, which had a strong urban presence in the neighborhood. The construction of this road had been considered during Council design workshops, and had been just completed one month before the disaster. Right after the earthquake, this skeletal space served as a temporary evacuation site for residents who, following the instructions of local leaders, escaped from the fire that spread from the east. The road and park also opened the congested urban tissue and acted as a firebreak, which stopped the fire from spreading within living areas.

Added to this, the Noda-hokubu Machizukuri Council received great support from the local residents, and thanks to this, in the following weeks, the reconstruction process progressed significantly.

In any case, the preexistence of the renovated Daikoku Park and the community road contributed greatly to mitigate the effects of the earthquake, almost as though the reconstruction machizukuri process had started in advance. These kind of efforts would be called later "pre-reconstruction machizukuri."

These series of very iconic events conformed to the modern "history of machizukuri." Beautiful and powerful stories about reconstruction spread and made machizukuri establish as an effective resource in the events of a catastrophe.

Before the Great Hanshin-Awaji Earthquake, it was a period during which it was difficult to maintain the goals and models set by the first generation of machizukuri. Besides, during the bubble era, machizukuri had been overshadowed by the new bright urban development. At the time, the second generation, even though effective in engaging communities and creating a fun atmosphere through workshops, etc., was not able to promote autonomous decision-making models for the improvement of living environments. At this point, the reconstruction machizukuri that emerged from the Great Hanshin-Awaji Earthquake opened up new possibilities and prospects for community development.

In order to coordinate the reconstruction efforts after the great earthquake and at the same time, facilitate the revitalization of declining central urban areas, the third generation of machizukuri had to manage and solve diverse issues in a comprehensive way. This meant integrating and coordinating the different local organizations as a whole area-management system, and linking individual machizukuri projects with the diverse goals that had been born during the second generation.

Preparation system to promote machizukuri as a series of linked projects

Three main goals motivated the development of comprehensive systems for the development of machizukuri during this period: the revitalization of central city areas, the support of welfare services, and ecology.

During the same period, the decline of historic urban centres in provincial cities had become a big social problem in Japan. Here, various efforts were carried out, not only addressing planning methods, but also promoting social systems and institutional development. In this way, machizukuri entered a period of original adaptation and evolution, and started being used more widely.

The system needed an organization that could serve as platform to encompass the different citizens' social activities and a mechanism for local governance in which they could cooperate. In 1998, the Central City Area Revitalization Method was created for the promotion of projects. To do so, Central City Area Revitalization Plans were created by each municipality, supported by a system of national subsidies and the institutionalization of the Town Management Organization (TMO) for project promotion. This was an attempt to develop a cutting-edge support system for machizukuri activities.

On the other hand, in 1997, the Law Concerning the Promotion of Specific Non-Profit Organization Activities was established. It listed 20 specific non-profit activities, the third one being "activities to promote machizukuri." As of the end of March 2019, over 50,000 corporations had been certified, and about 40 percent of them included "machizukuri activities" in their work field (Cabinet Office, 2018). Indeed, if simply put, nearly 8,000 Specific Non-Profit Organizations are working in the machizukuri field. Among them, "activities to promote health, medical care, or welfare," "activities to improve child health," and "activities to promote academic, cultural arts, or sports" are the most numerous.

As for welfare, which is the largest field of activity of NPOs, the "nursing-care insurance system" (equivalent to long-term care insurance) was introduced in April 2000. This system was established with the purpose of reducing the burden of families and supporting care in an aging society. In this context, various corporations developed nursing care service projects providing housing for the elderly and neighborhood day-care centers. So, in a broad sense, these groups became somehow the leaders of machizukuri.

Furthermore, through the Limited Liability Partnership (2005) Japanese type Limited Liability Companies were institutionalized. This made it easier for union members to establish autonomous small corporations, and with it, the possibilities to develop leading residents' machizukuri projects spread.

At the time, various social enterprises appeared also around the world according to the different legal systems and social contexts. In the case of

64 *Shigeru Satoh*

Japan, the development of machizukuri projects was promoted through various organizational forms, including existing *shotengai* shopping area associations and co-ops. Rather than relying on public projects for machizukuri development, "machizukuri residents' projects" promoted by the local community were encouraged. With this, area management became possible.

We can say that this third generation of machizukuri focused thus, area and community management models characterized by the agreement of diverse organizations to join efforts inside community cooperation platforms to resolve problems in a more comprehensive way. In order to make the most of these effective initiatives, governments gradually improved their legal systems and bestowed more autonomy in problem-solving on non-profit organizations, helping them assist local citizens and support their movements.

Cutting-edge area management by the Kurokabe Corporation in Nagahama City

The impact that the first steps of the third machizukuri generation had in other parts of the country is visible from the first half of the 1990s. For example, Nagahama City, a castle town built at the end of the sixteenth century on the shore of Biwa lake in Shiga prefecture, is the first best-practice case of machizukuri applied to the revitalization of a declining historic town. In this case, the strong local merchant community, with more than 400 years of history, was responsible for establishing the machizukuri company "Kurokabe." "*Kuro-Kabe*" (in Japanese) refers to the black wall of the former headquarters building of the local bank. The construction was a symbol of the local merchant community, who bought it with the support of the local government to spare it from demolition. From this, machizukuri actions to protect the traditional aesthetics and spirit of the area were initiated by the third sector and co-financed by the municipal administration. From this, by linking repeated trial-and-error experiences for the renovation of traditional "machiya"[4] town buildings, the historical shopping district was renovated giving rise to a considerable tourism increase.

The first project attempted was the Kurokabe Square. Then, other facility and urban layout projects followed. The Kurokabe group gave a number to each one of them, opening Kurokabe No. 30 in 2014. Besides, not only streets and open space, but also shops were built inside the area. In addition, in 1996, the organization called "Nagahama Plan Co. Ltd" was created to control real estate management in the area. Later, in 1999, the NPO "Machizukuri Town Hall" was established along with other groups that followed, expanding the local network. Even though this was a private NPO, it was called "Town Hall," a fact that underlines the traditional spirit of local townsmen, their autonomy, and the 400 years of history during which they had been responsible for the operation of the "machi."

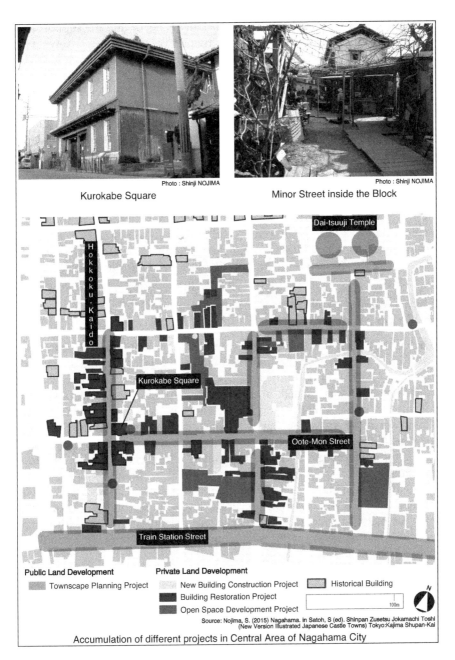

Figure 5.1 Kurokabe Machizukuri projects.

66 *Shigeru Satoh*

In 2018, machizukuri in the area celebrated its thirtieth anniversary. The current situation relies heavily on urban tourism. But at the same time, the local groups are working on urban resilience and the support and creation of jobs. When machizukuri activities began this was a town area where "in an hour, four people and one dog" would walk along the street; now, it has developed into a very popular place visited by two million people every year (Nojima, 2015).

This is a clear example of how a corporation dealing with a first machizukuri project gradually gets involved with area management, including various local organizations in a shared strategy. This case has thus become an iconic reference example of the third generation of machizukuri.

As described in detail in the case of Furano, in Chapter 14, there are many cases in which Machizukuri Companies became the center of revitalization projects for central city areas. Cooperation with the administration is indispensable for machizukuri activities related to regional/area management, especially in central urban districts, which are normally strong business areas. However, for many successful examples the private sector took the initiative and voluntarily developed various ideas.

Environmental machizukuri and its groundwork in Mishima City

The United Nations Conference on Environment and Development (UNCED), also known as "Earth Summit," was celebrated in Rio de Janeiro in 1992. As a result, the "Rio Declaration on Environment and Development" was issued and selected plans for its execution were resumed in the "Agenda-21." At the time, a special focus was put on global warming and other environmental changes that harm the global ecological system. The topic required immediate research, plans, and actions to protect the global environment and prevent further environmental disasters. Specific actions were detailed in the non-binding action plan "Local Agenda 21," which was supposed to be legislated and implemented at national, regional, and local levels on a voluntary basis. The plan advocated for citizens' participation in each nation, for without the citizens' willingness to personally support these objectives they could not be accomplished.

In Japan, based on the care of communities for their own living environments, the preservation of natural and ecological systems through a wide-range of participatory projects became a major theme for machizukuri. Thus, the "sustainable development" and the "circular economy" were proposed as basic concepts of machizukuri – which may also be claimed as the global ideals of the twenty-first century.

The idea of creating autonomous communities based on such ecological principles is not new; rather, it is a reflection of the 1970s' ideals on the one hand, and the local visions that had been rising in Japan. Both of them

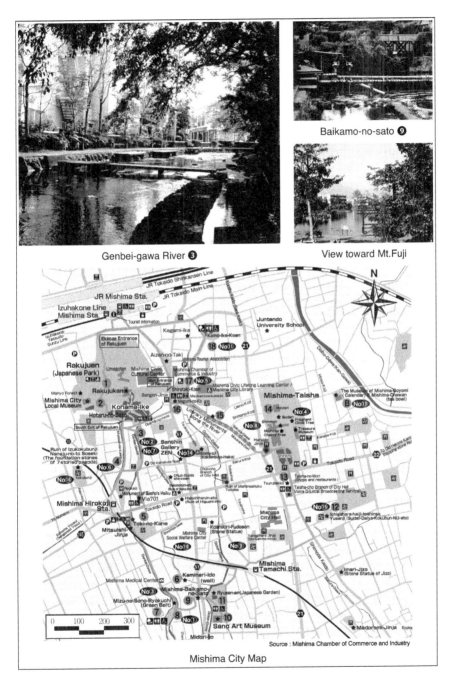

Figure 5.2 Genbei-gawa river projects and trail map.

68 Shigeru Satoh

contributed to form a vision for development from within the community based on local tradition and in symbiosis with the surrounding ecosystem.

In parallel, we can say that human beings have become separated from nature by abusing the natural environment and modifying it to meet other purposes (e.g., river embankments). Consequently, a sense of crisis arose and motivated people to act in symbiosis with nature, reconsidering daily life and going back to its roots. In Japan, since the 1980s ecosystem rehabilitation activities have been conducted. A relevant example is the protection of the "*tonbo-ike*" (dragonfly ponds). In them, Japanese fireflies restlessly hover around the waving reeds around ponds and along riverbanks to provoke "*suzumushi*" (bell crickets) to ring in summer nights and autumn evenings. This was a very typical scene that had a strong presence inside the Japanese imaginery and motivated citizen activities for the rehabilitation of natural life. Such activities have spread ever since and Japanese society has become aware of the environmental crisis: pollution, deforestation, shrinking lakes, rivers, and disappearing marshes.

The Mishima project and the expansion of machizukuri

The ecological system of Mishima City, located on foothills of Mt. Fuji, is conditioned by undercurrent water flows and the narrow Genbei River, which runs through the city. In this context, the project for the regeneration of the water environment was significantly symbolic of the cooperation between the citizens and the Mishima Administration. This project clearly represents the teamwork spirit of machizukuri, as through it, both shared the responsibility for river maintenance and landscaping, and contributed to a fresher environment.

From the 1960s, underground water had ceased due to the location of industries in upstream areas. Besides, domestic grey waters flowed into the Genbei river causing water pollution. As a consequence, citizens also lost pride in their city, which had once been called the "Water city."

To face this, in September 1992, eight citizen groups, such as the Mishima *Yusui* (play with water) Association, the Mishima city government, and local companies gathered to launch the Mishima Groundworks Steering Committee (later NPO Groundworks Mishima, which involved 20 organizations). Activities that encouraged locals to analyze the local environment and to clean up and embellish river areas by their own efforts took off under the slogan "a scoop in the right hand and a can of beer in the left," referring to the joy of this volunteer work.

Under these circumstances, the country, which has the final responsibility for river management, proposed a model project for the improvement and maintenance of the Genbei River, whose water is also used for agricultural purposes.

Taking this opportunity, in addition to experts, Groundworks Mishima and other civic organizations joined the projects, and through citizen

The third generation 69

participation, a strategy for river maintenance was drafted. Various plans based on the restoration of the local ecosystem, such as reverting the concrete riverwalls, returning to the traditional soil and lava stone embankments, and creating biotopes in some places. After that, with the cooperation of the upstream companies, cooperation strategies aimed at a fair distribution of groundwaters, which had been monopolized by them. Thanks to these, the water quality recovered, and by 1998, an entire area of 1,500 meters along the river was upgraded (Watanabe, 2004).

The subsequent activities of Groundworks Mishima, while still based on environmental restoration and conservation of biodiversity, expanded their scope to include local promotion, shopping district promotion, and the regeneration of the regional culture. The range of activities expanded according to river connections and water-related infrastructures in the city, developing a new local charm (see Figure 5.2). Various types of events and machizukuri projects were developed, such as eco-tours, the rebirth of local food culture, international exchanges, capacity building and training, and working on the management of wider areas[5] (Watanabe, 2004).

From here, the base for environmental machizukuri in Japan was set, and a new ecological order supported by the action of local communities was born.

Chapter conclusion

The method called "machizukuri," which has evolved throughout half a century since its birth, has proven itself capable of not only improving the living environment of local communities, but also playing a vital role in solving problems of diverse nature, such as welfare, education, regional economy, and environmental problems, while at the same time channeling and materializing visions for the future of a whole region.

The evolutive process of machizukuri, from its birth, to today's practice, through its three generations, has produced methods, systems, and tools, to respectively develop unique machizukuri projects. These generations have not substituted each other over time, but have accumulated and created plural possibilities for action.

Now, at this stage, the goal is to create a mechanism to motivate new forms of governance for the local community in which multiple agents can cooperate. Therefore, based on this mechanism, in order to improve the built environment, it is necessary to develop specific planning techniques, some of which will be discussed in following chapters.

Notes

1 Japanese terms usually bear an additional nuance that can be lost in translation. For example, the kind of ambiguous spatial domain or holistic vision we are discussing here is called "*chiiki un-ei*" (literally "regional management"). "District

70 Shigeru Satoh

Management" ("*chiku un-ei*") refers to an administrative scope, "regional management" ("*chiiki un-ei*") entails a wider range, and "community management" ("*komyuniti un-ei*") bears a stronger individual community nuance. Here, we have used the term "area management" to refer to the organizations and people who voluntarily gather in various forms and ranges of machizukuri.

2 Parallel and different from project-based Machizukuri Councils in other examples; dedicated to coordinate reconstruction efforts.

3 In addition, the Takatori Christian Church community in this area, which was a strong member of the Machizukuri Council, became a base for various volunteer activities. Student volunteers were dispatched every day from their provisional accommodation areas to their different work sites. Also, a mini FM radio station was opened to connect wide areas and offer multilingual broadcasting.

4 The "*machiya*" is a traditional type of Japanese merchant house composed of a shop, living spaces, warehouse, and workplace.

5 www.gwmishima.jp.

References

Naikaku-hu (Cabinet Office). (2018). *Tokutei Hieiri Houjin ni kansuru Jittaichousa (Survey on Actual Situation of Non-profit Organizations)*. Tokyo: Cabinet Office.

Nojima, S. (2015). Nagahama. In Satoh, S. (ed.) *Shinpan Zusetsu Jokamachi Toshi (New Version Illustrated Japanese Castle Towns)*. Tokyo: Kajima Shupan-Kai.

Satoh, S. (ed.) (2017). *Machizukuri kyousho (Textbook of Machizukuri)*. Tokyo: Kashima Shuppan-kai.

Watanabe, T. (2005). *Seiryuu no Machi ga Yomigaetta (Machi with Clear Stream Recovered: Challenge of Mishima Groundworks)*. Tokyo: Chuou Houki Shupan.

Part II
Method and Tools

6 Machizukuri methodology and tools

Shigeru Satoh

Introduction: six methods for machizukuri

In the beginning, a clear definition of machizukuri did not exist. In the second half of the 1970s, a blurred dreamlike image of "machizukuri" spread, various trial-and-error experiences were repeated and, from them, fundamental machizukuri principles, aims and methods became clear. This means that machizukuri was somehow discovered through practice. As each of the different machizukuri experiences grew, new practices were born inside them, overlapping and giving birth to new relationships between them. In any case, what is more important to machizukuri is that through its practice, places are able to redefine and develop themselves in autonomous ways, without a fixed formula.

This chapter describes six methods common to most machizukuri projects, and the tools related to them.

1   The "method of discovery" refers to a way to discover and share the unique conditions and potentials of a particular place and, with it, to define a clear direction for its improvement.
2   Machizukuri can take the form of a co-creation process based on gaming and simulation tools. The idea here is to simulate and get feedback prior to a reality that will certainly take shape in the near future.
3   Through "machizukuri citizens' enterprise" local citizens and various stakeholders engage in machizukuri projects by themselves. It allows the promotion of machizukuri on the local community's own initiative.
4   Through a multi-stakeholder governance method various citizen and community organizations, companies and the public sector, each of them with different objectives and behavioral patterns, are put together inside a planned system. This allows their collaborative schemes to improve and results to be boosted.
5   The "interactive editing" method refers to a system which aims at allowing various actors to influence each other as a way to redefine each one's objectives and programs, to cooperate and assemble efforts,

74 *Shigeru Satoh*

so as to achieve better results. To do so, specific tools and techniques are developed and used to put this idea to practice.

6 Machizukuri can be development through a series of consecutive initiatives linked by a unifying story or vision. Here, diverse complementary strategic flows combine to create, share and add value to a holistic comprehensive story.

The "method of discovery"

By the time machizukuri was about to take off, in 1965, Akio Chii, who was one of the first machizukuri supporters, standing in the middle of the burnt fields after the Oshima Motomachi Great Fire, understood the importance of the method of discovery. Taking Chii's words: "First of all, try to walk. Stand up and watch over, pay attention to [the sounds that reach] your ears. Leave your heart empty and try to accept phenomena as they are. That is the starting point" (Chii, 1975, p. 12, lines 3–5).

Through the carefully evolving machizukuri process an ideal vision for the study area is unveiled. This process cannot be reduced to simple design or analytic methods, which often become dry ways of expression that cannot connect to vivid images of the local lifestyles. On the contrary, residents by their own means must work together with experts to discover the essence of their shared places and community. This puts them in a place where they are able to feel and perceive what the place needs, on the basis of the mutual relations of the elements that compose it. Then, taking as a basis the problems and potentials discovered, while thinking of the true meaning of the "machi," participants approach the strategic design process in a cooperative way, which awakens the value of co-creation among them.

As machizukuri practice focuses on solving particular problems in a dedicated way by the local people and for the local people, it is essential to first discover and develop a common understanding of what machizukuri and "machi" are. Machizukuri activities first started in neglected districts where pollution problems and a high risk of disaster were generalized issues, such as the "old wooden densely built-up areas."[1] Even if many issues are patent in such areas, intangible strong community bonds and attachment to living areas has given them a unique cohesion, charm and quality that negate their flaws.

Such areas shared the same constitutive principles as traditional Japanese towns, similar living spaces, community structures and spirit, and yet, the high urban density gave rise important environmental deterioration problems. For example, winding narrow roads structure the urban pattern, entailing a high disaster risk. However, at the same time, traditional semi-private "roji,"[2] intermediate alleys, "michi," narrow human scale roads, and "tamari,"[3] small spaces inside superblocks, feel cozy, familiar and safe from heavy traffic of main roads. "Shoten-gai" neighborhood shopping streets and quarters[4] as well usually benefit from a busy vibrant environment, in

Machizukuri methodology and tools 75

which strong bonds between locals, merchants and customers are created. These unique spaces and human relations are the product of long processes of constant interaction and experience of communities in their living environment. Yet, such a complex and organic configuration is not difficult to grasp, but rather leaves a positive memorable impression on users and visitors thanks to the personal accumulation of rich experiences in them.

Bird's-eye view of "machiya" town houses

Expanding internal space to outer street

Decorating the space covered by roof eves

Transformative space for relaxed use

Figure 6.1 Ma: blurred boundaries and intermediate shared areas.

76 *Shigeru Satoh*

Box 6.1 "Ma": Blurred boundaries and intermediate shared areas

Concerning the physical structure of Japanese traditional living environments, various examples of intermediate space and transition areas exist. Let
me refer here to some of the most characteristic.

In traditional commoner and merchant quarters in urban historical centers,
like Kyoto merchant downtown areas, *machiya* town houses were a widespread building typology. The *machiya* presents clear facades and partitions
along main commercial streets. The space in-between is called *inubashiri* (dog
run), an narrow open corridor that runs between the *machiya*. It provides a
space that mediates between the private house and the town, facing main
streets covered by the roof eves but not walled. This composition allows
machiya residents to appropriate it and make it their own, decorating it with
flower pots, benches, etc. Dark rooms of the house also look toward the outer
streets, creating a connection between the household and the bustling *machi*.

This clearly represents *ma*, intermediate space, and the ambiguity of
Japanese urban space. Besides, these spaces have also been widely used in
Japanese traditional and modern architecture to emphasize the connections
between architecture and surrounding gardens. These threshold spaces,
between "inside" and "outside," are rather well-known in foreign contexts
and one of the most iconic features of Japanese architecture.

All these examples explain how the concept of *ma* materializes in the built
environment. In Japanese culture the *ma* makes reference to ambiguous
intervals and intermediate spaces.

In such places, even when functional needs were met through district redevelopment, the lives of the neighbors and their relations may be destroyed
by formal urban development projects. This motivated local communities
to look for sustainable development models that at the same time helped
preserve the local quality. To that end, it was important for local residents
to question themselves and clarify the meaning of the place they lived in,
how it had evolved historically, the values created in the process, and thus,
what to take care of and what to improve.

During this period, studies were conducted on the configurative principles of Japanese urban space with a special emphasis on the elucidation
of its historical processes and cultural significance.[5] This also required
observing how people were actually using their surrounding physical
environment. Social behaviors in traditional neighborhoods were recorded
and studied as a way to identify the special quality that the accumulation
through history of social activities lent to the built urban fabric. The most
important thing here, beyond sharing the results of the research, was that
local residents could also rediscover and become aware of the local value,
awakening their own confidence. This was thus a process of deciphering

the configurative principles of traditional living areas that were not only based on traditional academic or scientific observation and research. In this case, the process progressed thanks to the mutual influences and exchanges between experts and neighbors following the rediscovery of the areas. Thus, the process of discovery in machizukuri practice is neither individual nor isolated, but a collective experience. Machizukuri focuses on sharing different experiences of local discovery between neighbors, experts, stakeholders, etc., to help people realize what they desire and what should be implemented in the place they inhabit. This collective discovery process makes use of diverse tools to develop a common awareness of the targeted urban area, to then proceed with interactive design through discussion and exchanges of ideal images for the town or the neighborhood. These processes do normally bring enjoyment to the people involved and stimulate hope and motivation for machizukuri. This means that, through constant interaction and exchanges, these future ideals are collectively conceived. Throughout the discovery process, goals and values become gradually clearer until the participants finally understand and agree on a desired image for the "machi" (shared community and its place), and can proceed to define a machizukuri plan. In this way, the method of discovery guides experts and residents along the machizukuri process.

Machizukuri co-creation through gaming and simulation

Machizukuri processes have to face various contradictions and overcome diverse conflicts. To mediate in these situations, machizukuri games help support each participant, influence each other, negotiate and get better results. Such games lead always to a win-win situation where there are neither winners nor losers. However, if the machizukuri process does not go well, it would be extremely difficult to reformulate and repeat engaging the same participants. For this reason, to secure the success of this heterogeneous process, mutual editing and action scenarios must be simulated in advance, and feedback must be used to improve the real machizukuri process.

Through tools such as collaborative design and workshops stakeholders join simulation games in which they recreate real-life interactions. Along with the preparedness that the simulation brings, workshops allow experiencing the machizukuri process in advance in a playful manner, which also helps share ideas and find better solutions. The methods obtained from them are reflected later in real machizukuri practice and the selection of various types of project. Thus, different types of workshop must be devised so that the opinions of all the participants are reflected.

Tools for co-creation – machizukuri design simulation game

One of the first steps for machizukuri was to develop methods that enabled direct participation of residents and landowners in the planning and design

78 *Shigeru Satoh*

processes. This was also a way for them to get involved in the implementation and management of the project through a continuous commitment to it. The second generation of machizukuri, while keeping the experiences of the first generation in sight, encouraged people to take part in the "machi," live it, and get to understand it through their own physical senses as a way to discover what their own expectations were. This motivation stimulated the creation of simulation tools and design games to encourage the collective discovery process. In other words, to replace the mere discussions of the previous machizukuri generation and achieve long-term personal involvement and better understanding, it was necessary to introduce more engaging co-creation processes (Satoh, 2005).

In this context, simulations can confirm and strengthen the aims of the various machizukuri activities, visualizing the process and results, and providing feedback on the proposed plan in advance. Moreover, this is a powerful method to facilitate communication and agreement between various entities, to foster consensus, and to assist in the formation of new partnerships that will be necessary to carry out the agreed development ideals. The simulation of the machizukuri process includes an action process and the future lifestyles in the area, not merely the simulation of the modifications on the physical environment; this makes it possible to imagine the appearance of local life, trading and business exchanges, children's play areas and the activities of local people.

For that purpose, in order to simulate the both the shape and the activities of a future living town, Satoh laboratory of Waseda University developed a simulation device to visualize a 1/100 model from the position of the human eye. This device uses a microscopic camera that is remotely controlled by a manual remote control and monitored on a computer. The camera can move inside models and generate images on a screen to allow participants to recreate the future neighborhood. Through the images participants can experience the same sensations they would feel in their neighborhood after the completion of the machizukuri project, discuss and evaluate each other's impressions (see Figure 6.2). On top of this, the fact that the participants are able to move the camera, play with the model, and modify the proposals by themselves in an analogic way is extremely relevant to a successful co-creation process.

The previously mentioned research team developed three kinds of simulation devices. The first type of equipment can be easily carried around, used by hand, and checked during the design game. The second is a movable device in which the camera is attached to an assembled frame, and is used to present the results of the design game during a workshop and so forth. The third piece of equipment is a large system installed in the research studio, connected to a computer, in which the camera moves via an automatic control inside the model so that it simulates walks around the streets and alleys while recording images of this walk. This type of machizukuri design game assists the participated design of the town through an interactive co-creation process.

Figure 6.2 Design simulation game workshop using landscape simulation system.
Source: Satoh, 2019.

Based on the experimental models and ideas assembled during workshops, the experts will present a new model that assembles these hopes and presents an alternative plan, which will be discussed during the next workshop. Again, the process of simulation and modification will be repeated, and the plan will gradually mature. In other words, this process incorporates the simulation of the future appearance of the town and the gaming process related to the creation of actual agreements on cooperation efforts. This means that if an agreement is formed in this way, the actual process of project development, including the implementation of the agreed design and ideals, will proceed smoothly.

Through these processes, machizukuri participants are not only encouraged to think about their living environments on the desk, but to actively engage in promoting and implementing machizukuri.

Machizukuri citizens' operations

To facilitate the active engagement of the local population in redevelopment processes, the "machizukuri citizens' operation" method was created.

In many cases, the improvement of physical space is required for machizukuri to produce visible results. When a Machizukuri Plan is stipulated in a Machizukuri Ordinance, it is then possible to develop locally designed

80 *Shigeru Satoh*

community roads and green paths as public works. However, the budget for public works is often limited. Under such circumstances, what individual residents can do for machizukuri is limited to the improvement of their own properties, such as buildings. At the same time, private companies do not usually invest in machizukuri projects unless such projects will bring them profit. Linking both sides, what is important for machizukuri is the creation of "commons" between local residents and private companies through the development of joint projects. New actors who do not belong to either the government or private companies have become the engines of machizukuri practice, which has expanded from the improvement of living environments to the creation of public spaces, services and economic cycles within the local community (e.g., employment support). In recent years, during the third generation of machizukuri, citizens, local business operators and volunteers from outside the community started to gather in various machizukuri citizen operation groups in cooperation with community organizations and with public assistance and funding. Such methods for the preparation and implementation of machizukuri projects are collectively called "Machizukuri Citizens' Operations"; it can be defined as a collection of machizukuri activities implemented by a cooperative organization of citizens based on a local community through the use of potential resources and demands in the community.

The following three major methods have been developed for the implementation of such operations.

Cooperative redevelopment

In this method residents and landowners cooperate in the small-scale redevelopment of densely populated urban areas. Through the "cooperative redevelopment operations" method, mixed-use buildings, in which apartments co-exist with local commercial and other facilities, can be constructed through the exchange of property rights of residents and landowners. A cooperative redevelopment project does not attempt large-scale redevelopment endeavors, but smaller projects that enable residents to continue living in the same community while improving the livability and profitability of the areas. At the same time, such projects allow the creation of rich community spaces and improvement of the overall quality of a neighborhood by linking them and introducing common development goals in each of them (e.g., adding greenery or opening up new paths). Projects implemented through this method are referred to as "cooperative redevelopment projects" (Satoh, 1995, 2019).

Many densely built-up urban areas in Japan developed by the repeated and disordered subdivision of land. In old shopping areas, while shop owners had clear property rights to the narrow strips of land facing the main streets (normally, with the shop-house at the front occupying the front line), to the back, the lots were subdivided and complex rights (such

Machizukuri methodology and tools 81

as leases) appeared. These patterns have continued up until today, and nowadays, as these parts of land at the back of the lot are not compliant with the Building Standards Act, the buildings that occupy them cannot be reconstructed. This situation has caused several problems for older inhabitants with low incomes, who have to live in such old and dilapidated constructions.

In these densely built-up wooden housing areas it is difficult to fully tackle the improvement of the living environment by rebuilding individual houses or wooden apartments. Instead, so far the strategy has been to gather several houses, shops or land lots under cooperative redevelopment projects, which can leave a more fruitful impact on the urban fabric. Such projects enable residents to continue living within the same community by the exchange of property rights implemented by a cooperative of residents and landowners. By incorporating this activity in the official "machizukuri" category as defined by the public administration, these cooperatives can receive government funding as they contribute to solving social problems and creating commons for the community, such as small plazas or meeting spaces. For example, if new rental housing was constructed on the plot occupied by an old wooden apartment building, the low-income residents of the old building could not afford the rent of the new housing block. However, the low-income residents of the old building would be able to continue living inside the same community if some of the reconstructed apartment buildings were dedicated to public housing. In this way, the living environment would be improved, new public spaces would be developed, and housing for the elderly required by the community would be developed. Thus, such projects provide welfare services and community activities that can be considered "machizukuri" and, at the same time, the implementation of cooperative projects through the investment of residents and landowners for a mutual benefit contributes to the achievement of the general goals set by machizukuri practice in cooperation with various other machizukuri organizations (Satoh, 2011).

Yet, the implementation of such cooperative projects requires the consensus of all the residents and landowners in the targeted areas and their contribution to funding the projects. The stability of the shared ideals and spirit of machizukuri, along with its rationality and understanding of benefits in the long run, are definitely required to overcome obstacles in consensus building and funding.

The Machizukuri Company, towards Machizukuri Business

The second method responds to the implementation of projects through a Machizukuri Company established by local companies, individuals, the local Chamber of Commerce and Industry and/or public bodies according to each case. Machizukuri Companies work as third-sector limited companies partially funded by local governments (see Chapter 5) for the

82 *Shigeru Satoh*

implementation of social business. Such projects have become a global trend and new business have emerged all over the world aiming at contributing to society in various sectors, including the environment, education, health, poverty reduction and social inclusion, adopting different names in different countries in accordance with each social context (e.g., social enterprise) (Borzaga and Defourny, 2001).

Machizukuri is an activity that aims at solving the previously mentioned problems in local communities. In recent years, the responsibility for implementing machizukuri has fallen upon different groups or figures that have been recognized as leaders of the movement by local communities. Various types of figure bear such a responsibility. For example, the NPO Mishima and the Kurokabe Company, iconic examples of the third machizukuri generation mentioned in Chapter 5, were new machizukuri organizations established for the implementation of social business. These types of social businesses normally develop community business as an extension of their machizukuri activities.

Micro-initiatives

The third operational method focuses on the implementation of projects that provide for community activities, welfare places for various residents including the elderly, children and the disabled, and employment opportunities. Various small-scale companies and organizations, including NPOs, are at the forefront of this kind of initiatives. A representative example of this is the social business in Takaoka described in Chapter 8. In this case, a small *machiya* townhouse renovation project adapted the traditional building as a multipurpose space for the local community. From this, the *machiya* became a sort of community hub and incubator of new social business and local initiatives. Other micro-projects appeared and spaces around the neighborhood were transformed to provide social services (child care, common meals, etc.). Thus, from a first informal project, the community activated, projects appeared and linked motivated by a common image of the area. Later, this gave way to the establishment of an official organization in charge of such actions.

Micro-initiatives did not only operate in urban contexts but also in rural areas. The countryside has also incorporated agritourism and ecotourism social businesses, and has set cooperation schemes with machizukuri projects in neighboring cities, expanding their action scale to wider territorial management.

Through the combination of these three different methods Machizukuri Citizens' Operations take place nowadays. The emergence of these different types of social business conducted machizukuri into a new phase. Now, machizukuri practice has focused on setting networks and developing mechanisms for the collaboration of multiple stakeholders and the creation of project partnerships.

Multi-stakeholder governance

Takamasa Yoshizaka presented the concept of "discontinuous continuity/unity" (Yoshisaka, 1975), which portrays the world as a heterogeneous discontinuous reality in which autonomous colliding parts simultaneously belong to and constitute a comprehensive whole. This can be equally applied to social structures. It is possible to find as many different types of collaborative structures as different types of community. Thus, rather than trying to integrate different local community groups into one closed association, it is essential for the machizukuri process to recognize the coexistence of diverse actors. Based on this, multi-stakeholder collaborations for machizukuri practice should be fluid to allow different types of interactive editing, encouraging their mutual support under common objectives.

Besides, when allowing such discontinuity, it is also important to envision the formation of new groups and systems to help channel possible points of conflict into new creativity and energy. For example, in some cases stakeholders might connect through a regional network, organize in a bigger platform or even establish new associations. Here, machizukuri must help to define a stable strategy for such collaborations, but at the same time, in response to the different issues that might appear in time, the strategy should be flexible enough to be gradually edited. With this, this system allows to set structures for local and regional governance and at the same time accompanies and assists different stakeholders involved through their edition process.

In Japan, numerous organizations have emerged from the simple self-governing groups that were created for each elementary school district or smaller areas under the support of the local government. Bigger area management is thus implemented through partnerships between these smaller organizations. In urban areas where commercial, business and residential functions coexist, it is possible to find the most disparate self-governing organizations operating at the same time and in the same area. In consequence, when mechanisms to assist all these organizations fulfill their own goals while complementing one another are put in place, machizukuri practice can produce optimum results. But because each context presents particular social and power structures, deciding on the form of these mechanisms is an important point for machizukuri. Rather than waiting for such organizations to form networks spontaneously, machizukuri tries to design an appropriate system in advance and to share it with the organizations included in it. This is necessary to effectively include all the different stakeholders in an area and to optimize their collaborations. In this context, four basic patterns for multi-stakeholder collaboration appear (Aiba, 2005).

The first type is the network-type partnership. In it, although various citizens' organizations do get in touch with each other and sometimes do even cooperate. However, connections between network members are

84 *Shigeru Satoh*

weak and are almost limited to information exchanges. Thus, network-type partnerships are normally formed to enhance communication. In residential areas in many cases neighborhood associations are at the core of such networks and are in charge of organizing regular events through such a partnership. However, if machizukuri activities are to be implemented in a continuous way, other types of organizational structures must be developed.

The second type is the arena-type partnership. This type of partnership refers to a decision-making organization that is put in place to respond to urgent detailed discussions and exchange of opinions. Thus, this type of group aims at drawing conclusions on a particular matter. In consequence, discussion, study and decision-making are the three essential elements of this partnership, but these partnerships may also focus on one of these three elements in accordance with their particular nature. The Machizukuri Council, for example, composed by representatives of various community associations and individuals, is a clear case of an arena-type partnership. However, this type of group has no power to act, and needs either delegate to other bodies, or to gain the support of other groups to see its decisions implemented.

The third type is the platform-type partnership in which various stakeholders gather to design and implement a practical project or action. Even though decisions on individual projects and tasks are made through the platform, the partnership is formed with different independent members, which maintain their individual legal and administrative status. The Town Management Organization stipulated in the City Center Revitalization Act is an example of this type of partnership described in Chapter 5. This partnership will only be fulfilled if the interested parties participate in it freely under a membership or similar system. If stakeholders agree on specific actions, new project partnerships appear for their implementation.

The fourth type is the project partnership. Limited liability partnerships or NPOs are examples. This does not always have to be a permanent corporate organization, but one formed connecting various other organizations and individuals under a single legal entity for the purpose of achieving a specific goal. Thus, here, a variety of actors coming from different backgrounds gather to plan and design the machizukuri project and work together throughout the implementation stage after transforming into a corporate group.

While neighborhood associations and citizens' organizations such as NPOs are normally core members of local multi-stakeholder partnerships, private companies and school organizations (PTAs) and even public bodies, such as social welfare councils, may sometimes be members of the partnerships as well. Besides, in many cases, a local governance organization is formed by combining the four types of partnerships mentioned above, gathering the different possible members mentioned above in various combinations. From this, "holonic" relationships may also be formed when an organization composed by partnerships becomes a member of another partnership organization. For example, a platform-type group established for the conservation of the natural environment in a certain area can be also a member of an arena by becoming a member of the Machizukuri Council. As the structure of these local governance partnerships is normally fluid, it is important to always visualize and keep a close eye on it so that members of the organization share the same whole picture and confirm their roles inside this structure. Each individual community along with selected groups should decide on the types of partnerships and the structure desirable for machizukuri design and practice. For example, a multi-layered structure in which each different stakeholder occupies a particular position, plays different roles in the partnership, implements various activities and makes decisions is generally considered desirable for machizukuri practice. However, as it may take time and money to maintain the partnerships whenever too complicated, these multiple layers, relations and functions are often simplified at a certain stage of the machizukuri process. In any case, it is clear the machizukuri has produced important methods for the development of multi-layered local governance structures.

The challenge here would be to make these multi-stakeholder partnerships progress smoothly; to do so, the main tool is the interactive editing method.

The interactive editing method

Embracing diversity

Through this kind of process of discovery of the "machi," it is possible to understand the many different values and realities that coexist in it, things that have evolved along with local history, or things valued and cherished by locals, which have accumulated through time creating a historical layering difficult to isolate or divide. For example, in the exchange of impressions that Gulliver map (see Nakamura, 2003, Chapter 7) activities promote, everyone's desires and inclinations are expressed, different types of appeals are recognized for the "machi," and the participants get to realize that this diversity and variety is precisely one of the main potentials for the areas. This process thus makes clear that the coexistence of diverse realities, even if sometimes in apparent contradiction, contributes to a rich society and enhances local sustainability.

The recognition of diversity also means accepting discontinuities and contradictions in some cases. As the machizukuri process goes on, the goal is not to "tolerate" such diversity, but to recognize that a special vitality originates in the interaction of very different activities that develop in a discontinuous manner in various places, and the unavoidable collision of such opposites. Thinking about it carefully, it is possible to clearly understand that this discontinuity provides further charm and vitality to the urban society. Machizukuri can thus channel and contribute to the appearance of

86   Shigeru Satoh

multiple situations as such. If we tried to unify and organize these different realities under a single set of values, the original meaning and the vitality of each one of them would be lost. Parallels can be found, of course, at a bigger scale in general society, pushed forward by very diverse motivations and circumstances, all in continuous collision and equilibrium. Inside the city as well, different elements and realities coexist. These neither respond to mechanical behaviors nor do their links follow perfectly defined equations. Each one of them exists with autonomy while at the same time coexists, without much order and in constant collision, with the others.

Allowing and integrating "contradiction and discontinuity"

On some occasions, it is evident that in reality, rather than facing ideal harmonious scenarios, one must address situations in which inconsistencies and discontinuities stand out, proving that contradictions make part of the essence of the "machi." A special effort would be required to harmonize these, and yet, instead of thinking that inconsistencies and discontinuities should be avoided, it is important to find ways to recognize that collisions and conflicts can also generate a new energy. Here, machizukuri works with the conviction that, while enfolding the different discontinuities, integrating them in one strategy or scenario, a special vitality and interactions are born. Thinking about these clashes in a positive way would help sprout and grow various meaningful initiatives, which might appear from the collision of previous realities.

Recognizing the existence of such contradictions and discontinuities is at the base of machizukuri, which has focused on developing ways to better assemble them.[6] This led to the definition of specific methods for mutual interactive editing that will be described next.

Methods for assimilating discontinuities and allowing interactive editing

As said before, Yoshisaka's concept of "discontinuous continuity/unity" (Yoshisaka, 1975) defends the coexistence of discontinuities, collisions and interactions. Nevertheless, "editing" means neither unification nor elimination of discontinuities. The interactive editing method can be represented by the efforts to recognize diversity and the existence of eventual discontinuities, to tie them together, and to create new value out of them. When diverse things are assembled together, it is better not to force unification but to allow them to coexist while keeping their own independence. If a strong assemblage was forced, the meaning of each element would be weakened, and the different participants involved in the process would perceive its negative influence. Taking this into account, this method provides machizukuri with a way to recognize the autonomy and self-organization of the urban areas targeted by its activities and to mutually agree on common objectives, creating new value from the different existent relationships in the area. Machizukuri can be thus defined as a process in which diverse projects involving diverse actors are interactively edited.[7]

More specifically, this method corresponds with an "interactive editing of living space." The ambiguous place where private and public realms overlap enables interactive editing. Instead of advocating for a pyramidal society, various attempts are made to theorize and define strategies that enable the recognition of the coexistence and autonomy of diverse entities. These ideas are common in contemporary philosophical theories, as for example the holonic theory, complex systems, assemblage theory, etc.

This, applied to the machizukuri process, is reflected in the many different types of project and activities that are born throughout the machizukuri process. They often appear mixed with each other in a discontinuous way. Machizukuri does not exclude any of them carelessly, but works on achieving a new harmony through their mutual interaction. In return, such dynamic edition processes give shape to machizukuri and, whenever successful, help it progress more easily.

Scenario planning and multiple narratives

The management of unpredictable time flows

Discontinuity does not only apply to space and place. Time flows discontinuously and the future cannot be predicted with certainty either. Even so, in parallel to different events, as the machizukuri process advances, it must be able to manage change, integrating it and moving forwards while editing its original strategies. In this context, the scenario planning[8] method allows linking together sequential elements inside the spatial and temporal discontinuity, giving them a certain order. This broad comprehensive vision leads to better results in practice. Here, both experts and residents become intrinsic parts of the machizukuri process. This means going beyond the boundary that lies between those who make plans and what is planned, or between those who design and what is designed. Planning experts recognized that machizukuri presented an alternative reality, especially different from what city planning and environmental design had been trying to achieve so far. These scenarios assemble a wide variety of actors that carry out diverse types of machizukuri, and create a whole image for the area by combination of all these efforts and future potentials. Then, to assist the process toward this ideal image, flexible area management strategies are designed. To make this possible, it is essential that these ideas are understood by actors inside and outside the targeted areas, shared, and supported. For that purpose, it is necessary to express all the information related to the progress of the machizukuri process in an easy-to-understand manner. This must involve the evaluation, correction and further development of the machizukuri scenario, precisely, through a process of interactive editing.

88 *Shigeru Satoh*

However, it is difficult to completely plan and control the uncertain future in which discontinuous machizukuri actions will be assembled. To achieve more stable results, it is effective to draw a scenario to visualize the progress of machizukuri, this means, the ways in which various entities intertwine, and the different partnerships and projects that might appear. Later, this scenario must be shared with the different parts involved in the process and the community, to strategically edit each of the actions proposed by this future scenario.

Scenario planning in machizukuri can be thus defined as "a method to assemble machizukuri activities of various related stakeholders into a future area management vision, forecasting changes in the socioeconomic and physical environments in the area targeted by the machizukuri activity." In other words, this means to portray machizukuri as a "series of scenarios" consistently evolving from the past to the present and towards the future.

In order for machizukuri to bring a greater social contribution, it is important to represent whole stories in a scientific and visual way. Besides, understanding machizukuri as an action research, it is clear that illustrating the process and visualizing it as a scenario for past, present and future actions, acquires an extreme importance. Usually, these scenarios are represented in the shape of spiral diagrams, as shown in Chapter 8 (Satoh, 2019). The main spiral represents the whole project vision and flow. From it, sub-spirals are drawn for each individual project, and are connected to the general nexus. Furthermore, each of the events represented in the spiral map must be properly linked to archival materials or correspondent project databases. This allows to keep detailed track of the process and to use the model in an even more effective way, providing complementary specific project data.

Chapter conclusion

The six methods detailed above present ways that allow machizukuri to discover the "machi," to channel collaborative efforts to examine its essence, and with it, to later establish systems to promote related projects and partnerships for its effective development. These methods also help define specific actions within the machizukuri process, arranging structures to integrate various discontinuities and creating links between them. At the same time, these methods are flexible enough to allow continuously editing such plans and assimilating the different events that take place along the way.

Thus, these methods assembled together are the engine that promotes and brings effective results to contemporary machizukuri practice.

Notes

1 *Mokuzou misshuu shigaichi* is a Japanese term coined largely to define such areas, which concentrate a high density of old wooden small dwellings. These characteristics make them dangerous and prone to fire, which created a very

Machizukuri methodology and tools 89

negative image in Japanese culture. Nevertheless, the term *"mokumitsu"* represents also a potentiality, interest, and image of closeness to the urban context. This positive nuance comes from its rich energetic social context, which brings a special potential for developing art festivals and outdoor arts in urban area (in the case of Mukou-jima in Tokyo for example, the traditional commoner *"chou-nin"* town-people culture of much energy which was exciting for young artists).

2 The term *"roji"* was translated as "alley" and presented to the English-speaking audience by S. Barrie in *Learning from the Japanese City* (1999). He referred to the small "alleys" of about 1–2 m wide between city row-houses which hosted part of the daily domestic activities and outdoor life. Besides, I would like to add that the *"roji"* has a strong presence in Japanese urban tissues and a positive meaning, implying a place that is taken care of and can be used by the close community.

3 While bigger streets might be crowded and not welcoming for neighbors wanting to socialize, the *"tamari"* represents small spaces, corners, open areas, etc. that allow a small number of people to safely stop by and chitchat.

4 The "shopping street" concept is also presented by Barrie (1999). He describes the areas as groups of streets of about 5–10 m wide marked by gates or representative elements and decoration conferring on them a special commercial character. In such spaces the shops normally display products, occupying part of the street space in front of them, creating a kind of transition zone between the shops and the open route or road.

5 Many studies focused on deciphering the structure and configurative principles of spontaneous organic urban spaces and *"machi"* at district and neighborhood levels so as to obtain clues for urban planning and architectural design. For example, the architect Maki (1980) coined the term *"oku-sei"* (or innerness) to describe both the inner spatial position and the transcendent intangible character of spaces in Tokyo's *"machi."* Further, the author of this chapter analyzed the historical records of six different historical areas in Tokyo and studied their machizukuri development methods (Satoh, 1990).

6 At this point, we must start by referring to the philosophical approach presented by Kitarou Nishida, which defended the "absolutely contradictory self-identity," or in other words, the recognition that tensions between contraries exist, coexist and make part of dynamic wholes. Rather than finding this a problem, this way of thinking recognizes the essence of human nature in these various contradictions and identifies them as opportunities to produce vitality.

7 "Editing" is a concept coined by Matsuoka (2001).

8 Specific terms such as "scenario planning," "scenario design," "scenario writing," and so forth, are used to refer to such a method. It is used, for example, to examine future implications and specific reactions to business, industry or environmental problems, among others.

References

Aiba, S. (2005). Partnership Donyu no Handan (Decision for Introducing Type of Partnership), in Sato, S. (ed.). *Chiiki Kyoudo no Kagaku* (Science of Community Collaboration). Tokyo: Seibunsha, pp. 58–70.

Barrie, S. (1999). *Learning from the Japanese City: Looking East in Urban Design.* London: Routledge.

90   Shigeru Satoh

Borzaga, C. and Defourny, J. (2001). *The Emergence of Social Enterprise*. London: Routledge.

Chii, A. (1975). Hakkenteki Houhou (Method of Discovery), in Yoshisaka Laboratory. *Hakkenn teki Houhou – Yoshisaka Kenkyushitu no Testugaku to Houhou (Method of Discovery or Heuristic Method – Philosophy and Method of Yoshisaka Laboratory). Toshi-Jutaku*. Special Issue 7508, pp. 12–13.

Maki, F. (ed.). (1980). *Mie-gakure suru Toshi – Edo kara Tokyo he* (City Hidden and Revealed – From Edo to Tokyo). Tokyo: Kajima Shuppankai.

Matsuoka, S. (2001). *Chi no Henshu Kougaku (Editing Engineering of Knowledge)*. Tokyo: Ashahi Shupan.

Nakamura, A. (2003). Machizukuri Heno Sanka no Atarashii Kyokumenn to Sono Dougu Tositeno "Garibah Chizu" (New Aspect of Participation in Town Planning and "Gulliver Map" as its Tool). *City Planning Review*. Special Issue. Papers on City Planning. vol. 38. no. 3. 1989. October 25, 2003. pp. 235–240 (in Japanese).

Satoh, S. (1990). *Tokyo no Kako, Gennzai, Mirai (Past, Preset and Future of Tokyo)*. Tokyo: Shokoku-sha

Satoh, S. (ed.). (2005). *Machizukuri Design Game*. Kyoto: Gakugei-Shuppan.

Satoh, S. (ed.). (2011). *Machizukuri Shimin Jigyou (Machizukuri Citizens' Operation)*. Kyoto: Gakugei-Shuppan.

Satoh, S. (2019). Evolution and Methodology of Japanese Machizukuri for the Improvement of Living Environments, *Japan Architectural Review*, vol. 2, no. 2, pp. 127–142, doi: 10.1002/2475–8876.12084 https://rdcu.be/bIe4b.

Setagaya Machizukuri Center. (1993, 1996, 1998, 2002). *Sanka no Dougu bako Part 1. 2. 3. 4 (Toolbox for Participation)*. Setagaya Machizukuri Center.

Yoshisaka, T. (1975). Hurenzoku Touitsutai (Dis-Continuous Unity), in Yoshisaka Laboratory. *Hakkenn teki Houhou – Yoshisaka Kenkyushitu no Testugaku to Houhou (Method of Discovery – Philosophy and Method of Yoshisaka Laboratory). Toshi-Jutaku*. Special Issue 7508.

7 Machizukuri and planning

Shin Aiba

Introduction

One stage of machizukuri involves design and the formulation of plans; the other stage entails the actual implementation of the project. It is also characteristic of machizukuri that these two stages can be reversed or repeated or that they can occur in parallel, on occasion. Of these two stages, the former is an act called *planning*, and machizukuri follows one kind of collaborative planning method whereby specialists and citizens engage in dialog with one another in some form to coordinate plans and design.

Hypothetically speaking, if we were to call this method "machizukuri planning," how would it be defined in comparison to other collaborative planning methods, and what kind of "planning system" and "city master plan" are necessary?

Advocacy planners and the community

The planning method that arrived in Japan at the dawn of the machizukuri movement was *advocacy planning*, a planning theory proposed and implemented by the American planner Paul Davidoff. It came to Japan in the 1970s and became a guidepost for specialists dealing with machizukuri and citizen participation. According to this way of planning, a planner becomes a representative of the people in an area, organizing their thoughts and feelings to refine a plan, and pits that plan against other plans, such as the plan created by the government. As Davidoff was also a lawyer, this approach is based on the way a court verdict is ultimately decided by a judge between opposing arguments put forth by lawyers representing the defendant and the plaintiff.

Certainly, there are cases in which it is effective to pit conflicting values against each other in an arena to decide the winner, as in cases when there is a structural wealth inequality in a community, when local communities are divided by ethnicity or religion, or when values are polarized in regard to a given issue. Indeed, such was the state of local communities in America

92 *Shin Aiba*

when advocacy planning was conceived. People on one side of poverty, inequality, and polarization lack the financial resources to hire an urban planner. That is where a specialist comes in. This motive also resonated with many specialists in Japan and prompted them to shift to advocacy planning.

However, in the end, advocacy planning was not an effective strategy in Japan in practice. There are two reasons for this: *the absence of disparities and differences*, and *the absence of mediation*. In Japanese cities, tangible spatial disparities are rare. In addition, with little difference based on religion or ethnicity, it is also rare for communities to be divided along such lines. Even if a community was divided in opinion over a certain issue, it would be uncommon for such a division to be connected to hard-to-bridge gaps such as religion or ethnicity, and since it is not connected to a fundamental conflict, it would often disappear with the passage of time. Furthermore, even if there had been a plan that polarized values in the way that advocacy planning assumes, there was not yet a court-like mechanism in place to decide its strengths and weaknesses.

Machizukuri planners and the community

The essential involvement of advocacy planners with the target community lies in the integration of the specialist and the local people. Strictly speaking, of course, a specialist from outside acts as a spokesperson and thus cannot become integrated with the local people (the people being spoken for). However, it was considered desirable for the specialist to become as closely integrated as possible. As such, the yardstick for a planner's work was their "distance from the local community" – i.e., the extent to which they became a member of the community by living with them and associating with them, both officially and privately – and the shorter that distance, the more highly they were regarded as a planner. However, instead of this approach, what kind of approach *should* we take with regard to a community?

If we think about the ideal way for a specialist to relate to a community, then (1) given the absence of disparities and differences, they should collect information from various actors to bring subtle differences into relief and use the differences discovered therein as a guide to facilitate discussion among different actors, and (2) given the absence of mediation, those discussions should be used to decide on things as a community. This is the definition of "machizukuri planning." To put this in extreme terms to highlight the contrast with advocacy planning, machizukuri planning is an approach that (a) is not excessively biased toward those in the community who are most visibly disadvantaged, (b) does not involve integration into the local community, (c) brings subtle differences into relief without trying to use a single structure to identify differences, and (d) does not yield decision making to a higher system.

Machizukuri planning approaches

I would now like to discuss a few different kinds of machizukuri planning approaches that have emerged through involvement with the community.

"Gulliver Map" is a method of workshop to collect information from residents using a large map on the floor of a room. In this approach, which is commonly used to collect information about the community in the initial stages of machizukuri, spontaneous "chit-chat" among citizens develops around the map as their thoughts and feelings about their experience on the map (i.e., in the community) collect like waves. Data for picking out subtle differences in the community are gathered by writing each sentiment on individual sticky notes of equal importance.

The Machizukuri Notebook is a method I created as part of the machizukuri process in Tsuruoka City, Yamagata Prefecture. The Notebook is a compilation of information for machizukuri gathered from workshops and surveys, intended for sharing with citizens. The aim was to summarize the historical meaning of the space, which cannot be understood merely from living in the community, as well as incidental sentiments gleaned at workshops, in order to provide citizens who read the Notebook with a guide for machizukuri.

"Machizukuri Hub" was converted from empty shops in downtown Tsuruoka. In this so-called "Downtown Laboratory" approach, which can be seen in action at universities across Japan, a specialist stays in the community and gathers information through dialog with visitors. If the Gulliver Map-style approach to data collection is like a "temporary exhibition," this would arguably be the "permanent collection."

These three approaches are intended to collect information in the initial stages of machizukuri, in which the planner gradually enters into the local community, picks up subtle differences that can serve as a guide for machizukuri, and makes them tangible.

"Machizukuri Design Game" is a method of workshop for local residents to examine the organization of urban facilities in a district. In this game, a specialist and residents use meticulously prepared cards and model parts to explore future directionalities for a city. What results is a "shared vision" for the city, as well as spatial and visual forms of that vision. The participants move their hands to coordinate with each other and create a vision that will serve as a guide for future machizukuri efforts or a landmark that can always be revisited.

Repeatedly holding such workshops or other face-to-face discussions will eventually lead to a situation in which some kind of decision is to be made. In the case of public works projects, it would be the chief or legislature that has the final say; if a private building is to be rebuilt or renovated, it is the individual owner who has the final say. While the process and approach to be followed depend on what it is that must be decided, in any case, they are not decided by a court or through heated parliamentary

Figure 7.1 Design game in Tsuruoka.

debate, as is assumed in advocacy planning; rather, weight is given to decisions accumulated in the community. Figure 7.1 shows the process of deciding on a proposal for the design of a park in Tsuruoka. Here, three proposals that developed through multiple workshops were presented to the public, and the winning proposal was ultimately decided by a vote among participants. The workshop attendees were not the ones who had the final say, but the winning proposal was given a great deal of importance in the actual development of the space.

It is also true that designing a park is a public works project, which is rarely subject to extreme complications, but in the case of private developments that involve development or restrictions on people's land, the expectations and requirements of the people involved can sometimes become entangled and unyielding to compromise, leading to complications. Once, there was a major discussion about developing or conserving an area in front of a train station in Tokyo, in which people were divided into five groups based on their opinions. Each group made a proposal and presented it to the others for assessment. No final decision was made here, but the participants used the experience and information from this discussion to finalize their opinions, which would contest with each other at a subsequent explanatory meeting. Thus, information was shared and opinions

Machizukuri and planning 95

were exchanged within the community without simply yielding the decision to a higher institution, such as a legislature or urban planning committee.

To this series of processes, specialists contribute their expertise, investigate differences, make them tangible and show them to a wide audience, use that to open dialog, and compile the content of that dialog. I hope I have clarified this approach, which follows a way of relating to the community that (1) is not excessively biased, (2) does not involve integration, (3) brings subtle differences into relief, and (4) does not produce decision making.

Planning system and city master plan for Machizukuri

What do you think of when you hear the words *planning system* or *master plan*? In very large projects, such as the development of New Towns, planners frequently draw up documents called master plans. These plans specify land usage, the placement of public facilities, such as roads and parks, and the placement of residential buildings. For large developments in Japan, it takes much time to construct, and public and private planners are involved in it. A development's master plan functions as a coordination tool to show the goal to the many engineers involved in the development. In this chapter, I will use the words *master plan* to refer to the thing that shows the goal and serves as the basis for discussion and coordination in the collaboration of many actors, and the term *planning system* to refer to the organizations that share a master plan.

The people concerned in a particular development project are limited to engineers. The master plan for such a development project can be called a *project master plan*, then what I would like to focus on in this chapter is a *city master plan*, which includes simultaneously the community's machizukuri, and the planning systems consisting of the organizations that share that plan.

In traditional city master plans, the government's urban planning policies are conveyed to citizens as a static future image for the city, and the role of citizens is limited to that of stating opinions for the plan. However, if we plan a city master plan for machizukuri, in which citizens are responsible for the plan's implementation, then a city master plan would comprise a dynamic future image for the city, drawn through a process in which multiple organizations discuss and occasionally implement ideas. Rather than just being a direct planning process with the goal of realizing the government's plan, the planning process of a city master plan for machizukuri would be a double-tracked process that also includes the goal of citizens' machizukuri. In this process, discussion would cultivate citizens' awareness and shape citizen organizations, and its planning documents would accumulate in phases as machizukuri expands.

96 Shin Aiba

Creating a planning system and city master plan for machizukuri

To show how one planning system and master plan for machizukuri was created, I will now examine an initiative in Tsuruoka City, Yamagata Prefecture, in which I was involved as a specialist.

The request from Tsuruoka City was to introduce citizen participation in urban design policy, which had until then been the responsibility of the government, and to construct a planning system in which many actors could be involved in machizukuri. As a small city in which the administration and citizens were not far from each other, Tsuruoka was not a city where citizens were detached from the government. However, there was a lack of experience and methods relating to citizen participation in urban design. To overcome this, the city started by introducing citizen participation one by one in several of its projects to gradually accumulate machizukuri experience among the government and citizens. The main system at this time was the City Master Plan (CMP) established in 1992. The projects started in 1996, and a planning system gradually came to be organized through the introduction of citizen participation one by one into each project.

The first citizens' workshop to create CMP brought together citizens and government, who were somewhat skeptical of unfamiliar words like "machizukuri" and "workshop." The projects started with walking around the city to collect information and then sharing it. In addition to the workshop for CMP, other citizens' workshops were held concurrently to discuss issues such as renovation of canals running through the city or development of the government district in the city center.

After accumulation of citizens' workshop in two years, the first planning document of CMP, the "Machizukuri Notebook," was published. Machizukuri Notebook compiled information about the city obtained through workshops and various surveys. In the workshop where the Machizukuri Notebook was unveiled, all the citizens who had participated in past two years' workshops were invited and they discussed various issues in machizukuri. While Tsuruoka is a small city, there were many citizens who discussed the shared topic of machizukuri for the first time in these workshops, which resulted in new connections.

More machizukuri partners came to be discovered through the repeated process of collecting information, holding a workshop, and gathering different actors to have discussions. After the projects started out, the goal of the workshops was to dig up and share information during the first two years, then their goal transformed into contribution and discussion of concrete ideas in the third year, transformed into refining specific projects in the fourth year, and transformed into drafting plans for tentative experiments and reviewing and starting machizukuri projects in the fifth year. After year five, projects were realized one after the other: a festival produced jointly by an association of shop owners and citizen organizations; a DIY literature center created in collaboration with citizen organizations; the design for a new park and the development of an organization to manage it sustainably; the development of residences for the elderly; and the creation of design rules for the commercial district townscape.

Over the five years since the beginning of the projects, a planning system in which many actors were able to become involved in machizukuri took shape. The Tsuruoka city master plan was decided with the formation of this planning system in 2001. Various workshops at different stages of progress and with different goals had already been taking place concurrently, so the city master plan was made to unify all the discussions that had taken place up to that point. This is evident from the structure of the table of contents. Traditional city master plans are divided into an overall plan and district-specific plans, which specify detailed plans for districts. However, in Tsuruoka, plans were not shown for districts where the discussions with the lead actors had not yet reached a mature stage. Since collaborative planning systems assumed specific partners, the idea was to create the district plan after the partnership was formed.

Conclusion

Society has truly become decentralized in Japan, with each local government developing its own unique planning system. The city master plan developed in Tsuruoka was created to support the planning system created over five years of machizukuri work. The most significant characteristic of machizukuri is that the government decides on the plan not by inviting any and all citizens to participate in a program but by forming a partnership with an organization of specific citizens. In the case of Tsuruoka, citizen organizations were developed over five years, partnerships were formed with those organizations to decide on policies, and the detailed city master plan was formed with those policies taken into account. For those who believe that a wide range of citizens' opinions should be considered in the creation of a city master plan, this method may seem unfair. The only way to overcome this unfairness is for the government to hold workshops on a continuous basis at various opportunities, in which it can discover and develop new citizen organizations. This way, new partnerships can continue to be formed between the government and citizen organizations. Such continuity is absolutely necessary for a city master plan and planning system to support machizukuri.

Part III

Experiments and Case Studies

8 Regenerating the urban structure in historic districts

An approach through projects representing traditional culture and crafts, created by entrepreneurs and craftsmen in Takaoka City

Yosuke Mano

Regeneration of the historical city in the context of the sustainable development of urban areas

The role of the regeneration of the historic city has changed greatly in the small and medium provincial cities of Japan. During the post-World War II period of high economic growth, conservation movements against rapid urban renewal were instigated spontaneously by the citizens, having a huge effect in terms of the conservation of historic buildings and landscapes.

However, from the late 1990s onwards, the decline of the Old Town is prominent in many cities, and seems likely to continue in the long term. The issue of regenerating the old districts of historic cities has become a structural problem, going beyond the conflict between conservation and development in the city. We need to present new perspectives on those problems that cannot be resolved using only the conservation and community development methods that have been established up to now.

For the regeneration of the historical city, we need to address future changes in social networking, mobility and quality of life, and to think within the framework of sustainable development based on the premise of activity on the wide scale. With regard to the remaining architectural environment and natural environment, we need to think about not only the preservation of their historical value, but also the role they play as a hub of cultural and economic activities. There is also a need to gradually adapt these environments to future changes.

Takaoka City, described in this chapter, has followed the typical process of transformation seen in provincial Japanese cities in the early modern period following the Meiji Restoration, the post-World War II period and the end of the twentieth century. The environment of the historical urban area, formed in the early modern period from the combination of areas of high-density economic activity and housing, changed

102 Yosuke Mano

significantly at the end of the twentieth century. This decline is clearly evident in the current urban structure.

On the other hand, it is also an unusual city where the traditions of the townsfolk's culture and crafts that have their origin in the Edo period can be seen in the buildings, products, festivals and lifestyle of the people. Through the fostering of new projects and communities based on the architectural environments symbolic of each era and building on the diverse human resources gathered in the area, and on local historical and cultural resources, the process of rebuilding the environment is gradually getting under way.

The context of the historic city of Takaoka

Takaoka, a core city in the western part of Toyama Prefecture, is an area that retains much of the culture and environment that from the early modern age on have traditionally connected town and village, the city and nature.

Takaoka Old Town had its beginnings in the early Edo period (1609). An ideal castle town was built as a post-retirement residence by Maeda Toshinaga, the second head of the Maeda clan which ruled the Hokuriku region, mainly the Kaga Domain around the city of Kanazawa.[1] After the death of Maeda Toshinaga, Takaoka Castle was abandoned, and the samurai residential areas were converted to residential areas for merchants and craftsmen. Since that time, the fusion of urban and rural cultures have brought prosperity to the area. Traditional crafts such as copperware, lacquerware and woodworking, local culture such as the Hikiyama Festival and the lion dance (*shishimai*), remain strong. As a result, the Takaoka area comprises a full set of environmental and cultural resources that have been formed after the Edo Period, including the roads and historic streets that run through the heart of the old town, rural villages and temples; and many of these are extant to the present day.

With these rich historical resources at its core, the area remained as a physical environment; but after the war the urban functions that had come together were broken up with the movement to economic growth and regional development, and were scattered to the outskirts of the town. As a result, most of the historic city was unable to adapt to the shift to a modern city, so that in recent years there are a growing number of places that do not match the modern lifestyle of the people.

At the same time, many of these historical resources are valuable resources not found elsewhere. A regeneration of the environment is required if the value of these historical resources that have been preserved thus far are to be passed on to future generations.

This chapter describes the various activities and projects fostered by local citizens and the private sector in the process of rebuilding a town that was fragmented in the midst of historical change, and the practice of urban planning by multi-sector partnerships.

Historical assets of Takaoka, city of culture and crafts

The environment of Takaoka Old Town that remains to the present time is characterized by two historical assets.

One of these is the castle ruins of the early modern age, the tombs of the feudal lords and temples, which form the northern and southern edges of the old city. The remains of Takaoka Castle, where the outline of the castle including the earthworks and the moat remain almost complete, were designated for conservation, and in the Meiji era they were maintained as a park.[2] The approach road built by the lord running east–west connecting Zuiryu-ji Temple (National Treasure) and the lord's tomb is called Hatcho-michi, and together with the castle forms the southern boundary of the old city.

The other asset is the two historical areas on either side of the river to the southwest of the castle. One of these areas is Kanaya-machi, a residential area for foundry workers invited at the time the castle town was established (Takaoka City Board of Education, 2011). The other is Yamacho-suji, a merchant district formed along the Hokurikudo Highway. Most of the historic city area was destroyed in a great fire in 1900. During the rebuilding process, the townhouses were reconstructed in the "Dozo style," in which the walls and under the eaves are painted with stucco, and the streets were widened (Takaoka City Board of Education, 1986; see Figure 8.1). Many of the townhouses built during this period had tea rooms and inner courtyards, which also became the stage for cultural activities such as the tea ceremony and flower arrangement. After its recovery from the great fire, the city of Takaoka welcomed in an era of prosperity lasting about 30 years until the time of the Great Depression and the period of World War II.

After the Meiji Period, what first led Takaoka to prosperity were its craftworks. In 1873 a copper trading company that had started trading at the Yokohama foreign settlement at the end of the Edo period, for the first time exhibited copperware at the Vienna Expo and won a prize. After that, at the World Expos held in Philadelphia and Chicago, riding on the popularity of *Japonisme* the company gained high acclaim and made progress in the export of copperware as arts and crafts items (Takaoka Copper Cooperative, 1988). Takaoka lacquerware, with its unique techniques including engraving and patterning and decoration using shells, established a trading company in the late Meiji Period and lacquerware was exported overseas via Kobe (Traditional Crafts Takaoka Lacquerware Cooperative, 1996).

In the middle of the Meiji Period, shipping businesses known as *kaisendonya*, that during the late Edo period had made a fortune on the transportation of goods around the Sea of Japan, established in succession banks, spinning companies, railway companies, power companies etc.[3] The Taisho Period saw the rise of rice exchanges and the financial industry.

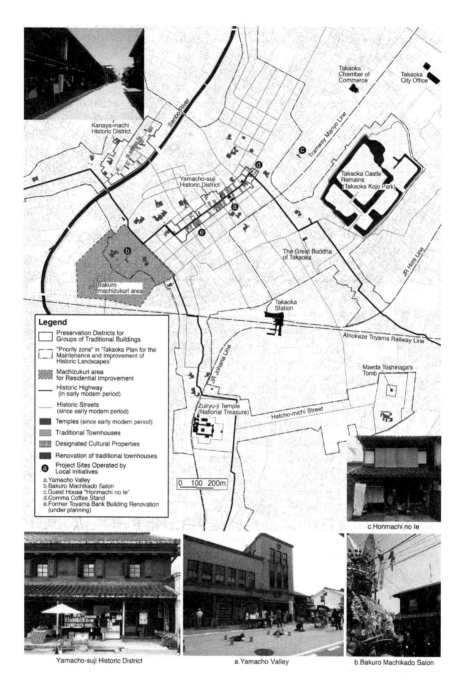

Figure 8.1 Historical assets, and places operated by local initiatives in the Old Town of Takaoka.

There still remain many buildings that symbolize this former prosperity, such as town houses where the merchants both lived and carried on their businesses, and bank buildings. It also remains in the cultural activities and entrepreneurial spirit of the region.

The transformation of Takaoka City after World War II

Many cities in Japan suffered air raids by the US military during World War II, but Takaoka, like Kyoto and Kanazawa, came through the war without catastrophic air raid damage. However, during the period of high economic growth, the remaining historical urban areas hindered the functional change to a modern city. From the late 1960s as suburbanization progressed, as a result of the establishment in the suburban areas of new distribution areas and a new market, the wholesale traders who had been established in the commercial area of the Old Town began to relocate and the economic status of the Old Town declined. Most of the metalworking factories that had grouped together on the north side of the Senbo River also moved to new industrial parks.[4]

After the war, in the area around Takaoka Station, retail specialty shops gathered in and around the shopping district, and until the early 1990s these played the role of the central commercial area. From the 1990s on, large-scale commercial facilities opened to the south of the station and in the suburbs, and the decline of the central commercial area of the Old Town began.

In contrast to the decline of these central commercial areas, two historical districts were designated "Preservation Districts for Groups of Traditional Buildings" as a result of energetic townscape conservation movements led by local residents.

While there are many historical buildings in these areas, more and more buildings are becoming vacant, with absentee owners who are not residents and who do not occupy the properties long-term. All kinds of historical buildings, such as the buildings of the former wholesalers and textile industry office buildings, stand vacant, and they need to be assigned new roles and be given a new planned strategy.

Urban planning to regenerate a city of culture and crafts

I would like to mention two themes for the regeneration of the Old Town of Takaoka in view of the above-mentioned changes the city has undergone.

The first theme was the conversion of the central commercial area, that to date had mainly served the purpose of distribution and consumption, into a center for knowledge economy and cultural capital, complete with a cultural and educational environment and entrepreneurial support. The second theme was the progressive improvement of the existing urban area

106   *Yosuke Mano*

between the preservation districts and the core development zone into a sustainable residential area.

The urban planning master plan formulated in 2019 shows the future urban structure and zoning for urban functions and residential areas. Within each zone, citizens and private sector organizations are expected to continuously create projects that are rooted in specific places and districts.

As a specific approach, first of all, it is important that public investment and development be concentrated around the Shinkansen Shin-Takaoka Station and Takaoka Station, and along the tramway. Second, there needs to be introduced a new program to preserve and regenerate the area of the Old Town that includes the two traditional building preservation districts, and to create spaces for diverse residences, start-up offices and cultural experiences.

The vision and public image of the town

Takaoka is one of the few provincial cities that continues to have trams. From 2010, the restructuring of public transportation and improvement of public spaces around the central stations of the Shinkansen and conventional lines were advanced with the maintenance of the Hokuriku Shinkansen.

From 2010 onwards, in development for the preparation of the opening of the Hokuriku Shinkansen, the public transportation system was reorganized and improvements made to the areas around the central Takaoka Station and the Shinkansen station. In the planning associated with the opening of the bullet train line, in addition to the planning for infrastructure development by the administration, a proposal was also put forward by young members of the Chamber of Commerce and Industry that focused on the restructuring of the town and was given the title "Transport Vision." In this proposal, it was suggested that by restructuring the public transportation system, such as extending the tramlines, the situation in the sprawling urban area would be changed, providing in the central urban area housing for the younger generations and places for their activities. In 2012 several proponents of this proposal formed a project team, "Takaoka Machikko Project," to promote shared houses and cultural activities in the community, making use of idle real estate. Members of the project team become owners and tenants of vacant buildings in the central urban area and turn them into low-rent housings for students and young people, workshops and studios, thus promoting the recycling of real estate.

As a turning point in urban development relating to the traditional crafts, in 1985 Takaoka City and local industry adopted the "Takaoka City of Crafts Declaration."

The following year, young business operators engaged in the traditional industries, in cooperation with the Chamber of Commerce and Industry, started the Takaoka Craft Competition, a competition to foster young designers and artisans. Since then, new product development has been carried out in cooperation with a local university, and every year a number of events have been held; the craft market "Kanaya Raku-ichi" in the Kanaya-machi historical preservation district (2008–), and the "Takaoka Craft Ichiba-Machi," a traditional craft experience and city promotion event (2012–). In addition to the traditional culture originating in early modern times, such as the "Takaoka Mikurumayama Festival" attempts are also under way to create a new public image of Takaoka City that will foster civic pride.

"Micro-initiatives" fostered on site

Converting the central commercial area and residential area of the Old Town in line with the proposals mentioned earlier and creating a new public image requires the manifestation of various wishes based on the sense of everyday feeling, and the coming into being of sites based on those wishes. Also needed is a process to bring such sites together and link them to the reconstruction of the town.

With regard to the establishment of the sites, of importance during the review process of the project is the formation of micro-initiatives to build partnerships concerning the preparation of the site, its management and programs (Mano, 2018). In addition, in order to enhance the sustainability of the site, it is important to increase the value of the area by building relationships at both the neighborhood level and a wider area that supports services and networks. From this perspective, I will introduce some examples that we are working on in Takaoka City.

Case 1: The Yamacho Valley Project, a complex of spaces in which to experience local culture, and shopping complex (Figure 8.1a)

A town development company became the business owner of this regeneration project, forming in the traditional building preservation area a complex of shops and spaces for a cultural experience, by renovating the building, warehouse and courtyard of a former stationery wholesaler which had become vacant. The space facing the main street, the warehouse behind the inner courtyard and the tea room are leased as shops, traditional craft workshops and corporate showrooms. Public areas, such as the entrance hall, the reception room and the courtyard can be used in combination for various events. The company that manages these events was launched by local entrepreneurs, and it manages the complex in cooperation with tenants and the town development company. In addition, this management company collaborates with universities and young local designers to exhibit panel and visual displays of the historical changes

108 *Yosuke Mano*

occurring in the district and the culture inherited by the people, arranged in maps and images.

The public spaces, such as the courtyard, hall and reception room, which are another characteristic of this facility, are used as venues for cultural activities in the city, gatherings of citizen groups, events related to food and health, etc. Every summer, the "Dozo-Zukuri Festival," an event organized by the Yamacho Town Development Committee, is held. In the autumn, the "Takaoka Craft Market Street" is held, featuring mainly crafts exhibitions and hands-on crafts experience. Craft-related events are places that attract citizens from the wide area and tourists from outside the prefecture.

Case 2: Reconstruction of the living environment and a new neighborhood starting from the creation of new sites: "Bakuro Neighborhood Plan" and "Bakuro-machi Machikado Salon" Initiatives (Figure 8.1b)

The Bakuro area, which consists of eight neighborhood associations and corresponds to the northern half of the elementary school district, is a district chosen as a model area for Takaoka City's policy for disaster prevention measures to cope with flooding due to heavy rain, earthquakes and fires. This policy also aims to stop the increase in the number of vacant houses due to the aging of residents and the deterioration of buildings, and to strengthen the community.

Since 2014, each neighborhood association has drafted its own unique plan through a series of workshops, and the eight plans were organized into the "Bakuro Neighborhood Plan" (Kanoh *et al.*, 2017)

In the planning process, first through a series of three workshops, neighborhood issues were looked for in each community association with from 25 households to 100 households and the sites brought to light, then the possibility of improvement and means of bringing about the improvement were considered. Next, conceptual plans were put together at the neighborhood level, a project drawn up once the potential for use of the site and its needs were settled, and the feasibility of the project was studied. Each project was started after operating teams were formed, funds procured, skills reviewed and the agreement of the owner obtained.

As a result of this kind of parallel study and project development, from the third year a number of achievements began to become apparent, such as the provision of side ditches in the roads that form the framework of the district, the demolition of old vacant houses and the creation of community spaces. In Bakuro-machi, the neighborhood association acquired a vacant property that had formerly been a stationery shop, renovated it including earthquake proof reinforcement and renovation of facilities, and established the concept of setting up a base of activity where multiple generations will gather. In the project given the title

"Bakuro-machi Machikado Salon," a series of processes from concept, planning and development to operation was brought about through a partnership between a project team of volunteers from the neighborhood association and the support team. The site, which opened in April 2018, is still in trial operation, but it is becoming established as a place where different generations can have a good time, with a salon that is open on weekends and circle activities for residents.

Together with these visible results, progress is gradually being made with the demolition and rebuilding of vacant houses in the vicinity. How to put together a program for the reconstruction of the neighborhood environment and extend it to the surrounding area on the basis of the results of the formation of the local bases and the building of relationships through improvement of the environment, is a challenge for the future.

Characteristics of regional partnerships and initiatives in Takaoka

The characteristics of the Takaoka town development partnership and initiative, including some of the projects mentioned above, can be summarized in the following two points.

The first point is that the projects were planned and put into effect in a short time through the partnership of multiple local private-sector companies with individual business owners. Each project started from an idea by an individual, with funding and business income and expenditure studied and the project put into practice within as little as two years, and within five years at the most. Although there are concerns regarding operation sustainability and improvement of management methods, it may be considered to be one of the methods suitable for the gradual regeneration of a historical city.

The second point was for the entire project to be made public, including the process of remodelling and conversion of small buildings, and for operation of the site to continue before and after the renovation. For example, not only were opportunities linked to the planning and renovation of a building, such as idea workshops, flooring and wall-finishing, shared; but the sharing of experiences of the environmental changes in the neighborhood, such as open houses and city walks, also led to urban planning partnerships. In addition, the reward of combining a diversity of approaches through the location, including traditional crafts, old town houses, antiques left in old houses, remaking culture, etc., is the driving force of partnership formation.

New role of the historic district centering on openness, creativity and cultural experiences

Takaoka envisions itself as a city of culture creation, and part of its historic building reconstruction program is implementing the creation of sites

110 Yosuke Mano

where the emphasis is on the experience of crafts and culture and on communication. Recent initiatives in the city are entering a new phase.

Partnerships, led by local individuals and civic organizations and supported by the administration, financial institutions, companies, etc. are gradually taking shape. At the same time, many historical buildings, craft products, historical archives, etc. remain unused, and a variety of movements are needed to raise the utility value of this cultural heritage.

Meanwhile, in the renovated buildings that have been updated and new programs installed, spatial complexes and networking through culture and craftsmanship are being developed, in the form of workshops with space for craftsmen, artists and designers to create and manufacture, where amateurs can try their hand at production; craft museums and archives; and showrooms where craft items and products can be held in the hand for inspection. These programs play a role in strengthening connections with creators from within and outside the region, and with supporters who visit the area regularly. In addition, for two years starting in 2017, a team initiative named the "Craft Hackathon" was implemented, with the aim of fusing craft techniques and IT technology. Essential to these developments is the need for support in human resource development, design management and housing, through the establishment of businesses and workplaces. I am convinced that the ongoing initiatives to fuse art, space and lifestyle set in the Old Town will clear the way for the future of this city.

Notes

1 The Maeda family held the second highest rank among the feudal lords of the Tokugawa Shogunate.
2 In 1875, Takaoka Castle Ruins were designated a park. In 2015, it was recognized that it was an environment in which the castle foundations and moat remained almost complete, and the site was designated a National Historic Site.
3 The *kaisen-donya* made a fortune by transporting to Osaka and Edo rice and cotton produced in the Tonami plain in the hinterland of Takaoka, and bringing back the products of those places.
4 Takaoka City's statistics show that in terms of value, copperware production peaked in 1990.

References

Kanoh, R., Tanabe, K. and Mano, Y. (2017). Chiisana chiku tani no keikaku to basyo no image keisei wo tsujita machinaka saikouchiku no kousou to jissen (Concept and practice in rebuilding the old city area through small-district planning and spatial image building). *Proceedings of annual meeting (Urban planning and design)*. Tokyo: Architectural Institute of Japan. 1097–1098.
Mano, Y. (2018). Chiiki kyoten no keikakuron to machi saikouchiku, Toyamaken Takaoka-shi no keikaku to jissen (Planning theory for local bases and rebuilding

of urban neighborhoods in the historical urban areas: Case study in Takaoka City). *Discussion papers from panel discussion on urban planning.* Tokyo: Architectural Institute of Japan. 21–26.

Takaoka City Board of Education. (1986). *Takaoka-shi yamachosuji dentouteki kenzobutsugun chosa houkokusyo (Takaoka Yamacho-suji traditional building group survey report).*

Takaoka City Board of Education. (2011). *Imoji no machinami, Kanayamachi Naimen dentouteki kenzobutsugun hozon taisaku chosa houkokusyo (The townscape of the metal casters: Kanaya-machi and Naimen traditional building group survey report).*

Takaoka Copper Cooperative (1988). *Takaoka douki shi (The history of Takaoka copper products),* edited by Minoru Yoda and Taketoshi Jozuka. Toyama: Katsura-shobo.

Traditional Crafts Takaoka Lacquerware Cooperative. (1996). *Takaoka urushi monogatari (The story of Takaoka lacquer products).* Takaoka: Sogokikaku Insatsu.

9 Discovering the authenticity of the historical landscape and the original urban context through small collaborative design projects in a local castle-town city, Tsuruoka City

Keisuke Sugano

Introduction

The historical urban area of Tsuruoka City, Yamagata Prefecture, located in northeastern Japan, is formed based on the early modern castle town[1] of Tsuruoka. Since the late 1980s, urban design projects that incorporate the authenticity of the historical landscape and the original urban context of the castle-town city[2] have been promoted by collaborative work within public-sector urban planning and private-citizen directed machizukuri.[3]

This process was carried out through a variety of activities by various stakeholders, in parallel with the typical urban planning in local cities of this time, as well as machizukuri, which was organized by private citizens and landowners (Satoh, 2017). A new urban design method has been developed that encompasses machizukuri alongside urban planning. This has been promoted while repeating the process of confirming the results of urban planning and machizukuri together with stakeholders and mutually offering feedback to one another. This is depicted by the spiral diagram (see Figures 9.1 and 9.2). In this chapter, this series of activities is taken as a model case that has been steadily advanced with mutual influence between urban planning and machizukuri, and is explained according to the following three periods.

In the first period (late 1980s to mid-1990s), the authenticity of the historical landscape and the original urban context of the castle-town city was reexamined by the local government and private citizens, and existing urban planning was reviewed to incorporate machizukuri into the future plans for the historical urban area.

In the second period (mid-1990s to mid-2010s), by renewing the existing urban planning,[4] the big picture – as well as individual projects which combined public projects featuring private-citizen participation with projects organized jointly by private citizens and landowners – was discussed for realizing the shared goals of the first period, and some of these projects were realized as machizukuri projects.

Tsuruoka City   113

In the third period (2015 to present), revitalization of the historical urban area was handled largely as a place where the diverse lifestyles of citizens could coalesce by residence promotion. Subsequently, regional management was developed, including the historical urban area and surrounding agricultural and mountain villages.

Sharing the ecological principle of a castle-town city as a framework for new urban design (Phase 1)

In the early 1980s in Tsuruoka City, redevelopment projects were being carried out around the train station located at the outer edge of the historical urban area, but the historical urban area itself was in decline. The late 1980s was a time to move from redevelopment around the train station to improvement of the historical urban area. At that time, urban landscape design was starting to become a subject of greater consideration in Japan, and Tsuruoka City was selected by the national government as a model city, prompting the "Landscape Design Guide Plan."[5] This plan showed how to design landscapes for promoting machizukuri and triggered the machizukuri of the historical urban area. In formulating the guide plan, a project team was established in the government of Tsuruoka City which worked to design the unique urban landscape of the historical urban area based on the castle town ahead of all else. During this process, the reasoning behind Tsuruoka's original design became better understood, including factors such as climate, environment, the early inhabitants' spiritual foundations, and elements of local history, all of which were to play a role in the current urban design. Urban planning up to this point had blindly applied a function-oriented method of modern city planning over historical urban composition, with little understanding of the authenticity of the historical urban area. In the project team, it was agreed to consider the landscape from the perspective of the authenticity of the historical landscape and the original urban context, and its incorporation into the present through the modern age.

Establishing and sharing the Landscape Design Guide Plan as a general principle for planning

The early modern castle town Tsuruoka is located on a plain formed by the Akagawa River and is surrounded by mountains which are the object of "mountain faith."[6] The townscape in the castle town was designed in harmony with the mountain scenery in an effort to elicit a resonance between the inhabitants and the natural setting that surrounds them (Sugano, 2017; Tanaka *et al.*, 2016; Satoh, 2015). Many of the officers who participated in the project team were native to this region, and some had been instructed in childhood to use the locations of the mountains to navigate when lost. Suffice it to say, the natural environment plays an important role in the lives of the inhabitants of Tsuruoka. The adoration

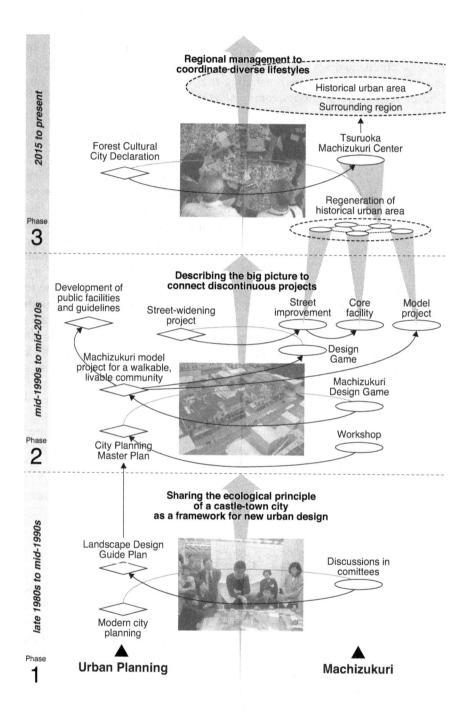

Figure 9.1 Spiral diagram showing the process of machizukuri in Tsuruoka City.

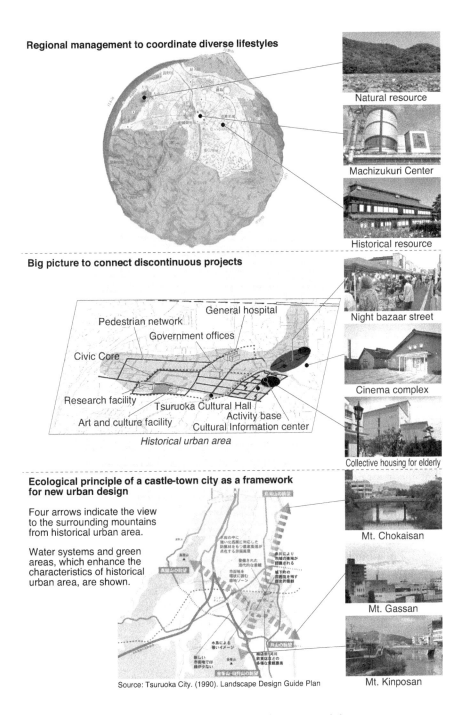

Figure 9.2 Project map of each phase corresponding to spiral diagram.

116 Keisuke Sugano

of and closeness to nature, which is also related to mountain faith, makes up part of the spiritual identity of the citizens. The officers rediscovered the importance of the authenticity of this landscape after making clear the ecological principle of the castle-town city united with the rich environment of the Akagawa River basin. This shared image was formed which emphasizes the ecological principle as well as the preservation of the view of the surrounding mountains, all of which was incorporated into the Landscape Design Guide Plan.

Public space improvement as the framework of urban development

Based on the above, much of the existing urban planning was reviewed. Until the 1980s, the formation of a purely functional urban structure was the top priority (Satoh, 1997), and the historical landscape was in danger of being lost. However, much of the straightening and widening of the roadways was reviewed to preserve the view of the mountain scenery. In addition, the plan to change the cross-sectional shape of the river was reviewed, and the historical landscape – composed of the existing wide river with its sandbank and reeds – was also preserved. Through this process, changes in the plan were amended and confirmed through discussions with private citizens in various committees.

Describing the big picture to connect discontinuous projects (Phase 2)

The Landscape Design Guide Plan, based on the ecological principle of the castle-town city, was the starting point for considering the machizukuri that incorporates the historical landscape and the original urban context. Subsequently, the discussion proceeded to the formulation of the City Planning Master Plan. The City Planning Master Plan required the inclusion of private citizens in the design process, and the introduction of private-citizen participation became the driving force of the new machizukuri at this point. In addition, the big picture in conjunction with individual projects was conceived in order to realize the ideas presented in the Landscape Design Guide Plan and the City Planning Master Plan in a historical urban area project. Also, a machizukuri project in which residents took the administrative initiative became concrete, and a machizukuri enterprise and its intermediary organizations were gradually created which would eventually realize several projects.

City Planning Master Plan through citizen participation

The main goal from the beginning was to create a livable environment in the historical urban area of Tsuruoka City, and plans were drawn to improve public facilities, rebuild the general hospital, and provide maintenance of the civic core that houses public offices. This was a political decision by the government, and in the course of local government planning, examination of the City Planning Master Plan began to generate discussion about urban planning and machizukuri with citizen participation. Discussions and workshops were held with the aim of setting up various organizations for promoting machizukuri projects launched by private citizens, nonprofit organizations, machizukuri enterprises, and local companies. In particular, the community council within the elementary school district organized the preexisting local shopping street association and an architecture association, each of which was important to the end product, and various symposiums and workshops were held.

Machizukuri in a compact historical urban area to design a walkable, livable community

In parallel with this, in 2000 when discussions on the City Planning Master Plan were stagnating, the national government called for a model city to provide a "Machizukuri model project for a walkable, livable community,"[7] and Tsuruoka City was selected as a result of the examination. This was precisely the machizukuri that Tsuruoka City had intended to produce from the beginning, and the method and design were further examined to fully realize the ideas raised in the Landscape Design Guide Plan and the City Planning Master Plan. The "Machizukuri Design Game," in which citizens participate in collaborative design and examine specific aspirations for the project, was conducted repeatedly by forming various local groups. During the Machizukuri Design Game, the importance of common spaces – such as the narrow streets within a city block and the open spaces within that block – was discussed. Such human-scale common space existed in the early modern castle town, and pedestrians were able to move freely through the streets. It was considered that main streets and individual projects should be linked by a continuous pedestrian network to revitalize the historical urban area via foot traffic (Satoh, 2000). The aspiration was shared by private citizens to form a new pedestrian network to emulate the historical street culture.

Development of a machizukuri project by private citizens and its organizational system

Based on this, the public project with private-citizen participation and the project organized jointly by private citizens and landowners started moving toward their realization. As a public project, the development of public facilities was considered, and guidelines for restricting the height of facilities were proposed in order to preserve the view of the surrounding mountains. The project organized jointly by private citizens and landowners was

118   *Keisuke Sugano*

conducted mainly in the two adjacent central shopping streets: Ginza and Sanno.

First, a model project was organized in Ginza. A complex was developed which preserved and utilized two adjacent historical warehouses – which serve as the activity base for a nonprofit organization and space for local restaurants – alongside a newly constructed facility which provides collective housing for the elderly. This project was carried out by two doctors (a married couple) at their properties, including a clinic where they practiced that also served as their housing. Within a city block, there had formerly been a space closed to the public behind two buildings, separated from public foot traffic on the street. This was reworked into a street-facing square surrounded by buildings on three sides, with the garden of a former home also incorporated into the space. This area became a walking area for a nearby nursery school, and common space connected to the street was also created.

Second, a shopping street improvement project was developed in Sanno. The main concern for the Sanno shopping street was how to deal with a street-widening project which had been planned by the government. Through the Machizukuri Design Game, the goal of a combined-use commerce/residential area using the existing shape of each lot was shared, and eventually, it was decided to abandon the street-widening project and maintain the street's original width. Instead, the pedestrian walkway was improved so that stalls and stages could be set up for a monthly night bazaar – a tradition in Sanno. Along this shopping street, each store had also begun its own renovation project, and several examples have been realized that provide space for galleries and events.

Third, following the previous two projects, the core facility in the Sanno area was created and connected to the shopping street. Through this project, the wooden spinning factory located behind the Sanno shopping street was converted into a cinema complex.

To oversee the machizukuri project in which private citizens start their own businesses, it was determined that an additional business entity would be necessary in order to organize their efforts. To this end, a machizukuri enterprise and an intermediary organization were established.

Regional management to coordinate diverse lifestyles (Phase 3)

In 2015, when the author participated in this process, Japan's birthrate was continuing to decline – spurring population decline and the aging of its population. Due to this phenomenon, vacant land and abandoned houses had increased in the historical urban area, and this was viewed as a significant problem. On the other hand, the lifestyles of private citizens were diversifying, and they had started taking up multiple residences in various locations in the historical urban area and the surrounding area, using them seasonally, on certain days of the week, or otherwise infrequently. In addition, a circular economy had developed in which food and building materials were purchased locally, and environmental preservation activities that manage historical and natural resources were undertaken via cooperation among agricultural, forestry, and fishery enterprises.

As for the third phase, it was considered first that the historical urban area should be regenerated as a place where the diverse lifestyles of citizens could coalesce, and to revitalize the area by residence promotion.

Second, regional management was considered in which the historical urban area and the surrounding farming and mountain villages would be integrally managed with respect to the environment and the regional economy.

Third, it was considered that the central facilities of this regional management should be developed in the historical urban area.

Regeneration of the historical urban area by residence promotion

Targeting Ginza and Sanno again, regeneration of the historical urban area was examined. The living environment adapted to various lifestyles was examined with the participation of local companies (e.g., construction and real estate) as well as the local government and private citizens. The plan presented was to reorganize the vacant space inside the block as a continuous common space which was guided by the design principle discussed in Phase 2.

Regional management for realizing the public regional plan

Tsuruoka City merged with neighboring local governments in 2005 to become a regional government and developed a "Forest Cultural City Declaration" which included hilly and mountainous areas. This declaration was enacted to preserve the ecological principle and historical environment of the region and to develop industry and the area's livelihood. In order to promote such a local governmental plan, it was deemed essential to cooperate with regions with diverse resources. The future goals of regional management, in which multiple stakeholders work together to build the machizukuri platform, were established.

Development of a base for new regional management

In order to promote this new regional management, a vacant public facility located in Ginza was renovated to house the regional management base called the "Tsuruoka Machizukuri Center." Here, a space was created for private citizens to discuss future machizukuri projects. The space includes a 1/300 model of the urban area and a display explaining the history of machizukuri as well as the area's natural and historical

120 *Keisuke Sugano*

resources. In addition, various offices were installed to promote regional management, such as offices for shopping streets, the management of real estate and other governmental functions.

Since 2017, based on the Tsuruoka Machizukuri Center, new regional management is beginning to be practiced within urban planning and machizukuri via multi-stakeholder collaboration.

Conclusion

In the collaborative design project that began in the late 1980s in Tsuruoka City, urban planning and machizukuri influenced each other and began to feature the interconnectivity of various spaces. Since each project was designed in response to the ecological principle described in the Landscape Design Guide Plan, these were created as one urban space from the gradual accumulation of several unique places. The key was to connect spaces that had tended to be discontinuous via the ecological principle that had been discovered by the private citizens at the beginning of the period. This process led to concrete projects at each stage, and various stakeholders were organized via this platform and the expansion of various business entities.

Japan is still facing a declining birthrate and an aging population. In particular, the decline of local cities, including Tsuruoka City, is remarkable, and there is a need for a future of establishing sustainable communities and organizational systems. As collaborative design projects accumulate in which urban planning and machizukuri are linked, it is thought that the authenticity of regionally unique historical landscapes and the original urban contexts will be prioritized by an area's citizens, and designs of the future will retain the said heritage.

Notes

1 In Japan, about 300 early modern castle towns were built nationwide from the late sixteenth century to the early seventeenth century. During the transition from a war-torn era to a relatively peaceful era, these towns were built as a political-economic base to manage the newly established region and bring about stable prosperity.
2 A "castle-town city" is a city which is formed based on the early modern castle town.
3 The Laboratory of Urban Design within the Waseda University Department of Architecture, as well as the Institute of Urban and Regional Studies, both represented by Shigeru Satoh, the editor of this book, were involved in this series of processes as an expert group, of which the author of this chapter was a member.
4 Existing urban planning was reviewed based on the new content of the "City Planning Master Plan" – which established urban planning policies for municipalities – newly established after revision of the City Planning Act in 1992. The City Planning Master Plan obliged the inclusion of private citizens in the design process.

Tsuruoka City 121

5 In 1987, in order to promote comprehensive landscape design, the national government institutionalized the "Landscape Design Model City." A city with candidate districts focusing on promoting landscape design is designated as a model city by the national government. Selected local governments created Landscape Design Guide Plans, and implemented street projects, park projects, etc., to improve the comprehensive landscape.

6 "Mountain faith" refers to the religion that treats mountains as sacred and gives them religious meaning as the objects of worship.

7 The machizukuri model project for a walkable, livable community is an attempt at realizing a safe, secure, and comfortable life in a familiar place that takes into consideration low birth rates and the aging society. By using various ideas and innovations in this region, this project aimed at realizing a city in which the various functions for daily life and work come together in a compact space, and in which a wide range of generations can interact and help each other in a barrier-free environment.

References

Satoh, S. (1997). Jōkamachi no toshi design wo yomu (Reading the urban design of the castle town). *Zōkei*. 12: 135–158.

Satoh, S. (2000). Tyūshin shigaichi ni okeru yūdō kūkan no sōsyutu (Creation of yūdō space in historical urban area). *Zōkei*. 30: 28–59.

Satoh, S. (ed.) (2015). *Shinpan zusetsu Jōkamachi toshi (New edition; Illustrated castle town city)*. Tokyo: Kajima Shuppankai.

Satoh, S. (2017). Scenario making toshite no Tsuruoka no Machizukuri (Machizukuri in Tsuruoka as a scenario making). In Shigeru Satoh, Shin Aiba, and Naomi Uchida (eds) *Machizukuri kyōsho (Textbook of Machizukuri)*. 192–200. Tokyo: Kajima Shuppankai.

Sugano, K. (2017). *Yamaate no keikan kōzō kaiseki ni motoduku kinsei jōkamachi no kōsei genri no kaidoku (A study about the principle of urban composition of pre-modern castle towns through analysis of landscape structure with "Yamaate")*. Ph.D. dissertation, Waseda University.

Tanaka, Y., Sugano, K., and Satoh, S. (2016). Kinsei jōkamachi ni okeru dentō teki suikei kōzō to keikan kōsei to no kankei ni kansuru kenkyū: Yamagata ken Tsuruoka shi wo taisyō toshite (A Study on the Structure of the Traditional Whole Water-system and the Relation with the Landscape Composition in Castle Town: Focusing on Tsuruoka, Yamagata). *Journal of the City Planning Institute of Japan*. 51(3): 305–312.

10 Revitalization of the central urban area by local residents in Nabari City, Mie Prefecture[1]

Kenjiro Matsuura

Introduction

In this chapter, we will introduce the application of machizukuri in Nabari City, Mie Prefecture in order to show how that paradigm can be applied in small cities. The use of machizukuri, which can be roughly defined as community and neighborhood planning and action in response to local needs and desires, has grown in popularity in recent years both in urban planning and in more general usage. In Nabari City, machizukuri efforts started by local resident organizations in the Shinmachi District swept aside top-down planning efforts by civil administrators, thereby resulting in an effective river refurbishment and the completion of a river embankment road.

The improvements to the embankment road and the environment spurred efforts that spread throughout the central urban area of the city. Simultaneously and in response to those efforts, the city administration created an area budget system to support such community-based town management, and machizukuri based on the desires and visions of the residents gained popularity. However, since both the residents' organizations and city administrators realized that there were limits to what could be accomplished by resident-oriented machizukuri alone, both sides came together and formulated action plans for reconstructing the central urban area via collaborative efforts. Among those projects was the renovation of a traditional townhouse known as the Hosokawa Residence, which became the centerpiece of the local historical exchange space and is now independently managed by residents' organizations.

Speaking of the generational theory of machizukuri in Japan, as administrative arrangements have been made for a financial system based on the second generation of "experiments and themes" that took place in each area, the third generation of machizukuri of "regional management" spread throughout the city.

This chapter introduces the above-mentioned process of machizukuri. In addition, the Urban Planning Laboratory in Mie University, to which I belonged, supported planning for the alternative embankment road proposals and future planning (e.g., holding workshops and summarizing the contents of discussions) in the Shinmachi District as part of efforts to formulate an action plan for reconstructing the central urban area, as well as to create the basic plan for the redesign and renovation of the Hosokawa Residence.

Spread of community-based machizukuri that started with Shinmachi District river improvements

Failure of redevelopment plan ignoring urban context

The central urban area of Nabari City is based on the castle town that was constructed by Daimyo Takayoshi Todo from 1635 to 1636. Until the 1950s there was a problem with river overflows along Hase Highway, the main street of the city. Additionally, as part of efforts to develop a suburban residential area for Osaka commuter families, the construction of numerous large-scale shops began in the suburbs, and the central urban area began declining in the 1960s.

Various redevelopment plans were conceived in the 1980s aimed at revitalizing the central urban area, but the one thing those plans had in common is that they made no effort to conserve the historical and cultural inheritance of the targeted urban areas. Many of them simply aimed at developing, dispersing, and interconnecting commercial spaces in those areas. However, none of those plans made any significant progress because they were not supported by the landowners and citizens of the area.

Expansion of machizukuri by residents' organizations

In contrast, residents' organizations have shown that machizukuri can produce results. First, in the Shinmachi District, which was outside the range of the 1986 Nabari City Revitalization Plan, machizukuri by residents' organizations focused on a section of the Hase Highway that had long been plagued by river overflows such as the flooding accompanying the 1959 Ise Bay typhoon that caused significant damage in both Aichi and Mie Prefectures. In addition to the negative effects caused by the hollowing out of commercial areas, the declining population of the area was also making its impact felt, and the local residents felt that there were limits to benefits that could be achieved by commercial revitalization alone.

Under these circumstances, the "Community Development Committee for Good Living" was organized within the self-government association in 1987.

It was the refurbishment of the Nabari River embankment that provided the first opportunity to show Shinmachi District the effectiveness of machizukuri. In 1983, the Ministry of Construction (MOC) issued a proposal for embankment improvements to district residents in which they

124 *Kenjiro Matsuura*

offered to construct and maintain an administrative road and concrete revetment within the public domain. After receiving the proposal, the Shinmachi District residents' organization established a river improvement committee to evaluate the proposal. Then, after a series of meetings among local residents, they made the following three counterproposals to the MOC:

1 The government would purchase a parcel of land from a private owner and provide it free to Nabari City, after which the city would improve the land and maintain it as a community road.
2 Instead of a plain concrete seawall, they would create a multi-nature type revetment[2] where grass and flowers would be grown.
3 The local residents would assume responsibility for maintaining and managing the multi-nature type revetment.

This alternative plan was accepted, and the residents' proposals were realized. After the new embankment road was completed, a flower-planting event was held by area residents, and the multi-nature type revetment has been maintained and managed by the residents as a community garden ever since. In addition, potted plants have been emplaced along the embankment road and careful consideration to the landscape was taken as houses were rebuilt.

However, after noting that the creation of the embankment road did not result in the level of area improvements that had been anticipated, the Shinmachi District residents' organization entered into consultations with the Urban Planning Laboratory in Mie University and engaged in several workshops during which the district's future was contemplated. The result was a future plan centered on the four following project themes, all of which would be managed and advanced by the residents and their association.

First, in order to create a "town project that celebrates history and tradition," it was suggested that the historic townscape along the Hase Highway be preserved to the greatest extent possible. Specifically, this included the preservation and utilization of the Hosokawa Residence (a traditional townhouse/storehouse), repairs to the townscape, traditional heritage, and the renovation of the traditional townhouse as a historical museum.

Second, as part of the "vibrant town project," shops marketing locally produced goods, a restaurant serving local cuisine, and souvenir shops associated with the traditional townhouse renovation were proposed.

Third, as part of a "road project where people want to walk," the embankment road was repurposed as a pedestrian-oriented thoroughfare and considerable attention was paid to the vegetation to be planted and the colors of the buildings along the road.

The fourth was the creation of "a riverbed where residents can work and play outside of the box." In the years gone by, the Nabari River used to be a lively place where citizens enjoyed numerous activities, and scenes of children playing in the river were commonplace. However, in recent years the embankment had come to be seen as a dangerous place, and few people chose to spend time near the river. In an effort to break that mindset and to promote the twin concepts of a "Nabari riverside where we can stroll" and a "Nabari River where we can play," specific measures included riverbed weeding and cleaning, the installation of walking paths, the development of waterside sports playing fields, and provision of roadway access to the riverbed areas.

Introduction of area budgeting system and machizukuri by residents

It was also under these circumstances that in 2002 the newly elected mayor created the "Dream-Making Area Budget System" in which the city government abolished the traditional locked-in subsidies normally provided to each area and instead chose to allocate portions of the available budget to each area that the residents' organizations in those areas could use as they saw fit.

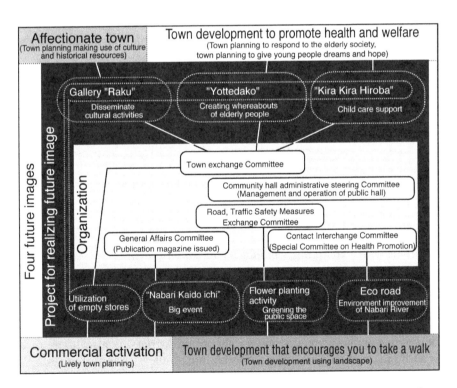

Figure 10.1 Approach of revitalization by the community management committee in Nabari area.

126 *Kenjiro Matsuura*

Community management committees were then organized into 14 community center areas (roughly following the primary school subdistricts) that were established as area budget receivers (Figure 10.1).

Those area budgets are characterized by *no subsidy rate or no limited business*. Regarding the target of the grant project, "area management business implemented by the agreement of local residents" is set up. For example, grant approval can be assumed when the efforts are focused on, for example, living environment improvement, social welfare activities, health promotion activities, safety/disaster prevention activities, cultural and lifelong learning activities, restoration/preservation activities of traditional events, and creative activities making full use of local characteristics. However, religious and political activities are excluded.

The roles of the community development committee are to examine, review, and decide on projects; to establish a three-year plan; to implement, settle, audit, and evaluate projects; and to publish a report on all those activities. In addition, the Nabari City government established an "Area Management Council" to help each area exchange information with the others.

Specific projects can be classified into the following five types from the balance sheet accounts of the 14 areas during fiscal year 2006:

1 "Area service business activities," such as crime prevention patrols/environmental beautification;
2 "Space improvement projects," such as flowerbed developments and park redevelopment;
3 "Fellowship projects," such as summer festivals and concerts;
4 "Surviving Projects, etc.," such as especially expensive projects (Respect for Senior Citizen's Day Events and Resource Waste Collection);
5 "Others," such as conference fees and administrative expenses.

The proportion of each project differs depending on the community management committee, and the Nabari area to be described later has the largest proportion of the "Space improvement project" budget.

Activities of the community management committee in Nabari area

Below, we will describe machizukuri activities in the central area of Nabari City. This area, while facing a variety of problems, such as the aging of its population base and the increasing number of vacant businesses due to the declining popularity of downtown shopping districts, is also home to a wealth of historical resources such as buildings, alleys, and waterways.

Accordingly, committee members visited all the residences in the area and created a "treasure map" after listening to the desires and intentions of the residents. Based on that treasure map, the "Nabari area activation plan" was formulated in November 2003. In this activation plan, they set out four goals along with specific visions of the projects needed to achieve them:

1 a town filled with amenity;
2 vitalization of commerce;
3 machizukuri for pedestrians;
4 machizukuri to promote health and welfare.

In order to realize this plan, they established four specialized subcommittees (General Affairs; Road, Traffic, and Safety; Communications Exchange; and Contact Friendship) and tasked them with developing projects corresponding to the four goals (Figure 10.2). For example, for the purpose of revitalizing commerce, the operation of the Silver Salon "Yottedako" was started in order to make the most effective use of vacant shops. Additionally, in order to create a place where elderly people living in the area would

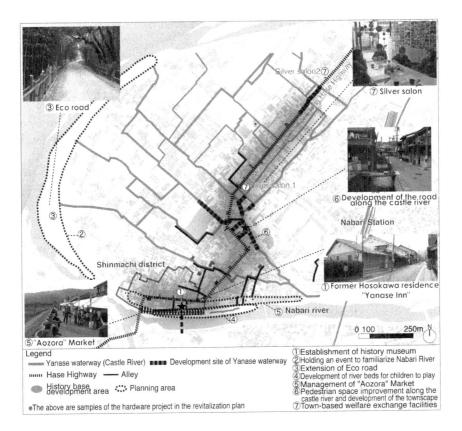

Figure 10.2 Project map of the revitalization plan for the central urban area in Nabari City.

128 *Kenjiro Matsuura*

feel free to drop in, nine different facilities were set up in the area in 2002. These facilities are operated by volunteer organizations in each district.

The improvement of the eco-road along the Nabari River, which was a machizukuri effort aimed at satisfying the need for walking paths, was made possible by purchasing a wild bamboo grove along the portion of the Nabari River flowing around the central urban area from a local landowner (Figure 10.2). In addition, the subcommittee operates the "Raku" gallery, which utilizes empty shops as locations in which local residents can engage in cultural activities.

As described above, these machizukuri efforts did not aim for conventional commercial revitalization targets; instead, their plans were designed to create environments in which people would want to live, attract visitors from suburban residential areas on weekends, and gradually change the tone, focus, and quality of living in those areas by utilizing area resources that were being neglected and ignored.

Revitalization plan for the central urban area by public–private partnership

Revitalization plan for the central urban area as "action plan" by public–private partnership

While community-based machizukuri were promoted in various parts of the city using the city resource budgets described above, there were also many cases where machizukuri efforts were undertaken by the residents alone. However, due to the necessity for coordination between administration public space development efforts and community-based machizukuri, both sides came together in 2004 to begin formulating a public–private partnership "Revitalization plan for the central urban area."

Reflecting on the fact that past redevelopment plans had failed to attract community support, the primary characteristic of this effort was the care taken to ensure that the administration and citizens clarified their responsibilities and aimed at rebuilding as a joint action plan. They also considered the roles of residents, the shopping district promotion association, and the Nabari area community management committee instead of simply leaving those decisions to the administration.

For example, among the items to be addressed by residents were the "construction of a system for utilizing empty shops," the "expansion of the eco-road," and "holding of events for familiarizing citizens with the Nabari River." Additionally as a matter to be addressed by the shopping district promotion association, "hosting an Aozora Market" was discussed.

In the revitalization plan for the central urban area, four major projects (improvement of historic spaces, improvement of exchange spaces, waterside improvements, and the improvement of living spaces) were proposed (Figure 10.2). In response to these proposals, a number of projects, such as the renovation of the historic Hosokawa Residence, which is the traditional townhouse mentioned above, were accomplished as both historic and exchange space improvements. The plan also resulted in improvements to the public space in the form of a road improvement project along the river near the castle, a public sign installation project, and redevelopment of the Taiko-mon road within the castle district.

Position of Hosokawa Residence in revitalization plan

The Hosokawa Residence was positioned as centerpiece of the revitalization plan. The residence, which is a merchant house located in the revetment of the Nabari River in the southern part of the city, had been abandoned for many years. It is said that the residence was built during the late Edo and early Meiji eras and it has come to be viewed as an important component of the Hase Highway townscape, which is the main street of Nabari City. In 2005 the residence was donated to Nabari City and was incorporated into the revitalization plan as a space for hosting resident events and as a historic exchange space.

Workshop for rehabilitating the Hosokawa Residence as a historical exchange facility

As the centerpiece of the historical exchange portion of the revitalization plan, the Hosokawa Residence was rebuilt using a town development grant. In 2006, a continuous workshop dedicated to the renovation of the residence was held. Workshop participants were members of the "Nabari executive committee" non-profit organization (NPO) which was created to manage the residence, Nabari City officials, and members of the Urban Planning Laboratory of Mie University.

Since the structure was very old, it had been partially demolished by the city administration. Additionally, the townscape along the Hase Highway that had been cut off due to the extension of construction activities in the east and west of the main building had also been demolished. As a result, in 2006, there were only three buildings (two storehouses and the Hosokawa Residence itself) remaining, all of which were abandoned and in a state of disrepair. At this time, some people said that the storehouse near the river should be pulled down as well.

Although it is easy to destroy buildings that are considered old and dangerous, other residents felt that such actions were bad, and that such historic buildings, where the memories of people's lives have been inscribed over numerous decades, should be leveraged to the greatest extent possible. However, it was difficult to convey the nuances of such efforts to the administrative side.

Therefore, in the second workshop, a simulation of the revitalized townscape simulation was prepared using the Charge Coupled Device camera.

130   *Kenjiro Matsuura*

Through this townscape simulation, it was successfully conveyed and recognized that (1) the first priority should be to protect the townscape along the Hase Highway, and (2) the deep perspective from the road along Nabari River was enhanced by the storehouse near the river.

In order to preserve and enhance an urban landscape, a vivid image of human activity is necessary. At the Hosokawa Residence, it was necessary to find ways to use the residence that would bring it into close contact with the citizens and encourage them to make repeated visits. In the first and third workshops, we examined various events, both large and small, in order to determine which could be held at the residence.

Those events were further classified it into three types: regular use events, mini-events held about once a month, and big events normally held about once a year. For example, the coffee shop and a Nabari City tourist information center could be seen as regular use, "pop-up" one-day restaurants could be seen as mini-events, and the Nabari Highway Market and Aozora Market could be seen as big events.

Later Hosokawa Residence

Eventually, the Hosokawa Residence was renamed the "Old Hosokawa Residence Yanase Inn" and opened in June 2008 under the management of the city residents. It has since been utilized as a location for one-day pop-up restaurants, classes of various types, gallery exhibition space, and many similar events. Stemming from the efforts of the one-day restaurants, there are currently six new businesses operating in Nabari City, including cafes that utilize empty shops. Additionally, the main building and two storehouses of the residence were selected for inclusion among Japan's registered tangible cultural properties in January 2009.

Furthermore, in 2012, the Hosokawa Residence was selected for the "Handmade Regional Prize" in the "General" category of the Ministry of Land, Infrastructure, Transport, and Tourism (MLIT) Awards "due to planning various citizen participatory events and an approach to area revitalization using the Nabari River such as the observation of aquatic life in cooperation with river rangers and environmental education such as firefly regeneration."

To create community-based machizukuri central city revitalization

In the Nabari City examples introduced in this chapter, machizukuri started by the residents from several districts spread throughout the city, thus leading to the formulation of an action plan for revitalizing the central urban area that was based on a public–private partnership. Community revitalization efforts by Nabari City residents are currently in progress, and will be carried forward over the next several decades after reviewing realized projects, reviewing current and adding additional plans, and other related activities.

The area budgeting system was inspired by the small-scale action of the residents in the central urban area, and the movement of machizukuri by residents spread throughout the city. After that, it was understood that the process of machizukuri, while alternating between the scale of the town and the scale of the city, progressed to the revitalization plan for the central urban area of public–private collaboration to further promote the machizukuri of the central urban area.

We will now outline the conditions that enabled these efforts.

Resident crisis awareness enhances the machizukuri momentum

In the Shinmachi District, the residents felt a rising sense of crisis because they could see that the survival of the district was in peril. Not only did they reject the scope of the regeneration plan for the central urban area proposed by the city administration, but they could see that the district suffered from periodic flood damage, a decline in the shopping districts, and an aging and declining population. Under such circumstances, with the creation of an alternative plan for renovating the riverside areas, the residents confidently took part in the revitalization of the district.

Future machizukuri through collaboration with experts

The Urban Planning Laboratory of Mie University was involved in the above-mentioned efforts and supported planning by the residents from a professional point of view. By organizing workshops that made it easy to examine future images using models, drawings, posters, etc., efficient planning became possible.

Transfer of resources to area residents by area budget system

In Nabari City, by transferring financial resources to the area residents, an environment was prepared in which the area residents could proactively proceed with machizukuri activities. Although not every idea succeeded, various machizukuri activities were promoted experimentally for each area.

Formulation of plan by public–private partnership

After the administration's plans for rebuilding the central urban area were abandoned, resident-oriented machizukuri was promoted in its place. However, it was said that the residents felt their efforts were restricted. Now they have learned that it is possible to formulate feasible action plans by having both the content to be addressed by the administration and the content to be addressed by the residents reach the same table for discussion.

132 *Kenjiro Matsuura*

Notes

1 This paper is a revised edition of Matsuura (2009) and Matsuura (2007).
2 "Multi-natural type revetment" means a revetment that is naturally incorporated with natural elements and close to nature.

References

Matsuura, K. (2007). Design Workshop ni yoru Seikatsukei no Hozen Keisyou Mieken Nabari shi wo jirei to shite (Preservation and Succession of Living Landscape by Design Workshop – The Case of Nabari City in Mie Prefecture), Nihon Kenchiku Gakkai Taikai Toshikeikaku Bumon Panel Discussion Siryou "Seikatsukei no Potential" (Architectural Institute of Japan Architectural Planning Division Panel Discussion Material "Life Landscape Potential"), 119–122, Tokyo: Architectural Institute of Japan.

Matsuura, K. (2009). Tiiki ni Yosan wo haibun suru torikumi Mieken Nabarishi "Yumedukuri Tiiki Yosan Seido" (Efforts to allocate budgets to the area, "regional budget system for community" in Nabari City, Mie Prefecture), *Jyuumin Shutai no Toshikeikaku Machidukuri heno yakudatekata (Resident-oriented city planning – How to use it for Machidukuri)*, 255–263, Kyoto: Gakugei Publishing Company.

11 The rebirth of mixed-use blocks in the decayed historic centre of Takefu in Echizen City, Fukui Prefecture

Shinji Nojima

Introduction

Many historic urban areas in Japan have old buildings such as *machiya*[1] (townhouses), *kura*[2] (warehouse), and *nagaya*[3] (tenement houses). These have a unique spatial composition and are an important part of the city, but they have many problems. Buildings are disused with closed shops and empty, decaying houses. Kura-no-Tsuji at Takefu in Echizen had this kind of problem, but it was rejuvenated as a community centre. A public square was built within the city block, storehouses were repaired, and shops were built. This attracted galleries, boutiques, and restaurants needed by the local community, and events were organized.

Often, when a block is redeveloped, large-scale work is carried out to ensure profitability of the business. However, this approach can result in a loss of historic scenery, resources, and attractions. In contrast, this case study shows a combination of small projects such as coordinating rights relationships, reorganizing the site, moving storage, and creating a common square. An internal pedestrian flow line is also designed inside the large block. The space was reorganized while saving and utilizing the historical landscape with its spatial features and resources.

In this case study, I will clarify this complicated development method. I will describe the process of machizukuri, where residents, landowners, the administration, and experts have repeated discussions, and residents and the landowners take the main responsibility.

The project background describing the characteristics of historical urban areas in Japan

Problems facing historical urban areas in Japan

The Takefu Echizen district of Fukui Prefecture had problems that are typical of historical downtown areas of Japan.

134 *Shinji Nojima*

Disappearance of retail businesses and shoppers

Many houses, businesses, and much commerce moved to the suburbs because of the increased use of cars and loose regulation of land use.[4] The fall in population caused a loss of retail businesses, there were fewer people on the streets, and the number of vacant shops increased. Decline followed in these historical areas of cities and city centres.

Street spaces are bad for pedestrians and are car-oriented

Formerly streets were attractive for pedestrians and offered beautiful townscapes, but after the motorization of society the streets were adapted mainly for cars.

For this reason, the town area became an unfriendly space for pedestrians, and crossing it was not an enjoyable experience. The pleasant, relaxing area was lost.

Destruction of historical buildings and landscape

Once, historical wooden buildings were lined up along the street, with roofs and town views aligned, making beautiful prospects. However, the unified landscape of these buildings was lost as the buildings were pulled down to make way for large-scale, fireproof buildings.

The spatial characteristics of historical urban areas in Japan

To start with, town design in historical urban areas in Japan is marked by the narrow fronts[5] and the long depth of the premises. House fronts were used as *machiya* shops opening onto the street, and there were *kura* storehouses in the interior of the block, where ancestral valuables were once stored (Figure 11.1, upper right-hand schema). The street front is considered public, and the interior part is private. Urban spaces in Europe are explicitly separated into public and private, but those in Japan are less clearly defined. The interior parts of a block are wooden buildings that are connected to the streets by narrow alleyways.

In recent years, many street front *machiya* shops have disappeared, while many private *kura* storehouses still remain. In this case study these remaining *kura* were incorporated into a community plaza in a joint venture between the local government and inhabitants. The construction of the community plaza was followed by the conversion of the *kura* along the plaza into the shops the community needed, for example a gallery, a boutique, and a restaurant. Then events such as antique fairs and local festivals were begun on a regular basis. This is an example of how a pedestrian-friendly, bustling location was constructed. The appearance was improved with landscaping and utilizing the spatial characteristics of this historical area.

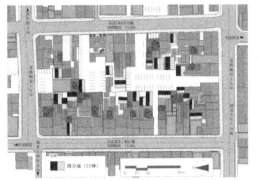

Placement map of the block before the project

Spatial composition of "Machiya" (town house) and "Kura"(warehouse)

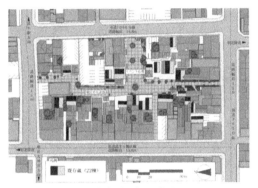

Placement map of the block after the project

Creation of public space (Plaza in the block built on the parking)

Creation of building continuity (Tea room made by house moving)

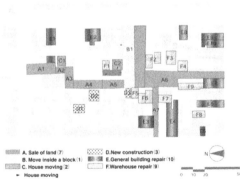

A. Sale of land (7)
B. Move inside a block (1)
C. House moving (2)
► House moving
D. New construction (3)
E. General building repair (10)
F. Warehouse repair (9)

Development by combining various maintenance projects

Exterior refurbishment and interior renovation
(Flower shop making use of warehouse)

Figure 11.1 Situation and development method of block area before and after project.

136 *Shinji Nojima*

The design process and relocation within the block

The target area is located in the Takefu district of Echizen City in Fukui Prefecture, known as Kura-no-Tsuji (meaning "crossroad with warehouses"). Takefu is one of the central urban areas of Echizen city, which is located about 100 km northeast of Kyoto City and has a population of 83,000. The area has a history going back over about 1,300 years. After becoming the Kokufu[6] in 646 it flourished as the cultural, economic, and political center of the surrounding Hokuriku region.

Despite its long history, Takefu is one of the areas affected by the problem of declining, central, urban areas. Between 1992 and 2006 the population in the central urban area decreased from 8,896 to 6,450, and the aging rate increased rapidly.

Kura-no-Tsuji is located about five minutes on foot from the main, local railway station. It extends over an area of approximately 170 m × 90 m, and is a historically significant urban block. Its old streets were constructed in the shape of a crank, which tells of its past as a vibrant centre in the area.

Urban area improvement project using large-scale redevelopment (1976–93)

The project began in 1976 with a locally organized seminar on revitalizing local shopping districts by harnessing their historical heritage (Sezaki *et al.*, 2001). This set the target area of the local business modernization plan and the station area as a primary focus for business revitalization. In 1981, a joint redevelopment conference between local residents, the local government, and a private consulting firm was established, and a proposal for a commercial system of redevelopment was made. The redevelopment plan had an ambitious aim to carry out three major and three medium-scale redevelopments, and to connect these by arcades. It was to develop the entire block, which was too large in the historical city area. The redevelopment project was abandoned in 1993, as discussions over strategies to invite tenants made little progress between 1990 and 1993, due to a decline in the world economy.

Urban area improvement project by individual building restoration (1994–)

The redevelopment conference changed into the regeneration project promotion council, which was launched as a government-funded redevelopment project. The previous plans were all reexamined and new plans created for communal walkways and a recreational plaza in the designated block, to be carried out by the city. Restoration of *kura* and renewal of each land sector was to be done privately in stages, aimed at keeping the

Takefu in Echizen City   137

continuity of the townscape. This avoided large-scale redevelopment which would destroy the characteristics of the old town, and used the retained historic space features. It revitalized the former bustle and vitality of the area, by combining small-scale alterations and restoring individual buildings.

Utilization of community space (2000–)

The plaza, where the hub of activities had been formerly, was created after the project was completed. This plaza quickly became the scene for regular, major events such as market fairs and festivals, and a recreational space for residents.

Market fairs were held monthly from April 2007. This was to encourage citizens' organizations to carry out activities and enhance movement. An antique market fair was held from April 2008, and it operated regularly every month.

In addition, the following events were held: a Central Shopping District Market Fair, a "Moonlight Café" (beer garden) in July, a Summer Festival run by the East District Autonomy Promotion Organization, an Echizen City Summer Festival in August, an Echizen Citizen Festival, a Citizens' Cultural Festival, and an Autumn Harvest Festival in November. Organizations such as shopping districts started to run these events in cooperation with the Kura-no-Tsuji Council, the Echizen-shi Mochizuki Centre, and others.

A design method for development based on combining small projects

In order to revitalize the interior of a private urban block and make it a bustling public space, three key design points had to be taken into account. (See Figure 11.1 lower left-hand diagram.)

Construction of public space

The parking lot inside the urban block was remade as a community plaza. Dead-end streets were then opened up by moving buildings[7] to create more decorative alleys, connecting the new plaza to the surrounding streets. Small landowners also agreed to sell as much of their land in the area as possible to create the public plaza. This is how the plaza, the alleys, the waterside space, the arbors, and the roadside trees, were arranged for pedestrians.

Reconstruction of building continuity

The city council purchased several *kura* inside the urban block. They kept building continuity by moving the *kura* to face the plaza, or by building new *kura*-style houses on vacant lots.

138 *Shinji Nojima*

Exterior restoration and interior renovation

Besides restoring *kura* and buildings, the outdoor facilities on the site, made visible by creating a public plaza inside the area, were redesigned and repaired.

This restoration was exterior, but the interiors of buildings were also redesigned and renovated to meet the needs of private landowners and new tenants who began to set up new shops in the area. A gallery, a craft shop, a gallery-cafe, a Japanese restaurant, and a bar were among the first to open. By the time renovation was completed a total of 11 new businesses had opened on the block.

The design method used for Kura-no-Tsuji does not have one large business owner carry out a big development project. Instead, many small-scale landowners, business owners, and local government administrators cooperated to do small designs and projects. It employed the following two methods.

The first method was to utilize Japan's historic urban areas where small wooden buildings were lined along an alley. This method used the characteristic, flexible spaces found in Japan to create passageways. It moved structures without changing the spatial composition and enhanced movement about the city, and it created a beautiful landscape through restoration. In this way beautiful views were created through restoration. It made use of the characteristic Japanese, flexible spaces by creating passageways and by moving houses, without increasing the spatial composition, and it enhanced movement about the city.

The second method was for various people to share roles and collaborate to advance the project. Local government administration bought parking lots and developed a square, and each individual small landowner cooperated by selling a small amount of land. Owners of buildings gained subsidies to restore the exterior of their buildings, and they opened new stores. Store operators also entered the market. It is a method of design where individuals cooperate over their plans.

Organization and systems to promote the project and its role

Which people and organizations came together to promote the plan in this project? The relationship between the people, the organizations, and their respective roles are described graphically in Figure 11.2.

Planning organization up to the completion of the renovation project

In the renovation project, the Takefu City, Horai-chou Area Regeneration Project Promotion Council, asked local architects to act as business coordinators, and the city, the local architects, and the council (landowners,

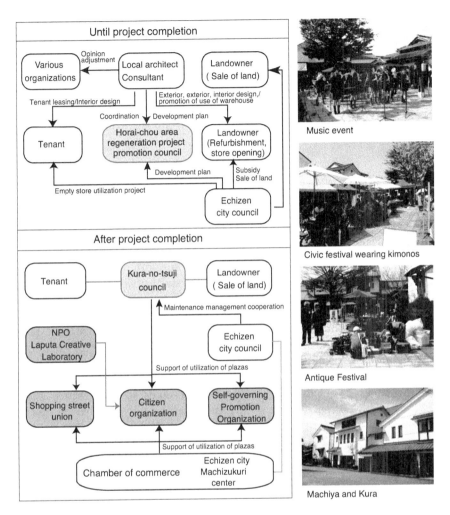

Figure 11.2 Promotion system of town planning during development and later.

residents) planned the project dividing up the roles. The councils, local architects, and the city formulated and implemented the renovation project plans in 1997.

In 1997, the city bought land from landowners, and developed streets and parks within the block. Experts coordinated the opinions of local groups and citizens who use the area. For residents' activities (such as building landscaping, and new construction), experts guided the use of buildings and sought new store operators who were to occupy the restored buildings.

The Horai-chou Area Regeneration Project Promotion Council, organized by the landowners of the district, was the central organization making

140 Shinji Nojima

decisions for the project, and it made decisions for the Takefu City (now Echizen City) renovation project plan and land acquisition plan.

Also, landowners who agreed to the sale of land, landowners who landscaped buildings and exteriors, landowners who opened shops and businesses, and tenants from without, played a part in deciding on each business.

As coordinators, the local architects put together advice on the design of public spaces, design proposals for renovation, the project profits, residents' consultation, and attracting stores.

Planning organization after completion of the renovation project

The Horai-chou area was named "Kura-no-Tsuji" by public choice, and this was a nickname for the plaza. The Horai-chou Area Regeneration Project Promotion Council also changed its name to "Kura-no-Tsuji Council" and promoted the utilization of the public plaza.

The Chamber of Commerce[8] gave active support during the bridging period from the project completion to the start of local activities, and various citizens' organizations, such as the Self-governing Promotion Organization and the Shopping Street Union,[9] acted as leaders in utilizing the open space and conducting events such as the antique market fair. After that, the Echizen City Machizukuri Centre was established and carried out these support functions.

A citizen group NPO is a community business launched by a landowner in Kura-no-Tsuji. In this way, after Kura-no-Tsuji created a presence in the city, organizations such as citizens' groups carried out town development activities there, and a network was established.

Achievements and issues

The project was evaluated as having the following merits.

Preservation of the historical context of the area

Large-scale redevelopment in urban areas can often lead to the destruction of the historical context, but since this project was conducted in a phased manner combining restoration and the creation of public spaces, the original landscape context was successfully utilized and preserved.

A community plaza was formed inside the block

In the old city centre, there were still several traditional *kura* buildings. Using these kura to create communal spaces was a good way to improve the atmosphere of the city center, but land in the interior of the block was originally private. Since space in Japan is very limited, that made it difficult to build a consensus among landowners who had

Takefu in Echizen City   141

strong connections to their land, and to implement the transformation of the space.

Integration of street redevelopment, building restoration, retail attraction strategies, and plaza utilization

In many cases, local revitalization projects in Japanese cities stop with the redevelopment of public spaces. Integrated design of building restoration and attracting new storeowners are almost always excluded, since reaching a consensus among the local landowners is difficult.[10] In this case, however, it was achieved, which allowed for a well-integrated design process.

A system of machizukuri organization was established, and later machizukuri activities were developed

Using the opportunity provided by the project, an organization was formed to carry out machizukuri such as special events, and the community square became a plaza full of busy activities. In this way, Kura-no-Tsuji was reconstructed and successfully turned into a vibrant space.

Currently, there are changes in store occupancy, but there are no vacant stores. But there is a problem as the number of events and activities is decreasing due to the aging of residents and landowners. In the future, in order to keep this open space as an exchange base for citizens, the management system for the open spaces must be strengthened. Also, careful machizukuri, mainly by residents and landowners, must be continued utilizing the historical resources such as Kura-no-Tsuji in various places in the future, and they must be dotted about busy locations. By networking these places, movement through the whole historic city area can be improved.

Notes

1 A traditional, merchant's wooden residence in the historical city area, with stores and dwellings united.
2 Traditional, stucco-made warehouse in the historical city area.
3 A rental apartment house with low rent. A wooden building, with multiple dwelling units sharing walls and in line.
4 The sprawl, due to suburbanization of retail stores and urban functions, is more severe than in the UK due to loose land use regulations.
5 After the townhouses were taxed by the length of their frontage, they were built narrow.
6 Cities where administration facilities were set up for the governors to direct the political affairs of each county from the Nara era to the Heian era (710 to 1185).
7 A construction method used when moving a building to another place without disassembling it.

142 *Shinji Nojima*

8 A public economic organization run by commerce and industry in areas such cities for the purpose of improvement and development of commerce and industry.
9 Organized by retail stores that are doing business in shopping streets. They develop infrastructure such as the construction of arcades and the maintenance of street lights, and events such as year-end sales.
10 This is because there is a tradition that land passes to children and selling land is disliked. There are cases where multiple people share land and buildings.

Reference

Sezaki, S., Nojima, S., and Tamaki, S. (2001). A Study on Method of Community Open-space Improvement in Residential Block of Local City – A Case Study at Horai-cho of Takefu City in Fukui. *Journal of the City Planning Institute of Japan*. 36: 127–132.

12 Reorganization of the local housing production system for maintaining and improving the historic landscape

Kosuke Masuo

Introduction

As our society matures and enters a period of acute slow growth, it is essential that we deal with the changes in the construction market, such as the scaling back of the market for new construction and the switch to a maintenance industry.[1] In addition, we are facing new social challenges, including frequent disasters[2] and increasing numbers of vacant houses,[3] that call for the management of existing urban areas in a form appropriate for handing on to future generations.

In response to these social changes, a greater emphasis is being placed in town planning and machizukuri on the maintenance and improvement of the historic landscape. "Historic landscape" is defined as the favorable urban environment formed in unison with the activities of people reflecting the unique history and traditions of an area and with buildings of high historic value and the surrounding urban area in which those activities are carried out. This perception of the historic landscape is at one with the concept of *fudo* (natural features of a region: human milieu) and the connection with the environment created through human action on nature (Watsuji, 1963). On the subject of *fudo*, Augustin Berque says that

> *Fudo* is not merely an object, that is, the land and the climate: it is the history of the people who live there. It is when humans and other living creatures come together that a particular *fudo* comes historically into being.
>
> (Berque, 2011)

Of the human activities that impact the historic landscape in this way, together with the actions of residents, there is an extremely close connection with the local housing production system that handles new construction, maintenance, repair, etc.[4] However, in the process of modernization and industrialization a huge gap has opened up between the maintenance and improvement of the historic landscape and local housing production systems. In our mature, low-growth society, the local housing production

144   Kosuke Masuo

system must break away from the scrap-and-build system of the period of rapid growth and be reorganized as a recycling system in terms of both resources and technology, and as a system that will contribute to the restoration, maintenance and improvement of the historic landscape.

In this chapter I would like to introduce some examples of local residents, producers, experts and local administration working together to restore, maintain and improve the historic landscape through the reorganization of the housing production system, in an area in which the historic landscape was lost at a stroke through disaster. Moreover, I would like to consider, from what can be learned from those efforts, the best system of housing production to restore, maintain and improve Japan's historic landscape in the future.

Machizukuri aimed at the restoration, maintenance and improvement of historic landscape lost though natural disaster

Post-earthquake reconstruction and machizukuri aimed at the restoration of the homeland landscape and mountain lifestyle

In recent years many areas of Japan have suffered from frequent disasters. One disaster that caused a great deal of damage is the 2004 Chuetsu Earthquake. This earthquake struck rural settlements in secluded mountainous areas of Niigata Prefecture, and the most badly affected region was the area of Yamakoshi. The earthquake cut off access by road, isolating many settlements, and an evacuation order was issued for the whole of the Yamakoshi area. As a result, the whole population of the Yamakoshi area was evacuated en masse to Nagaoka, the regional hub city, where people from each settlement were obliged to live as refugees in temporary accommodation.

In this situation, the recovery plan for the Yamakoshi area (Yamakoshi Village, 2005), put together half a year after the earthquake, was given the title "Let's go home to Yamakoshi." The plan begins with the words:

> There are many of us who cannot enjoy life except in Yamakoshi. Built up over long years and months, Yamakoshi is our spiritual home, the home on which we depend for our lives; and we are determined to work together to realize our wish to return home to Yamakoshi.

The characters used to write Yamakoshi in Japanese mean "old aspirations of the mountain"; it is an area where the traditional mountain lifestyle of the Japanese people has carried on for 1,000 years, where bullfighting performances are still held. The rice grown in the scenic terraced rice fields is Japan's top-class brand of rice, known as Uonuma Koshihikari. Yamakoshi is also the home of *nishikigoi*, the ornamental carp which have many fans both in Japan and overseas; they were bred in the irrigation

Reorganization of local housing system 145

ponds for the terraced rice fields. The Yamakoshi area is also known as the snowiest part of Japan; in winter the snow lies nearly three meters deep. The style of house, an accumulation of generations of wisdom in adapting to this harsh climate, is the style of private house known as *chumon-zukuri*. The historic landscape of the Yamakoshi area is the very landscape in which are interwoven the mountain lifestyle, the terraced rice-fields and the *chumon-zukuri* houses.

The central component of this recovery plan was machizukuri that would take advantage of the reconstruction to create a new mountain village culture and industry in the wake of the earthquake, while restoring the old scenery and way of life. On the basis of this recovery plan, the residents of Yamakoshi in the meeting room of their temporary accommodation split into their respective villages to hold repeated discussions. As a result of such discussion, it was decided that they would all return together and consider post-disaster machizukuri aimed at restoring the scenery of their home and their mountain lifestyle.

Deployment of self-reconstruction housing support by focusing on regional style housing

A natural disaster impacts many houses, and the historic landscape of the area is lost at a stroke. Further, in post-disaster machizukuri the call is for the swift reconstruction of large numbers of houses, and the further loss of local historic landscape in the process of rebuilding homes is a challenge. Recognition of this issue led in the Yamakoshi area to the development of a model for regional style housing[5] that would succeed the *chumon-zukuri* that is the local style of housing in this region;[6] the local housing production system was reorganized as a system to provide this housing, and initiatives were implemented to support those rebuilding their homes by themselves. This was the first time this had been tried in Japanese post-disaster machizukuri. This writer was also involved in the implementation of this initiative. This kind of initiative is called "Support for self-reconstruction housing," and since then has evolved as one method of post-disaster recovery in Japan.

The practice of self-reconstruction housing support in the Yamakoshi area

The Niigata Prefecture Chuetsu Earthquake that occurred on the October 23, 2004 inflicted severe damage on the Yamakoshi area of Nagaoka City in Niigata Prefecture: 328 houses, some 44 percent of the 747 houses in the area, were completely destroyed. Other houses were also badly damaged; there was not one house that escaped damage.

The basic policy of the Nagaoka City recovery plan was to return as many residents as possible to the Yamakoshi area that was impacted by

146   *Kosuke Masuo*

the disaster. Against their wishes, there were problems to be solved for both the residents and the administration; while the residents wished to return to their old familiar settlements, for many households old age meant that they were not able to rebuild their homes; at the same time the progressive depopulation of mountainous regions meant that if the administration were to build large numbers of public housing units, it would in the future be left with large numbers of vacant housing units on its hands.

Accordingly a committee was set up in Nagaoka comprising the relevant administrative agencies (Nagaoka City, Niigata Prefecture and the central government), academics and interested parties from the local construction industry. In order to enable as many residents as possible to return to the mountain and rebuild their homes by their own efforts, the aim of this committee was to develop regional style housing that would withstand the snow and be suited for the lifestyle of the mountain region, and moreover could be built at a low cost of around ¥10 million. This writer was commissioned by Nagaoka City to play a major role as a member of the team formed to develop and promote this regional style housing.

Development of the regional style housing

In the development of this regional style housing, as our first task, we carried out the following surveys in order to gain an understanding of the rural landscape of Yamakoshi and how local house construction was carried out: (1) a survey of the local climate and houses; (2) a survey of all 14 settlements in the Yamakoshi area and the degree of damage suffered by them; and (3) a field survey of the houses that had escaped damage. Next, based on photographs and data we analyzed the surveys together with local carpenters and timber suppliers in terms of changes to the floor plans, measures to cope with snow, way of life, housing provision system, local construction costs, etc.

On the basis of these surveys, regional style housing was developed in line with the following five concepts:

1   Housing suited to Yamakoshi that follows the traditional method of building of a family home;
2   Housing well able to cope with the heavy snowfalls of the region;
3   Locally-sourced housing making full use of local materials and carpentry skills;
4   Housing that imposes a reduced cost-burden on the victims of the disaster;
5   Housing that provides safe and comfortable living over the long term.

The plans were made public in the year following the disaster.

After that, in order to show the regional style housing that we had developed to those planning to rebuild, we actually constructed two types

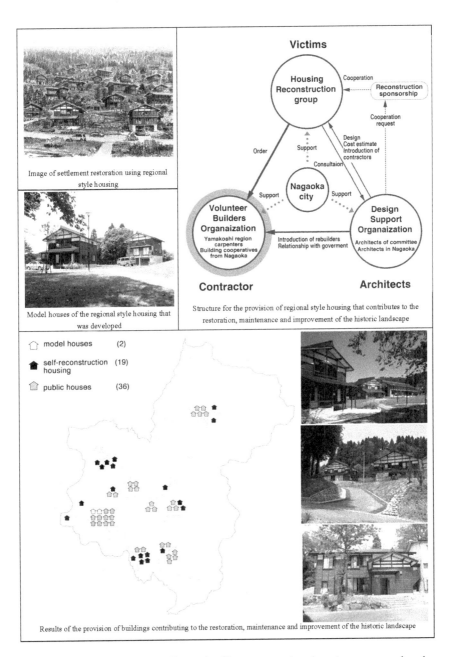

Figure 12.1 Approach and effect of self-reconstruction housing support by the regional style housing.

148 *Kosuke Masuo*

of local housing in Yamakoshi, one with a low floor and one with a raised floor. The construction of this kind of prototype building also served to provide building contractors and carpenters working independently with a common model.

The low-floor type with a total floor area of $90\,m^2$ and a cost of ¥12.5 million and the raised-floor type with a total floor area of $140\,m^2$ and a cost of ¥13.5 million were set as the minimal models. With Disaster Victim Livelihood Recovery funding of ¥1 million from Niigata Prefecture, donations of ¥4.59 million and support from the Disaster Recovery Fund for the Maintenance and Improvement of the Historic Landscape of ¥1.8 million, the personal capital required was ¥5.11 million for the low-floor type and ¥ 6.11 million for the raised-floor type.

In the Yamakoshi area many residents have earthquake insurance, so that insurance pay-outs helped reduce the amount of money that needed to be found.

Creation of a design and construction structure

Disaster recovery requires a lot of housing to be provided efficiently, at reasonable cost, and within a limited timeframe. In order to do this, we provided support in three ways. The first of these was the preparation of a house construction guidebook, standard drawings and specifications, rules for structural design, a rough construction cost estimate system, etc. Second, we formed an organization of interested construction businesses (Association of Builders Supporting Housing Construction in Yamakoshi) and design support organizations and formed into groups those wishing to rebuild. The third means of support was to approach construction materials manufacturers and set up a mechanism for buying in construction materials at a favorable price.

The interested construction businesses were formed into teams with carpenters from Yamakoshi and building cooperatives from Nagaoka, the local hub city, working together. A relationship of mutual trust between the owner and the builder plays a large part in the repair of a house damaged in an earthquake. For this reason most of the repair work was undertaken by local builders. However, this led to the situation of local builders being too busy to handle the construction of new housing, and thus support contractors stepped in to fill the gap. In such a case, instead of rebuilding the house in its completed form, at first just a minimum living space was built, with extensions to be added in stages at a later date. The thinking behind this, in addition to reducing the cost burden on the owner, was to enable local builders to take on the daily maintenance of the property.

The design support organizations were formed into teams comprising interested architects from Nagaoka with extensive experience in the design of timber housing and an understanding of machizukuri, and members of the regional style housing development team.

Reorganization of local housing system   149

Support for those wishing to rebuild in each settlement

There are 14 settlements in the Yamakoshi area, but the degree of damage from the earthquake differed in each settlement. In eight of the settlements there was relatively little damage to the infrastructure, and the restoration of individual plots of land and rebuilding by the owner was possible, while in the other six settlements the infrastructure was severely damaged; in these settlements a machizukuri council was set up, and a separate restoration plan considered for each settlement.

A general explanatory meeting was held for residents of the eight settlements, and those who wished to rebuild a mountain-region style home in place of the home they had lost to the earthquake were invited to come forward; lists were drawn up, and the owners formed into groups. Not everyone wanted to rebuild a simple residence, so that diverse reconstruction needs had to be met; some wanted to rebuild as a farming guest-house, others wanted to take advantage of the reconstruction after the earthquake to return from Tokyo to their home in Yamakoshi.

As for the six settlements where restoration plans were being studied, on the other hand, those wishing to rebuild were organized into groups by the machizukuri council. The machizukuri councils made use of the strong local community ties to urge the rebuilding of regional style housing after the earthquake, for example through the establishment of a landscape agreement based on the concept of the regional style disaster restoration model houses. In addition, planning was not restricted to the repair of infrastructure damaged by the earthquake and the rebuilding of housing: the opportunity presented by reconstruction was used to promote post-disaster machizukuri that would create a new mountain village culture and industry.

For elderly households for whom self-reconstruction was particularly problematic, public housing was provided. This public housing was provided in each settlement, so that residents could return to the settlement with which they were familiar and continue living there, and so that the restoration of the function of the settlement could proceed smoothly. So that it would provide future stock and serve as a model for landscape formation, the public housing was built following the concept, specifications and construction methods of mountain-area reconstruction housing.

The results of the restoration of the old landscape of the Yamakoshi area and of the mountain lifestyle

Three years on from the earthquake, of the 690 households that had been in Yamakoshi before the earthquake, 470 had returned. The rate of return after three years was 68 percent. Of the 470 households that had returned, 99 households (21 percent) had built new homes; 35 (7 percent) had moved into public housing, and 336 (72 percent) were living in homes that had been repaired.

150 *Kosuke Masuo*

Of the 134 new homes, a total of 54 homes had been built under the local housing production system developed on the basis of the regional style disaster restoration housing; 19 independently, the other 35 being the disaster-recovery public housing. Roughly 40 percent of new homes were built as regional style housing, and a variety of housing types were developed that followed the rules for regional style housing. In the case of repairs too, many houses were built in line with the rules for regional style housing thanks to the influence of the construction businesses. At the same time that support was provided for the rebuilding of homes, support was also provided for the rebuilding of the industrial infrastructure that had thus far sustained the mountain lifestyle; the terraced rice-fields, *nishikigoi* ponds, cattle sheds, etc., were similarly restored in three years.

After three years, once the first stage of the recovery work was completed, the Organization for the Restoration of the Mountain Lifestyle was established as an organization to continuously promote machizukuri to create the new mountain village culture and industry that had been under discussion throughout the post-disaster machizukuri. Thus a number of projects were implemented aimed at restoring once again the mountain lifestyle, such as the establishment of Orataru, a field museum. This will play a part in the transmission and development of the mountain village culture, including *nishikigoi*, which originated in the Yamakoshi area, and Yamakoshi bullfighting, with its 1,000-year history, and in the recollection, recording and passing on to future generations of the lessons learned from the earthquake; it will also invite visitors to learn about the mountain lifestyle; training/educational tours relating to the preservation of damage caused by the earthquake; the development of old private houses into farm guesthouses or direct-sales cooperatives; the creation and branding of new indigenous vegetable products of the Yamakoshi area; and restaurants offering vegetables grown in the Yamakoshi area.

Through machizukuri following the earthquake, to the old landscape of the Yamakoshi area, built up over long years, has been added a new mountain lifestyle, and the historic landscape is being restored, maintained and improved. (Figure 12.1)

In conclusion

The maintenance and improvement of the historic landscape relies not on simplistic solutions such as building construction or street restoration, but on the sustainability of a system of community-based construction. Based on this concept, in "machizukuri" activities themed on the preservation of the historic environment it is important to reconfirm the relationship between the residents, builders and architects, and to reconstruct a new local housing production system.

Finally, in promoting the creative recovery of the Yamakoshi area, reference was made to the industrial rehabilitation from an ecological

Reorganization of local housing system   151

perspective that makes the most of biodiversity as seen in Taomi Village, Puli Township, an area affected by the 1999 Chi-Chi Earthquake in Taiwan. I hope that in an age when disasters are occurring with great frequency all over the world, we will see the spread of thoughtful interactions permeated with the knowledge and wisdom of this kind of machizukuri following an earthquake.

Notes

1 From around 2010, Japan became a country with a declining population. This social change has also brought huge changes in the housing industry; in the post-war period the construction of new houses increased steadily, reaching a peak in 1996 of ¥70.3 trillion, but in 2013 this had fallen to ¥37.4 trillion, halving over a period of 20 years. With this rapid shrinking and decline of the new construction market, the role of maintenance and repair work has grown in comparison, and the situation regarding the housing industry in local communities has changed greatly.
2 The Great Hanshin-Awaji Earthquake (January 1995), the Niigata Prefecture Chuetsu Earthquake (October 2004), the Noto Peninsula earthquake (March 2007), the Great East Japan Earthquake (March 2011), the Great Floods in Kii Peninsula (September 2011), the Great Fire of Itoigawa (December 2016), the West Japan Heavy Rain Event (July 2018); from the Hanshin-Awaji Earthquake onwards, Japan has experienced many large-scale disasters, making disaster recovery an issue of great import in urban planning and machizukuri.
3 According to the Housing and Land Statistical Survey, as of 2013 there were some 8.2 million vacant houses in Japan, accounting for 13.5 percent of the total number of houses. Vacant houses that are ranked as historic buildings are treated in the same way as ordinary vacant houses, and the loss of the historic landscape due to their demolition is an issue.
4 A local housing production system is a social system comprising a number of entities involved in the production of housing in a region, including foresters, the lumber industry, timber merchants, parts manufacturers, architect offices, carpentry/engineering firms and clients.
5 Housing that satisfies the regional style environment (environment taken in the broad sense; the natural environment, resource environment, cultural environment, etc.)
6 Local housing newly developed through a reinterpretation of the regional characteristics of housing production hitherto existing in natural form, in the light of modern social and technological conditions, and built under the local housing production system.

References

Berque, A. (2011). Nihonteki hūdo no saikouchiku (Reconstruction of the Japanese fudo), www.wochikochi.jp/topstory/2011/11/restructuring.php
Masuo, K. (2015). An organic method of village rehabilitation through a reconstruction archetype based on vernacular architecture, 22nd ISFU 2015 Conference. Rome.

Masuo, K. (2018). Rekishitekihūchi no ijikoujō no tameno chiikijūtakuseisanshisutemu ni kansuru kenkyū (Study on regional housing production system for maintaining and improving historical scenic beauty), Ph.D. dissertation, Waseda University.

Watsuji, T. (1963). *Fudo*, Iwanami Shoten.

Yamakoshi Village. (2005). Kaerou Yamakoshi he (Let's go home to Yamakoshi – Main points of the Yamakoshi recovery plan).

13 The urban renewal method based on the community principle
The case of the Yuyuan area of the Shanghai Historical Scene Conservation District

Chengqi Zhao

Introduction

Characteristics of East Asian metropolitan cities

Large cities in East Asia are characterized by high density of residential population. Differences in land ownership and constraints result in various spatial forms. The majority of China's largest cities meet their living needs by constructing a large number of high-rise residential buildings. The resultant urban issues from large-scale development are homogenization of space, large scale of infrastructure, standardization of residential units, and fragmentation of social fabrics in neighborhoods. Under the process of systematic urban housing demolition, the original communities cannot be sustained and protected as they should be. On the other hand, Japan's metropolitan areas are characterized by large areas of low-rise, high-density residential districts. Its urban issues are the high density of buildings, insufficient public space, and fragmented urban space.

In comparison to the sophisticated urban redevelopment in Japan, the urban renewal discipline in China is still in the process of exploring its own methodology. During the last 50 years, Japan has gradually experimented and successfully implemented the bottom-up renewal model, the *machizukuri* methodology, which is supported by various renewal mechanisms. Its accumulated experience has attracted the attention[1] of Chinese planning disciplines attempting to address similar urban issues.

Characteristics of development and protection

Contemporary urban planning in China tends to employ the strategies of Development and Protection. Faced with a large number of Protected Areas, there seems to be a lack of innovative strategies and methodologies between Development and Protection. In addressing the renewal of Protected Areas within the inner city districts, both Development and Protection tend to lead to "sudden failure." While Protection is run by the government and

154   *Chengqi Zhao*

Development is operated through the market mechanism, renewal of urban centers requires a new system of mutual interest and collaboration as the main body of the project, aiming to protect and revitalize traditional communities. However, such a new system and methodology have yet to be established in China.

The methodology of *machizukuri* is based on the fundamental principles of the collaboration of multiple subjects. Although the land ownership policies of these two countries are different, *machizukuri* can be used as a reference for the renewal of China's regional fabric, sustainability of community heritage, and the formation of diversified, high-quality neighborhoods.

Bottom-up planning trend

Since the limitation of the traditional top-down planning approach is recognized to a certain extent, the new trend of bottom-up social planning approach has emerged in Chinese cities since the beginning of this century. Nevertheless, due to the lack of immediate change at the legal and institutional levels, public participation in urban planning still remains at the initial phase of soliciting public opinions. Consequently, the following issues arise in the urban planning: (1) destruction of traditional neighborhoods; (2) widespread creation of standardized urban space caused by short-term profit-driven development; (3) an unsustainable relocation and redevelopment model; (4) ineffectiveness of government-led and market-driven urban renewal.

Market-driven Development has led to an unusual spatial phenomenon in Shanghai: "Foreigners living in the inner ring, non-Shanghai immigrants living in the middle ring, and Shanghai residents migrating to the areas between the middle and outer rings, or beyond the outer ring." Although this is an exaggerated generalization, it somehow reflects the fact that the traditional neighborhoods have been severely damaged after 30 years of rigorous development in the city core. Under the guidance of the Development model, almost every housing estate unit has its enclosed walls, forming an independent territory within the urban environment. After the completion of the Development model, the undeveloped area becomes an isolated island.

The diversification of urban space simply cannot be realized by the top-down planning approach. The diversification created during the urban renewal process should be encouraged by various mechanisms (selectivity of system) and collaboration of multiple stakeholders. At the same time, it is essential to encourage the initiative of various undertakings. In addition to the government-led and enterprise-led undertakings, it is also necessary to foster local interest groups to set up their own ventures, to "redistribute the interest/gain after urban renewal," to nurture local residents' small businesses, and to encourage civic participation to improve urban space.

Proposal of urban renewal methodology for multi-stakeholders' participation based on community principle

Objectives and significance of urban renewal based on community principle

Generally speaking, urban planning has gone through two historical stages: the principle of top-down planning and the market-driven mechanism. With the philosophy of *machizukuri*, the principle of community breaks through the Development approach dominated by government and market. Aiming at protecting traditional neighborhoods, urban renewal encourages the collaboration of government, developers, and original property owners to develop their common interest, and promotes the renewal projects collectively.

Urban renewal based on the community principle is the third approach to urban renewal, different from the government-led or developer-led renewal. The responsible body for the urban renewal projects has changed from a single party to a joint coalition of government, developers, and original property owners. Consequently, a collaborative coalition of the main parties for the renewal projects can be established. Urban renewal with multi-stakeholders' involvement tends to have a positive impact on the diversification of urban space, sustainability of traditional neighborhoods, and the governance of society.

Residential district renewal method by "property right exchange"

At the methodological level, the residential district renewal method needs to address the following issues related to: (1) economic balance during renewal; (2) implementation procedures; and (3) establishment of a project-oriented association for urban renewal.

How to address the issue of financial resources needed by urban renewal is the most important prerequisite. In response to this issue, Japan specified "Urban redevelopment projects" in the Urban Renewal Act.[2] Through the joint reconstruction of an old building, a new building is allowed to be built with significantly more than the existing volume-to-land ratio. With the new volume-to-land ratio, the permitted additional floor space is shared by the joint stakeholders. However, in Chinese metropolises, the plan to increase the volume-to-land ratio of existing blocks will be in conflict with the superior regulations and thereby face these issues: (1) adjusting the regulatory plan; (2) how the development stakeholders can obtain the right to develop the piece of land; and (3) how to upgrade the subject's legalization.[3] With the above premises guaranteed, the original owner of the property, as one of the stakeholders, obtains certain rights and interests after the renewal through a "property rights exchange," and, hence, makes the traditional neighborhood sustainable.

156 *Chengqi Zhao*

Establishment of project organizations with multi-stakeholders' participation

When *machizukuri* is implemented in Japan, an important issue is how to develop an organizational relationship between the project subjects and stakeholders. Based on the principle of community, different types of project-oriented association will emerge due to different collaborations of stakeholders. Moreover, with the difference between Chinese and Japanese land ownership,[4] the design and development of the project-oriented associations should comply with Chinese laws and adjust to the actual circumstances.

Urban renewal case study in the Shanghai Old City Yuyuan area: research and exploration

Background and drawbacks of urban renewal in central Shanghai

As one of the most influential modern cities in China, Shanghai has gone through different development in different eras: influence of earliest old city, lease era, planned economy era, early planned economy era, and market economy era. The city shows the coexistence of urban spatial patterns characterized at different times by unique regional characteristics and features. In recent years, while facing the pressure of large-scale development in the central city area, Shanghai promulgated the *Shanghai Historical Landscape Protection Planning* in 2002, effectively preventing its traditional urban space from being damaged by the large-scale Development and reconstruction of traditional residential districts. In 2015, the *Shanghai Urban Renewal Regulations* were promulgated, and research and implementation of urban renewal has begun. Besides, the community planning system implemented in recent years has opened up the bottom-up renewal of the old urban areas.

Shanghai Yuyuan district is one of the 12 historical landscape protection areas in Shanghai. The potential and drawbacks of this district include: (1) historically rich district with historically significant architecture remaining intact; (2) unfavorable living environment with fragmented community; and (3) limitations and difficulties of building relocation. To achieve urban renewal based on historical landscape protection, Shanghai City made a long-term commitment to research and implementation. In December 2015, the city organized international bidding from international architectural design firms, and integrated the specialities of many firms. As a result, a statutory planning system was formulated.[5]

Solutions at the level of renewal mode and diversified renewal methods

In contrast to the other three architectural firms, in consideration of fostering a balanced economy and sustaining the traditional inheritance of the

Yuyuan area of Shanghai 157

community, the author proposed the following unique renewal strategies (Figure 13.1).

Renewal models and techniques

1 Property rights exchange;
2 urban space renewal from property rights exchange;
3 reserve the air space on top of the protected area (the remaining volume from maximum volume-to-land ratio) for the government to experiment with its allocation;
4 linkage of land parcels: develop the linkage between Development and Protection land parcels;
5 explore urban renewal with participation of diversified stakeholders.

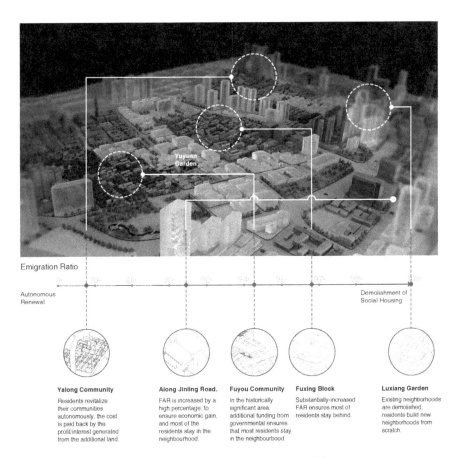

Figure 13.1 Horizontally expanded collective housing model.
Source: courtesy of Ting LU.

158 *Chengqi Zhao*

Programming of renewal process

Urban renewal is programmed to proceed gradually over time, with four stages. All districts are revitalized gradually.

Establishment of community association for urban renewal

The establishment of a community renewal association continues to be subject to some legal restrictions in China. When the organizational relationship for various targeted projects are set up, there are still considerable barriers and legal restrictions. Community associations at neighborhood level[6] have played a positive role in maintaining a safe living environment at the grass-roots level. To realize urban renewal with the participation of diversified subjects/stakeholders, community associations play an active role. Complying with the existing laws and regulations, they aim at revitalizing neighborhoods. They play a significant role in "establishing rules/principles for their organizations," "coordinating to organize project-oriented coalition," and "ensuring the individual renewal projects can proceed continuously."

Spatial planning of low-rise, high-density landscape and community protection area

Design strategies for low-rise and high-density residential districts

During the renewal of the northern Shanghai Yuyuan District, it was difficult to implement the "property rights exchange" within a short period of time. As a result, in the subsequent development of the southern Yuyuan district, a particular area was selected as the pilot study plot.[7] Based on the experiments on the study plot, the appropriate spatial design was implemented, targeting a low-rise and high-density residential district with the protection of the existing street lane system. This served as a model for sustainable renewal in the next stage.

For the redevelopment of landscape protected districts, under a certain floor-to-land ratio, the correlation between building height and density can be found with the reference index of gross open-space floor-area ratio (GOFR) (Satoh 1980). The open space that Japanese building law achieves may not be realized in China due to constraints of laws and regulations. How to achieve this vision through architectural design is a critical issue. To protect the street lane system, and overcome the constraints of "distance between adjacent buildings not less than 6 meters" (specified by China's Code of Design on Building Fire Protection and Prevention), the design strategy of "residential collective housing spread in a horizontal direction" is proposed. This kind of collective housing, spread in a horizontal direction, can maintain the spatial characteristics of Shanghai's unique street lane structure at the neighborhood scale, creating a "reconstructed street lane system"

Yuyuan area of Shanghai 159

and promoting the formation of "street" (Figure 13.2). Consequently, at the residential scale, a variety of types of living space with courtyards and terraces can be designed. (The planned floor ratio of the plot is 1.32.)

Spatial characteristics of residential district design integrated with historical landscape protection and neighborhood improvement

The residential district planning integrated with historical landscape protection has the following characteristics: (1) low rise and high density; (2) inheritance of the structure of the street lane system; and (3) horizontally spread housing with flexibility of future horizontal expansion.

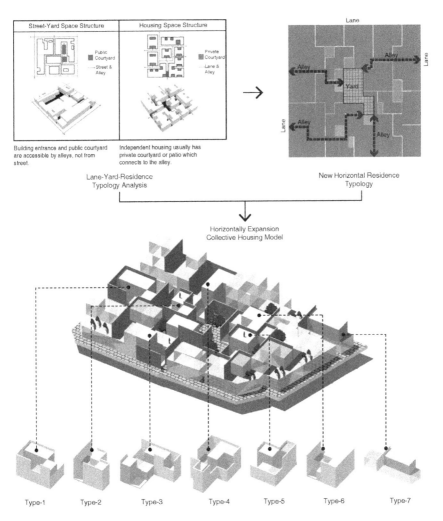

Figure 13.2 Diversified methods of district renewal.

160 *Chengqi Zhao*

Overcoming the constraints of laws and regulations, through the design of horizontally expandable collective housing, the spatial form of the "street lane" residential district was reconstructed.

Residential district planning: objectives of regional cycle with equilibrium age structure of population

The aging residents in old urban areas present a grave issue to cities. After urban renewal, a balanced age distribution of residents should be planned to live in the revitalized neighborhood. This healthy mix of residents of different ages would result in a diversity of lifestyles co-existing in the community. With the aging population and change of family structure of local residents, the renewed neighborhood can meet the diversified needs of housing for everyone at every stage of his/her life: single units, newly-married units, child-independent units, healthy elderly units, and units for severely impaired old people.

Conclusion

Based on the case study of the sustainable urban renewal model of the Shanghai historical landscape protection area, Yuyuan District, this chapter suggests urban renewal principles aiming at community protection and economic balance, and proposes the spatial planning scheme of low-rise and high-density horizontally expanded collective housing at the neighborhood scale. The proposed methodological approach addresses several critical issues commonly faced by historical landscape protection areas.

1 From the perspective of community protection, the original land owners should have the choice to "stay or leave" during the urban renewal process.
2 From the perspective of historical landscape protection, it is appropriate to design low-rise, high-density residential districts, and to develop corresponding indicators and evaluation systems.
3 From the perspective of neighborhood sustainability, local operational maintenance and social governance within the neighborhoods should be promoted.

There are still some obstacles in the implementation stage. Therefore, it is necessary to conduct more research and pilot projects to improve the existing regulations and systems; particularly, the regulations for urban renewal of old residential districts, the approval procedures for local planning, the development of project-oriented coalitions, and the detailed rules at the operational level.

Currently, the main issues encountered at the implementation level include:

a   The land transfer system is constrained in the urban renewal projects, especially the intervention projects in residential district. (new routes to acquire development rights need to be developed).
b   Renewal projects cannot mobilize private funds from private parties' participation through public financial subsidies (development of profit-oriented model).
c   The upper limit of some regulations should have the flexibility to be increased, permitting the volume-to-land ratio to exceed up to a certain range (according to the needs for renewal to modify the regulations).

The urban renewal of Chinese cities based on the community theory proposed in this chapter has the following characteristics:

- It is a process of multi-stakeholder participation and cooperative effort.
- There is no real sense of completion, it is a step-by-step dynamic process.
- The planning of renewal, program, and project-oriented coalitions is the premise of spatial planning and design.
- There is a need to establish a project-oriented coalition to smooth the progress of the renewal projects.
- There is a need to support the new planning technologies (consensus formation technology, virtual technology).
- It is necessary to formulate or improve the system, regulations, technical regulations, mitigation conditions, and approval procedures for urban renewal.

Notes

1 Tongji University Press published *Urban Regeneration in Tokyo: Key Urban Redevelopment Projects* by Yongjie Sha and Eiji Okada in 2019.
2 Urban redevelopment projects as stated in the Urban Renewal Act are a system of Urban Redevelopment in Japan based on the participation of original owners. The goal of economic balance and community inheritance can be achieved by increasing the volume-to-land ratio in the process of redevelopment.
3 These three issues can be addressed through the corresponding method under the existing legal framework. This chapter will not discuss them.
4 The land ownership system in Chinese cities is public ownership, where the land belongs to the state. In the process of development, the government transfers land ownership. Land ownership in Japan is private ownership, which is mainly by individuals.
5 In December 2015, the government of the Huangpu District of Shanghai organized the collection of the international urban design for the North District of Shanghai Yuyuan area. SOM, KPF, and EIH, as the finally selected three firms, took part in the planning of urban renewal in the area. Based on the above

results, the compilation of the Regulatory plan has been completed. The project is being implemented in the process of research.

6 A community association is a residents' organization for the community in the districts of urban streets and administrative towns in the mainland of China, i.e., an autonomous organization of local residents.

7 The right to land development of the plot is owned by Shanghai Shilin Company.

References

Mashiko, T., Zhao, C.Q., Uchida, N., and Satoh, S. (2014). Research on Improvement Methodologies for Living Environments in City Central Areas in China: A Case Study about Three Different Living Environment Quality Areas in Hangzhou city, 10th ISAIA, Hangzhou.

Satoh, S. (1980). A Study of Criterion about Density and Open Space, Part 1. *Transactions of the Architectural Institute of Japan*, 283: 167–177.

Satoh, S. (2004). To the Third Generation of Machizukuri. In Satoh, S. and Architectural Institute of Japan (eds.), *Machizukuri no Houhou (Method of Machizukuri)*, Tokyo: Maruzen.

Satoh, S. (2004). *Illustrated Urban Design and its Methodology*, Tokyo: Maruzen, 2006.

Shanghai Urban Planning and Land Resource. (2007). *Urban Planning Administration Practices in Shanghai: An Exploration of Urban Planning Administration under the Scientific Concept of Development*, China Building Industry Press.

Uchida, N., Mano, Y., and Zhao, C.Q. (2008). Reforming the Crowded Inner-City Residential Areas with Different Actors: Cases in Tokyo and Shanghai, IFHP World Congress for Housing and Planning.

Zhao, C.Q. (2015). *Yangxi, Jiande City, Hangzhou Multi-Stakeholder Participation in Urban Regeneration*, Urban Wisdom Advancing with China, Tongji University.

Zhao, C.Q. and Wang, S.P. (2019). Study on the Characteristics of Adjustability in Japan's District Planning System [J]. *Journal of Urban and Regional Planning*, 11(2): 76–91.

14 Development of the Furano Machizukuri Company connecting rural areas and urban core revitalization in Furano city

Katsuhiro Kubo

Business development in the urban center of Furano

The Furano Machizukuri Company (hereinafter called the Machizukuri Company) was accredited with revitalizing the center of Furano city, one of the most famous tourist cities on Hokkaido. This was part of the new Act on Improvement and Vitalization in City Centers.[1] Furano city is located in a major agricultural area, which was developed at the beginning of the nineteenth century. It was established as a hub city in the center of Furano Basin, which stretches 30 kilometers from the north to the south. The city area was formed as an integral part of the farmland at that time; therefore, the city is located deep in the agricultural area, and both city and farmland retain a high spatial continuity. Tourist spots in Furano are now mainly found in the rural areas and surrounding hilly areas. Attracting tourists from those areas to the center of the city is one of the Machizukuri Company's main aims. To date, city-planning in Furano has involved two projects, and both have targeted the whole region. The first project involved revitalizing the wider area in the 1960s. Traders and manufacturers took the lead in developing ski resort areas, which was sponsored by residents of Furano. They also started planning, executing and running the Heso Matsuri (Navel Festival), which has become a major event. The second project was developing the "Furano Brand" in the 1970s. "Local production for local consumption" became the key phrase, and wine, cheese and grape processing plants were built, fostering the development of local products. Following these projects, the Machizukuri Company was organized and the current project involving the center of Furano is regarded as the "third generation" of development.

Being capable of dealing with new local issues and reorganizing promotion systems, the Machizukuri Company has filled the role of a "public developer" in the city center. Through carrying out various promotion-related projects, the company is fast becoming the center for multi-business collaboration and regional management. In particular, wide-area town planning success has proven the Machizukuri Company's skill at promoting the "Furano Brand." The Machizukuri Company has the potential to develop the management of the entire cosmopolitan area.

164 *Katsuhiro Kubo*

Increasing its capital had a significant effect on the shape of the company. Hereafter, the company before the capital increase will be called "the former company," and the company after the increase will be called "the new company."

The improvement of the train station forecourt and establishment of "the new company"

Urban redevelopment project in Furano started with the improvement of the train station forecourt. A basic plan in 1999 was based on the Land Readjustment Project[2] and Urban Redevelopment Project,[3] then transferred to old City Center Basic Revitalization Plan (see endnote 1). The city of Furano became a commissioning entity and completed the Land Readjustment Project in 2008. The Urban Redevelopment Project started in 2007 introducing municipal housing, stores and indoor pools. The former company was established as a TMO (Town Management Organization)[4] to manage the redevelopment of buildings in 2003. The main reason for establishing the TMO (partly founded by the city) was to receive subsidies and obtain floor space within the redeveloped buildings. The company developed promotion-related projects, such as direct sales of agricultural products from local producers, and became the designated manager[5] of developed buildings in 2007. As there was only one full-time employee at the time, leadership was undertaken by the commerce and industry department of Furano city.

Relocation of the Central Hospital and increasing the capital of the new company

The relocation of the Central Hospital was a turning point for the central city revitalization. Although reconstruction of the hospital had been planned from the first, some problems arose such as the site location. It was finally decided to relocate the hospital to the east side of the station. At that time, private land was exchanged for city-owned land to make the reconstruction possible. As the new hospital plans had reconstruction taking place 600 meters away from the station, shop owners expressed their disagreement due to the fact that the original hospital location was a major factor in attracting customers to the shopping district and their shops. Therefore, a practical use for the site of the demolished hospital was considered, and it was proposed to the city government in 2005 that elderly welfare and medical care functions would be introduced onto that site.

In response to this proposal, the city government announced the policy on the site, utilizing private sector vitality after the Act on Improvement and Vitalization in City Centers (see endnote 1) was revised in 2007. At the same time, the Council for the Revitalization of Central Urban Districts (hereafter called the "Council") (see endnote 1) was established by the initiative of the shop owners. The New City Center Basic Revitalization Plan (see endnote 1) was formulated in 2008. This plan aimed to provide convenience and ease of movement for pedestrians downtown, and also to promote living in the area. Construction of customer attracting facilities and housing for the elderly was also planned. These projects were mainly implemented by the private sector and thus the former company increased its capital and became the new company in 2008.

The transition of investors in the Machizukuri Company to a town planning company (Kubo, 2013)

The establishment of a council to relocate the hospital in Furano city became a major turning point of business development. The Machizukuri Company expanded its local support after that. The following is a review of the way the former company and the new company changed members and investors (hereafter, called investors etc.) with the establishment of the council and increase in capital.

In Furano city, the master plan for urban planning was created in 1996 and five committee meetings for city planning, including civilian groups, were held before the establishment of the Council in 2007. In the following, the features of the investors for each phase will be highlighted due to their "history of participation in city-planning."

Status of the steering committee before the establishment of the former company

Before the establishment of the former company, many local and conventional organizations, such as the chamber of commerce, agricultural cooperative, shop owners' association and financial institutions, joined the committee. Membership was fixed and the committee had representatives from each organization. The committee was subject to evaluation by the local administration.

Investors in the former company (October 2003)

Nineteen organizations invested 10,350,000 yen. The city's investment was 1,000,000 yen, accounting for 9.7 percent of the total investment. Investment from affiliate organizations, the chamber of commerce, agricultural cooperative and shop owners made up 70 percent of the total capital. On the other hand, only 22.2 percent of the funds were raised from private enterprises. Thus, the former company was considered to be closely related to the public sector. The municipal government became the representative director. There was no investment from financial institutions at this time.

166 *Katsuhiro Kubo*

Composition of the Council's steering committee (February 2007)

One shop owner took the initiative in forming the Council. The purpose was to create a place to attract customers to the site of the demolished hospital under a private-sector initiative. The steering committee involves a substantial consultation system of Council members. The following are features of its composition. First, among the total of 23 members, nine new members that had previously never participated in past meetings related to city planning joined the committee. Eight out of the nine new members were company executives, making a total of 13 company executives in total. These members were recruited by local business owners, from which the steering committee chairperson and the new company's representative director were later elected. This steering committee was composed of four sub-committees and a New City Center Basic Revitalization Plan was considered. They then decided to increase the capital of the former company.

Capital increase for the new company (June 2008)

Forty organizations including local companies made fresh investments. Members of the steering committee were among them. The capital was increased by 73.15 million yen to make a total capital of 83.5 million yen. The capital from private corporations increased to 76.4 percent, while only 1.2 percent was from the city, which could not meet capital increase requests to the same extent as private corporations. In addition to corporate managers who were already participating in the steering committee, 14 company executives, who were not members of the committee, also invested. Half of these companies decided to participate in the committee dealing with this investment. Overall, there were 23 investors among the 40 new investors who had never participated in the committee. The board members were renewed, and two local company executives became representing directors. The two directors were also local company executives. They were members of the Chamber of Commerce and Industry, and exercised strong leadership qualities. There were six full-time employees, and eight part-timers were also hired (as of 2011).

Statutory reorganization of the Council's steering committee (June 2008)

With the transition from planning to the project implementation stage, the steering committee was reorganized from the four committees into the 5 PT system. Of 40 members, excluding municipal employees, 21 had never participated in the committee before establishment of the Council. On the other hand, the number of members who had participated in the committee before establishment of the former company increased. As described above, the committee shifted from organization centered on representative members to a place for discussion by volunteer citizens who had an interest in establishing the Council. More volunteers joined at the time of the capital increase. These members drew up revitalization planning while some representatives of the shopping district organizations, who had a certain influence in the local community, returned to the steering committee when projects were being carried out.

Business history of Furano Machizukuri Company

Development of construction- and maintenance-related projects by the new company as a non-profitable developer

The greatest feature of the new company was that the company became a non-profitable developer. The company developed construction and maintenance related projects described in the new City Center Basic Revitalization Plan as described below.

Furano Marche was completed in 2010 as the first phase of the project. This consisted of a facility attracting customers to a plaza under the theme of "food and agriculture." The new company rented the site of the hospital owned by the city, and constructed a building using a state-sponsored subsidy. After starting the business, the success of the company was published in local and other newspapers.

Possible factors that led to the success of the project might include the following: (1) convenient location to attract tourists; (2) the plan involved public interest which ultimately contributed to revitalization of the area; and (3) the site utilized city-owned land, which ultimately carried less financial risk.

The new company also plans, manages and operates the facility and earns rental income from tenants such as restaurants. It also manages events at the plaza. Securing such a place had the effect of encouraging new businesses by local citizens as described below.

The second phase of the project was completed on the north side of the site in 2015. This was named Navel Town and consisted of a commercial area and the medical welfare area. A child-care facility, a medical facility and senior housing were introduced in the medical and welfare area. Furthermore, an atrium of approximately 300 square meters was erected as a social interchange space. This was a part of the urban redevelopment project.

Strengthened cooperation in the city through the "Support Project"

Another role of the new company was to participate in various promotion-related projects and to build cooperative relations with related organizations.

The most distinctive feature was the "Support Project." This was to take a limited role in supporting projects of other companies or organizations.

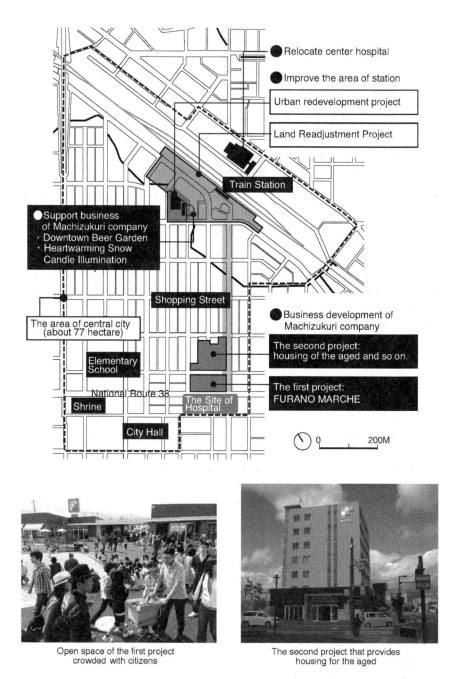

Figure 14.1 Plan of business development in Furano central city.

Such support includes business administration roles including PR assistance, licensing procedures, securing venues and the necessary equipment etc. Being an "intermediary" for business projects, the company helps citizens in consultation with new companies, utilizes diverse networks to support plans and gives advice on how to raise money etc. Once ideas and plans are realized, the company participates in the projects as administrative support.

As an example, the "Machinaka Beer Garden"[6] (Downtown Beer Garden) was held at the outdoor plaza of the building constructed along with the redevelopment around the station. Young volunteers working in the shopping district and the new company organized the executive committee, and created the "Machinaka Beer Garden" which has come to have a high turn-out over recent years. The new company secures necessary equipment, manages the budget and promotes the event. In addition, "Honobono Yuki Akari"[7] (Heartwarming Snow Candle Illumination) is held at the plaza in winter. The new company was also successful in illuminating Furano Marche and the shopping district. This helps to connect events in front of the station with the shopping district and created easy walking within the city. This was an example of trying to multiply the accomplishments of two projects held at two newly improved areas through support projects.

Such support projects are carried out within the limited role according to the scale of the new company. However, this project aims to link ideas, activities, associations and organizations in Furano city where there are many active citizens. This is presently functioning as a way to expand promotion-related projects proposed by citizens. During this process, a cooperative relationship centered on the new company is being established.

Possibility of wide-area business coordination, connecting agriculture and tourism (Kubo, 2013)

Furthermore, wide-area coordination is being seen not only in the city center but also throughout Furano city.

In the city, wineries, cheese factories and grape processing plants were constructed in the 1970s and developed the "Furano Brand." Utilizing these regional resources was seen as a way to connect agriculture and tourism in the central urban area with "local production and local consumption" as a key phrase.

The relationship between the Machizukuri Company and agricultural producers has continued since the establishment of a farmers' market organized by the former company. Product development has continued since the former company and the new company also has a hand in developing new products.

Examples of projects associated with mediating agriculture with tourism are the "Furano Wine Festival" and the "Autumn Harvest Festival." The

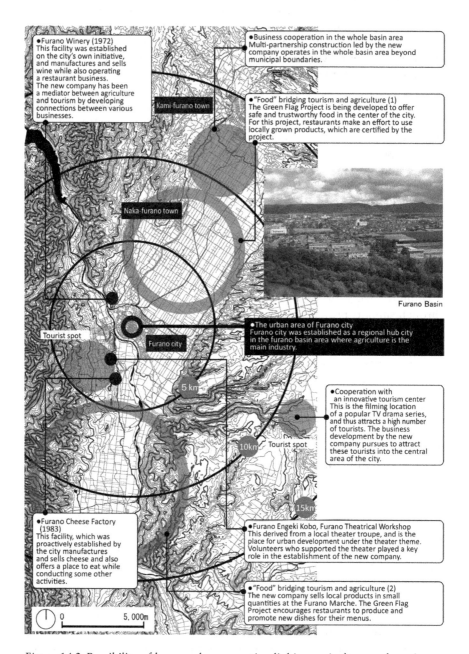

Figure 14.2 Possibility of large-scale cooperation linking agriculture and tourism.

new company hosts a flea market on the same day, which has a synergistic effect on attracting customers. In addition, the Furano City Tourist Association promotes the Green Flag Project. This project certifies restaurants, which offer safe and secure foods to tourists using locally grown products. The new company participates by being the selection and judging committee.

This movement was not a strategic approach by the city as a whole but was implemented fragmentarily. However, it is interesting to note that the city of Furano is seen as constantly conducting the approaches. The new company is involved in a variety of different projects. It provides a place where various companies and organizations in the whole Furano Basin area can meet beyond their municipal boundaries. Therefore, the company plays a role in mediation in a cross-sectional manner for many different businesses such as agriculture and tourism.

Creating a multi-agent collaboration framework responsible for regional management

As described above, the redevelopment of Furano City with Machizukuri Company at the center has been implemented by skillfully utilizing national policy measures related to it.

The former company, mainly made up of the public sector, was transformed into the new company, which is better supported by local communities to deal with new social missions in the area for business development based on revitalization around the station. The new company realizes projects proposed by citizens, and spreads citizen-based business and the projects by cooperation with diverse entities through its support services. All the projects which started with development around the station are mutually connected to each other through the second phase of the project and other promotion-related projects. Therefore, the next phase to build special contexts has begun to take shape.

Moreover, the agriculture–tourism initiative within the whole city of Furano is being realized beyond the city center framework. What is of most importance is that many different organizations with networks consisting of a wide variety of stakeholders do business using local resources. All work and projects by the organizations are connected directly or indirectly with the new company in the city center.

Behind such a background are the following important points which are paramount and cannot be omitted: (1) local company executives correctly understand the significance of national policy; (2) the situations in areas which are changing dynamically can respond flexibly; (3) the subsequent plans are independently described; (4) additional organizations or companies are welcomed at each turning point, such as increasing the capital of the Machizukuri Company; (5) the support of local communities is obtained.

172   *Katsuhiro Kubo*

The Furano Machizukuri Company is actively engaging projects proposed by citizens and has become an organization of Machizukuri Partnership. It is hoped that this will develop into management of the whole urban areas.

Notes

1 The Act on Improvement and Vitalization in City Centers was driven through in order to pursue a revitalization of city centers in regional cities that faced hollowing out in 1998. In addition to the establishment of the TMO, this act legislates a system by which municipalities and the Association for Regional Development formulate a master plan for city center revitalization, and state subsidies are given as necessary. The act was revised in 2006 when the Prime Minister certified the City Center Basic Revitalization Plan, and a system for subsidies which could be obtained for the purpose of urban development and improvement. The establishment of the Council for the Revitalization of Central Urban Districts was requested as the place for various non-official organizations to build a consensus. The participation of non-official organizations including developers, other than municipalities in councils, was expected. The participation of organizations like the Machizukuri Company, which promotes the enhancement of urban functions and also organizations like the chamber of commerce, which promotes the improvement of economic vitality, was imperative. This chapter refers to the act prior to the revision as the Old Act on Improvement and Vitalization in City Centers, and the revised act as the New Act on Improvement and Vitalization in City Centers. The former company is a TMO under the old act, and the new company is an organization which promotes the enhancement of urban functions under the new act. Participation of an organization, which promotes enhancement of urban functions, is required under the new act.
2 This is a project which includes changing a parcel of land and constructing new public facilities in order to improve them and facilitate the use of housing sites.
3 This is a project which plans and constructs a building that has received joint investments by several entities, and improves public facilities.
4 This is an organization which manages city planning in relation to commerce in the city center. It is expected to be able to manage plans with participation by many entities comprehensively and with a cross-cutting approach under the Old Act on Improvement and Vitalization in City Centers. However, it was initially limited to only the chamber of commerce and a joint public–private venture, so the anticipated results weren't obtained.
5 This is an organization assigned by a local government in order to outsource management of public facilities. The organization used to be only a joint public–private venture, however, recently private companies have been able to participate.
6 This is a summer event which started in 2007. Initially it began as a naturally occurring event which citizens held to celebrate the completion of the land readjustment project and the urban redevelopment project. Then "Premium Tickets" were sold with the cooperation of shop owners and others, which had a ripple effect in the district. People were attracted, and many came to walk about the shopping streets.
7 This is a winter event run by citizens which started in 2008. A lighting performance is created using approximately 3,000 candles covered with ice with support from a candle shop. Concerts and open restaurants are held in the hall of a redeveloped building.

References

Kubo, K. (2013). Machizukuri-shimin-jigyou no Tenkai to Tasyutai niyoru Kyoudou-Kankei no Koutiku – Furano-Machizukuri-Kaisya wo jirei tosite (Develop Machizukuri business for citizens and construct collaborative relationship through diverse entities. Based on the method of the Furano Machizukuri company). *Kikan-Machizukuri (Quarterly Machizukuri)* 33: 56–63.

Kubo, K. and Nakahara, R. (2013). "Evaluation of Community Development Company's Evolution Processes according to Its Investors' Individual Carrier," *Journal of the City Planning Institute of Japan*, 48–3: 255–260.

15 Post-disaster reconstruction of central Ishinomaki through the formation of local initiatives

Yosuke Mano and Akihiro Noda

Introduction

While area management covering the central urban area is of increased importance in the reconstruction following the Great East Japan Earthquake, planning to restore things to their former state or to implement the disposition/consolidation of functions only within the area cannot curb the deterioration of the central urban area that had already begun before the earthquake. We need to think about the creation of a space that will satisfy the activities and quality of life of people over a wider scope, that can cope with the housing trends and needs that have arisen anew after the earthquake, the evolution from reconstruction support efforts to entrepreneurship and employment, diverse interactions, and cultural experiences.

It is desirable that the system that will make possible the operation and management of this kind of complex program will evolve in the process of community development; an effective business partnership that is a combination of not only landowners but also residents, tenants, NPOs (nonprofit organizations) and other entities that have come into being since the earthquake, together with entities such as shopping street associations that were active before the earthquake and that continue to operate after: in other words, local initiatives (Mano and Noda, 2018).

Here we present a case study of participation in the configuration of this kind of local initiative in the post-disaster machizukuri of the central urban area of Ishinomaki City in Miyagi Prefecture, in an attempt to design various programs in combination with spatial design in order to rebuild the stricken urban area as a vibrant environment.

Damage from the Great East Japan Earthquake and the mission towards machizukuri

A port city situated at the mouth of the Kitakami River,[1] which flows into the Pacific Ocean, Ishinomaki is located on the southern edge of the Sanriku Coast of the Tohoku district. In the Edo period, by order of the Daimyo Date Masamune, who conquered the whole of the south Tohoku region, a new river channel was constructed to enhance the convenience of water transport, with rice granaries and shipbuilding facilities on either bank and on sandbanks in the river, to which large numbers of merchants gathered.[2] After the Meiji Restoration the fishing industry prospered, taking advantage of the rich fisheries resources off Kinkasan and Sanriku, said to be one of the world's three greatest fishing grounds, and the area prospered as a base for distribution and processing of marine products; but from the 1970s onwards there was growing dispersion to the outskirts of the city, and from the late 1990s the central urban area went into decline. This trend was further aggravated by the Great East Japan Earthquake (Mano, 2012).

Ishinomaki was the city that suffered greatest damage in the Great East Japan Earthquake. In the central urban area, many buildings were inundated to the height of the ground floor ceiling, and many buildings, both timber and non-timber structures, were damaged. However, a situation in which the whole area was lost was fortunately avoided; a certain proportion of buildings remained that could be used again with some repair or clearing-out. In the coastal area around the mouth of the former Kitakami River, on the other hand, the habitable area was greatly reduced, and in the year following the earthquake there was a marked exodus of population.[3] Added to the more than 3,000 who perished in the earthquake, in the following year some 10,000 people, approximately 7 percent of the population, disappeared from the town (Mano, 2016).

This was the starting point for the reconstruction of the central urban area of Ishinomaki City: in addition to setting in motion the reconstruction of the town itself, the great mission of building the momentum for restoration was assigned to the people who live and work in the town.

The context of machizukuri and the process of reconstructing the central urban area of the city through local initiatives

In the coastal area, which suffered particularly serious damage, in addition to such measures as the construction of seawalls, there was drastic revision of urban zoning, and there was no way large-scale relocations and a reduction of the city area could be avoided. This kind of revision of land use planning required an enormous budget and a lot of time, a large part of which was taken up by technological studies regarding tsunami protection. For this reason, while the government and local authority had overwhelming jurisdiction in consensus building with regard to urban planning and projects, the restoration of functions other than the development of such infrastructure as the seawalls, roads, etc., and how the town should be restored, was in large part left in the hands of the local communities.

The construction of seawalls in the coastal areas and the preparation of residential land by raising the ground level took a long time. During this

176 Yosuke Mano and Akihiro Noda

period, a means had to be found of guaranteeing the sustainability of the town. In the central urban area of the city, it was necessary not only to carry out large-scale urban renewal and the construction of river embankments that would take about the same amount of time as the improvement of the coastal area, but also to seek a means of development in the short term to allow people to start living and working there until the urban renewal was completed.

Meanwhile three factors formed a unique combination for the development of Ishinomaki: the ties between the traditionally formed industries (commerce, fisheries), the move towards the restoring the city to its pre-earthquake state, and the movement born from the volunteers and supporters who came and stayed after the earthquake.

The base with the longest history is the network of commerce and fisheries. With the construction of the fishing port and fish market, most of the fishing companies and wholesalers moved out of the central urban area, but a cluster of restaurants and fresh food shops, another core of consumption and distribution, managed, barely, to remain. This cluster of restaurants, which has supported a unique food culture with the concept "Ishinomaki: a gourmet town,"[4] took the lead in the move to reconstruct the central urban area and has played a major role in guaranteeing the QOL (Quality of Life) of the town. In addition the activities of the union of storekeepers[5] became a base supporting the move towards reconstruction.

Here we investigate the changes in the post-earthquake machizukuri environment in which the local initiatives were formed in this unique context, divided into two periods, in terms of the relationship between organizations, places, businesses/projects and networks.

First period (one year after the disaster): field design for the regeneration of the town

The process of reconstruction immediately after the disaster was based on the unprecedented inflow of human resources[6] in the year after the disaster. Immediately after the disaster, huge numbers of volunteers came to the town to work on cleaning up the damaged buildings, helping out at the evacuation centers, etc; during the four months following the disaster, support organizations and bases of operations were set up in the central urban area.

The reasons for the bases of operations being set up in the central urban area were that this was the intersecting point for traffic in Ishinomaki, plus the fact that clearing up the ground floor of damaged buildings created space and it was possible to borrow as bases of operations these places which would not be able to reopen for some time.

People gathered at each of the bases of operations set up along the main street of the central shopping area, and they became places where opinions could be exchanged. A new public space was formed based in the shopping area. In a corner of a damaged shop or in a building with space to rent, many places opened up in the town where people could consider solutions to local problems and interact with each other; this was something that had not happened before the earthquake.

The authors of this report also formed in May 2011 the volunteer project team "ISHINOMAKI 2.0," made up of prime movers from Tokyo and young participants from the central urban area of the city, and we set up a base of operations in a vacant space in a damaged building. The immediate aim of this project team was to involve young people both from within the central urban area and from elsewhere in experimental initiatives to put the damaged buildings and vacant spaces to good use. In these initiatives, attempts were made to set up an environment leading to rehabilitation in a short period of time, by involving young people in a variety of projects based mainly on a cultural approach. About four months after the earthquake the team published the free paper "Voice" and the "Ishinomaki Walkabout Map," showing shops that had reopened and the state of activities working towards reconstruction, held outdoor film screenings and live music performances, opened the Resilience Bar, and held a symposium on machizukuri.

Another feature that was not present before the earthquake was the establishment of business entities in new fields that were needed immediately following the earthquake. In damaged buildings and on demolition sites were opened one after the other such enterprises as the "Ishinomaki Laboratory" (from June 2011), promoting DIY and the making of household furniture; "Itnav" (from January 2012, incorporated in 2013), fostering professional skills in the young through app development and IT education; and "Makigumi" (from April 2014, incorporated in 2015), supporting the use of damaged buildings as real estate. These enterprises formed a project alliance with ISHINOMAKI 2.0. In the central urban area during the process of reconstruction, an environment took form that produced this kind of micro-initiative.[7]

Second period (from the second to fifth year after the earthquake): towards the reconstruction of a sustainable development environment

After the disaster the buildings and land came to attract the attention of a variety of people other than the original landowners and residents, and prompted new uses and sharing. From their involvement in the town, their sojourn in the town, interactions, etc., they developed ways of looking at things that differed from the way the residents and business owners saw things, and led to the creation of different places.

The first change to occur was in the year or so from the summer of 2011, when the number of volunteers coming to Ishinomaki had passed its peak. The volunteers staying in the town during this period and involved

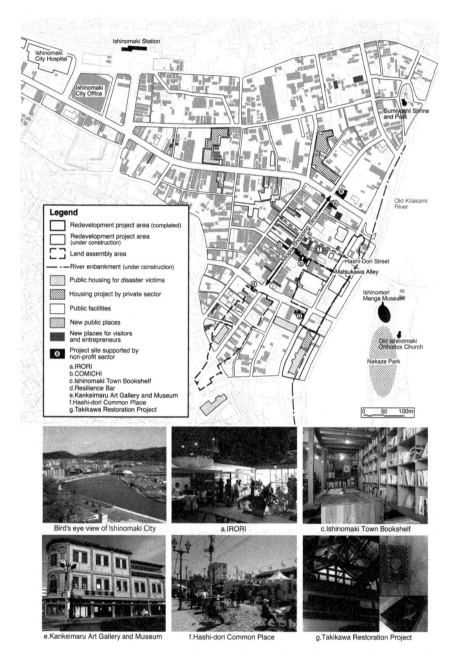

Figure 15.1 Projects of post-disaster reconstruction in central Ishinomaki.

in the reconstruction of the central urban area were people who for whatever reason had chosen to remain in the town and had taken to living in damaged shops or buildings. These people cooperated with the shopkeepers who were faced with the problems of carrying on and resuming business, forming a mixed community in the shopping area that worked on solving these problems (Watanabe and Mano, 2015).

In the period up to two years after the earthquake, there were formed in the central urban area roughly 20 community spaces of varying purposes, where supporters and citizens interacted. Some ten of these were located along Itopia-dori, the main street, which became a place that supported a unique approach to all kinds of cultural activities in the town, through books, modern art, newspapers, magazines, etc.

As this kind of environment was being formed, a number of the bases for reconstruction support activities began to develop into bases for social business. A shared feature of these spaces is the function of giving rise to new businesses or projects, for example, the co-working workspace IRORI opened in January 2012 by ISHINOMAKI 2.0, and Yahoo Life Design, Y-LD, the Ishinomaki reconstruction base opened by the IT enterprise Yahoo in July 2012.[8]

Construction of the COMICHI program

In the third year of the process of the reconstruction of the central urban area, the COMICHI Ishinomaki project was started. COMICHI Ishinomaki is a composite building brought into being through cooperative rebuilding by four landowners on a narrow, irregularly shaped plot of land with an area of some $450\,m^2$ facing onto the previously mentioned Itopia-dori and Matsukawa Yokocho, a side-street that intersects it, a project for which this author and his associates undertook coordination and design. COMICHI Ishinomaki is a building of a type not previously seen in Ishinomaki, comprising two housing units for previous residents whose homes were deemed to have been completely destroyed, a share house for young people, and rental premises for traders affected by the disaster. The following two strategies were employed in the configuration of the COMICHI program.

The first strategy was to make it a program that catered to the needs expressed in the research and workshops carried out in 2012 regarding commerce and housing for the young. Two needs came to the fore: housing in which the young people who came as reconstruction support volunteers immediately after the earthquake, and then as the next step found employment locally, could continue to live; and shop premises in which shopkeepers and business owners who after the earthquake restarted their business in temporary premises could make a serious capital investment.

The other strategy was to make it a program that would raise the value of the area through linkage to the functions that were beginning to take

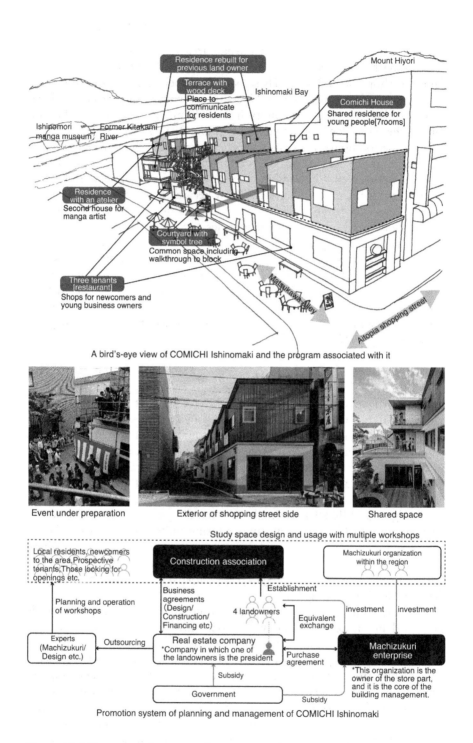

Figure 15.2 Features and systems of COMICHI Ishinomaki.

shape in the central urban area in the summer of 2013. On Itopia-dori there was a collection of small working offices, and long-established shops were being restored; but neither of these were satisfactory with regard to housing. It was a natural progression for housing for the people who worked in these offices and for the shopkeepers to be made a central feature of the project. With arrangements already in place for the provision of post-disaster public housing and blocks of private flats for local residents affected by the disaster, the plan was to incorporate a residential style other than those two choices.

On the basis of these two strategies, the project was being promoted by involving not only the original landowners but also a wide range of people, including prospective residents and tenants, local residents, shopkeepers, and young team members participating in community development.[9] Furthermore, a scheme was created so as to involve a diversity of individuals and organizations in the management of the project by setting up a joint venture company financed by the landowners, community development groups, and shop associations from the local area.

Even now that construction has been completed, experiments are continually being held to bring together for interaction a diversity of people including local residents by giving shape to the many different ways of utilizing the common space, ideas for which were shared at the discussion stage, such as events that are held taking up the whole of the Yokocho side-street.

Developments after completion of COMICHI: a new role for the town center in nurturing people and events

The COMICHI project was completed four and a half years after the earthquake, and now a turning point is approaching; it will soon be ten years since the earthquake struck. In the central urban area, the public and private housing provided for victims of the disaster, as well as commercial and tourism facilities have one by one reached completion. It is apparent that there are two ways, described below, in which, breaking free of its ranking as a disaster-stricken town with a symbolic role in reconstruction due to this kind of accumulation of public projects and facilities, the central urban area can play a new role in moving toward sustainable restoration of the urban area.

Its role as a hub for the local culture across a wide area

In the aftermath of the earthquake, action groups from within and outside of the community established spaces in the central urban area to enable people to have different cultural experiences, and a large number of programs were implemented. A lot of the programs were temporary, cooling off within five years of the earthquake, but a number of programs created a place for continued activities.

182 Yosuke Mano and Akihiro Noda

In 2018 the former Kankeimaru Shoten reopened for business after repairs and earthquake-proofing work, continuing the cultural experiences that post-earthquake activities had made possible temporarily, and promoting activities with the aim of becoming a hub for local culture.

In 2017 the first Reborn Art Festival, a festival of contemporary art held every two years, was staged in and around Ishinomaki through collaboration between a bank (an NPO engaged in environmental activities that was formed in Tokyo by musical artistes in 2003) and local government, business enterprises, and NPOs. The central urban area of Ishinomaki City was one of the venues, and with the visitor center and the offices of supporting organizations being located here, it became the base for people visiting the surrounding areas. This kind of integration of the environment, the arts, tourism, and other spheres of activity is giving rise to a move towards the formation of a multi-character network linking the city with the regions.

Its role as a platform to activities of young people who have started to get involved five years after the earthquake

In 2013 ISHINOMAKI 2.0 started the Ishinomaki School, which provides vocational education for the future and community activity planning for local high school students. From 2017, the fifth year since its inception, activities have expanded into programs aimed at young adults working in the area and the holding of symposiums connecting the local education sector.

Hagukumi,[10] a consortium providing support for start-ups and housing, was established in 2016, and offers a variety of programs to train human resources who will be a link between the big cities and the regions of the Sanriku coast, between urban Ishinomaki and the surrounding areas. These include a contest for pitching ideas for start-ups; internships with local businesses; worker dispatch programs; and practical workshops covering the utilization of real estate.

In conclusion: interpreting the changes to the town in the aftermath of the earthquake, and the role of machizukuri

Over and above the significance of its recovery from the disaster, the town after the disaster displayed the significance of the varied characteristics of the city and the regions, and brought many points to our attention. More than the gathering of new methods and techniques regarding planning and projects, the interpretation of new social characteristics and temporal changes has taken on a still greater importance.

In the process of recovery from the Great East Japan Earthquake, along with fixed goals and technical guidance, there seems to be something else other than consideration of the planning, that is, how to plot out the vision and plan, and which process will better lead to the achievement of that. Rather than guidance according to a plan, it seems that in terms of recovery design what is most important is practical fields and a variety of programs that will respond on a daily basis to the dynamics of the city as they change over time.

It has become clear that in the process of recovery from the earthquake, the urban areas affected by the disaster cannot be maintained as a living environment merely by maintaining and preserving the original buildings and architectural environment, but by taking up the challenge of trying out new technologies, programs, businesses, and services. As well as the functional design, namely what kind of space or design of shop or business to build, of greater importance is program design, namely, what new endeavors will be attempted in that place.

Notes

1 The Kitakami River is the fifth longest river in Japan, and has the fourth largest catchment area.
2 In 1689 the poet Matsuo Basho visited Ishinomaki with his disciple Sora and wrote in his travel diary *Oku no Hosomichi* (*The Narrow Road to the Interior*) of the prosperity of the port.
3 Approximately 30 percent ($73\,km^2$) of the plain area suffered flood damage, and over 75 percent of all homes were damaged. One week after the earthquake the number of displaced persons was as high as 50,000; over 7,000 temporary housing units were built, and one in ten citizens had no choice but to live in temporary housing (from the Ishinomaki City website, State of damage as described in its "Reconstruction of Ishinomaki" section (November 2018)).
4 Beginning in 2009 with its city manifesto, "A healthy Ishinomaki thanks to its food," Ishinomaki in March 2010 stated in its central city area activation plan, recognized by the national government, that the type of town it aimed to be was "a town known for its colorful food and manga."
5 In the central city area are eight shopping streets, centered on the main streets running east–west and north–south. Two of these, the Tachimachi-Odori shopping street and the Itopia shopping street, were incorporated as shopping street promotion associations. Of these, the Itopia shopping street promotion association was dissolved in 2018 due, among other reasons, to a fall in the number of participating stores.
6 Over the year following the earthquake the number of people who assisted in the restoration work totaled some 280,000 people, up to 3,000 people on some days (3.11 Future Support Association Ishinomaki, 2013).
7 Following the earthquake 20 NPOs (specified non-profit organizations and general incorporated associations) and ten newly established companies (limited liability companies and stock companies) were located in central Ishinomaki as of December 2018, and individual proprietors are also beginning to gather.
8 Other enterprises were Maki-biz, opened by AFH (Architecture for Humanity) in November 2012; Ishinomaki Future center Kohaku, opened by a private individual in April 2013; and Coworking@Ishinomaki, opened by the NPO Ishinomaki Revival Support Network in July 2014.
9 In building construction projects such as redevelopment projects, the person with rights to the land and building is the sole decision-maker; it is not normal for other persons to have a say in the spatial or business planning.

10 The organization forming this partnership has as its base multiple business entities that were formed in the search for a new style of reconstruction for Ishinomaki in the immediate aftermath of the earthquake. Having at its core the aforementioned Makigumi, Itnav, and IRORI, the consortium consists also of two other partners such as "ISHINOMAKI 2.0" that has been described in detail in earlier sections and the "Ishinomaki Tourism Association," which, having reached a new turning point, promotes the development of human resources that will take the extra step to bring about innovation. This consortium offers a variety of programs to train human resources who will be a link between the big cities and the regions of the Sanriku coast, between urban Ishinomaki and the surrounding areas. These include: a contest for pitching ideas for start-ups; internships with local businesses; worker dispatch programs; and practical workshops covering the utilization of real estate.

References

Mano, Y. (2012). Toshi fukko to chushin-shigaichi: Ishinomaki deno context no saininshiki kara (Urban resilience and the role of the historical city center – Rediscovering the context of Ishinomaki City after the Tohoku Earthquake disaster). *City Planning Review.* 61–5. 18–21.

Mano, Y. (2016). Chiiki initiative wo kiten to shita Chihou-Sosei no shikou to jissen heno datsu-kochiku (Deconstruction of thoughts and practices for regional revitalization based on initiatives by communities). *City Planning Review.* 65–2. 64–69.

Mano, Y. and Noda, A. (2018). Ishinomaki chushin-gai yokocho wo kiten to shita kankyo saikochiku: Comichi Ishinomaki no jissen (The reconstruction of the environment starting from the town center and side streets of Ishinomaki: the operation of COMICHI Ishinomaki). *Saikaihatsu Kenkyu.* 34. 72–81.

Watanabe, K. and Mano, Y. (2015). Shien katsudo wo kikkake to shite raigai shita siensya no teiju process wo toshite miru hisai-shigaichi ni okeru gaibu jinzai no kyoju-kankyo no kadai ni kansuru kenkyu: Miyagiken Ishinomaki-shi wo jirei toshite (A study of the issue of the housing environment of external human resources in the stricken city center seen through the process of the permanent settlement of support workers arising from their support activities). *City Planning Institute of Japan Essays on City Planning.* 50–3. 945–952.

3.11 Future Support Association Ishinomaki. (2013). *Ishinomaki saigai fukko sien kyogikai katsudou houkokusyo (Report on the Activities of the Ishinomaki Disaster Recovery Support Council).*

16 Regeneration of the cultural landscape of the fisheries city of Kesennuma through collaboration in machizukuri by multiple project-implementing bodies

Toshihiko Abe

Introduction

Since speed was a priority in the post-earthquake reconstruction of areas affected by the Great East Japan Earthquake, the development of urban infrastructure was initially carried out under the initiative of the government. Work to raise the level of the land was carried out in areas that had been inundated, and seawalls were built along the coast for speedy reconstruction of the urban infrastructure. In some areas, the historic cityscape was lost due to large-scale land redevelopment, and the sea and the town were separated by the seawall. This meant that the pre-earthquake context of the region, such as the landscape, the community and historic resources, was lost.

The earthquake victims had hoped that reconstruction projects would be implemented to redevelop the fisheries industry and fisheries-related commerce, as well as to restore their livelihoods. However, there was no collaboration between the reconstruction projects desired by the victims of the earthquake and the urban infrastructure redevelopment projects. As a result, even when the development of the urban infrastructure was completed, this infrastructure did not match the city environment that was desired by those affected by the earthquake: accordingly, many of them moved out of the area, leaving the vacant land bare with no buildings reconstructed on it. Such problems have occurred to greater or lesser degree in all the affected areas.

In the Naiwan District, in the center of Kesennuma City, Miyagi Prefecture, a large-scale urban infrastructure development including the construction of a seawall was set to be implemented, taking precedence over other projects as was the case in other affected areas. However, in this District, middle-aged and young entrepreneurs from the fisheries industry rose up and took the leading role in the opposition movement. Their fears were as follows:

186 *Toshihiko Abe*

1 Separation of the sea and the town by the seawall would make it impossible for the sea to be viewed from the city, depriving the city of landscape that was a tourist attraction.
2 Local communities and historic resources, which had been in place from before the earthquake, would be lost, and people and businesses affected by the earthquake would move out.
3 The fisheries industry, the key industry in Kesennuma, would decline because of the relocation of people and businesses.

The redevelopment of the fisheries industry would require the creation of the physical environment needed to support the industry and the restoration of high-quality coastal landscape: housing, tourism facilities, shopping streets etc. This chapter introduces a case study of post-earthquake machizukuri accomplished by a number of different project-implementing bodies that acted independently while taking advantage of their distinct attributes, and worked together in collaboration with each other to restore the cultural landscape.

The context of machizukuri in Kesennuma and the damage caused by the Great East Japan Earthquake

Kesennuma is located at the northernmost tip of Miyagi Prefecture in the Tohoku Region. The fish market of Kesennuma is famously the "largest in the Orient" and it boasts the largest catches in Tohoku. The Naiwan District, in the city center, is where the former fish market was located before it was moved to its current location. Having developed in the pre-modern period as a post station and a fishing town on the coastal road, the city center faces the original Kesennuma Port and is a symbolic place that is acknowledged by many citizens even today as "the face of Kesennuma." The poet Kotaro Takamura described his first impression of the city when he visited Kesennuma Port by ship in 1931 as follows: "Viewing Kesennuma Town from the ship, I was surprised at the glowing lights and when I landed, I was all the more surprised at how like Tokyo the town was, with the people unashamedly wearing non-traditional Western clothing." This gives us a picture of the night view of the sea and the town together, and the past prosperity of the town (Kawashima, 2012).

Later, in 1956, the fish market was relocated, and starting in the 1990s the city center went into decline due to the relocation of commercial functions to the suburbs. This was the situation when the Great East Japan Earthquake occurred on March 11, 2011. Kesennuma City has an area of 4,600 ha, of which 9.6 ha, or 20.5 percent, were inundated by the tsunami, resulting in 1,214 dead, 220 missing and the complete destruction of 8,483 houses. The Naiwan District (19.1 ha) suffered some of the severest damage; of the 410 houses there, 344 were inundated by the tsunami to a maximum depth of 7 m.

However, the District is backed by mountains, so that high ground to which people could evacuate was closer than in lowland areas where there is an expanse of flat land; and as such, fewer lives were lost. Accordingly, most local residents did not feel the need to build a new seawall. This is why there was a movement to oppose the seawall construction plan presented by the government after the earthquake.

Historically, machizukuri in Kesennuma had been led by the entrepreneurs of the fisheries industry, which is the key industry in the City. This history was also a factor in the rise of the opposition movement. More than 30 years before the earthquake, the entrepreneurs had started to work on machizukuri with a food theme, based on the "port city culture" that had formed as a blend of social and economic arrangements centered on the port. From their knowledge of fishing ports around the world, their ambition was to compete against the rest of the world from a global standpoint. Accordingly, two declarations were issued; the "Healthy City with a Fish Diet" Declaration and the "Slow Food City" Declaration[1] and facilities such as the *Umi-no-Michi* ("Marine Road") Walkway, the Rias Ark Museum of Art and the Shark Museum were built as a result of activities related to these declarations.

The Naiwan District Machizukuri Council for Reconstruction, which served as a discussion platform for the post-earthquake reconstruction process described in this chapter, was organized on the basis of the unique history of machizukuri in this fisheries city.

Process and configuration of the post-earthquake machizukuri

Background to establishment of the Machizukuri Council

In September 2011, six months after the earthquake, Miyagi Prefecture announced plans to construct a seawall 4.4 m in height in the Naiwan District. Local residents voiced their objections to this plan and filed a petition with the city government. In this petition, they asked for the government not to start construction work until they had approved the height and location of the seawall, and to draw up an appropriate design of a seawall that would conserve the landscape and the environment and revitalize the District. In December 2011, Kesennuma City held a competition for machizukuri, calling for alternative proposals to the seawall plan. Out of over 100 proposals submitted by universities and expert groups, three proposals, including the installation of an upright floating breakwater on the seafloor at the mouth of the bay together with development of the seawall and tourist facilities, were publicly recognized to be the best proposals.

In order to put these ideas into practice and to study the post-earthquake reconstruction projects to be implemented under the initiative

188 *Toshihiko Abe*

of local residents, the "Naiwan District Machizukuri Council for Reconstruction ("the Council") was established.[2]

The Council comprised 35 members in total, including the president of the neighborhood association, who was also a member of the competition judging panel, board members of the neighborhood association and entrepreneurs such as the presidents of local companies headquartered in the District; it was operated by a steering committee consisting of a total of five members, namely, the chairperson, the vice chairperson and the heads of three working groups. This author, who submitted one of the proposals deemed most excellent in the competition, was appointed coordinator.

It should be noted that the town regulation of machizukuri does not stipulate the establishment of the Council. However, with Kesennuma City assuming responsibility as Council secretariat, the Council functioned as the sole forum for official discussion between local residents and the government regarding the reconstruction project and district plans.

Building consensus regarding the seawall and land use plans

At first, the Council focused only on the issue of the height of the seawall. Accordingly, no agreement could be reached between local residents demanding the height be lowered and Miyagi Prefecture insisting on the initial height. In order to resolve the issue of the seawall, an integral, all-embracing study of town redevelopment was needed, broadening the scope of discussion to include not only the issue of the height of the seawall but also disaster hazard areas and building construction.

As such, three working groups were established within the Council, each working group putting forward creative ideas on diverse themes. The working groups were: "Working Group for Public Facilities and Tourism" for young members under the age of 40 to examine public facilities and tourism strategy; "Working Group for Commerce" for local merchants to study the restoration of shopping streets; and "Working Group for Housing" for board members of the neighborhood association to discuss housing reconstruction.

The ideas put forward by the three working groups were put together by the steering committee and assigned to specific projects, which formed a comprehensive reconstruction plan. The plan was presented by the Council chairperson at a briefing session for local residents to express their opinions, which were incorporated into a modified plan which was submitted to the government. This process was repeated four times in total to ensure thorough discussion.

With regard to the seawall, eventually, Miyagi Prefecture revised the plan and reduced the height from the initial 4.4 m to 1.3 m from ground level. In line with this, Kesennuma City revised the plan for disaster hazard areas and land redevelopment projects. Consequently, in March 2014, an

Kesennuma city 189

Figure 16.1 Projects realized by post-earthquake machizukuri.

agreement between local residents and the government was reached regarding the seawall and land use plan (Abe, 2017a).

In 2014, work began to rebuild damaged buildings through the implementation of multiple small reconstruction projects, which were included in the reconstruction plan developed by the Council and are shown in Figure 16.1. Local residents taking part in the Council formed a number of groups and established a machizukuri company to study the projects (Abe, 2017b).

The machizukuri company completed most of the reconstruction projects, such as the reconstruction of coastal tourist spots and post-disaster public housing with local community bases, in 2018, in accordance with the initial plan; and urban infrastructure development, such as construction of the waterfront plaza and roads serving as the main street of the town, is scheduled to be completed by the government in 2019.

Collaborative framework for post-earthquake machizukuri

What was important in proceeding with work on the post-earthquake machizukuri described above was the promotional framework, shown in Figure 16.2. In the Naiwan District, the Council served as a forum for discussion to formulate the post-earthquake machizukuri plan and served as a platform for sharing the progress of the projects. The Council held discussions on the landscape and the value of the connection with the sea, the lifestyle based on the fisheries industry and fishing, and new industries leading to the creation of new culture (Abe, 2017c).

Moreover, the machizukuri company responsible for the reconstruction projects participated in the Council, as well as Miyagi Prefecture and Kesennuma City, which were responsible for public works projects; and discussions held at the Council led to collaboration between the reconstruction of buildings and urban structure development. This collaboration included the following: (1) use of 1/200 models to coordinate the seawall with the tourism facilities to be reconstructed behind it; (2) use of 1/500 models to coordinate the development of urban infrastructure, such as road construction and preparation of residential land, with local community bases; and (3) use of models and CG (computer-generated) simulation in the development and modification of landscape guidelines (Abe et al., 2017).

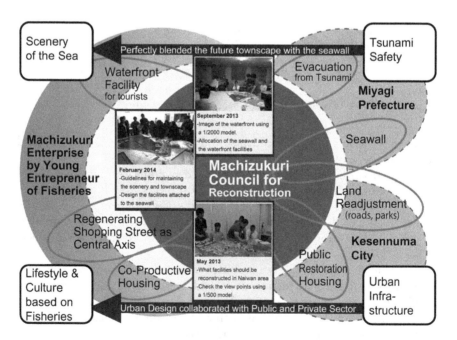

Figure 16.2 Collaborative framework for post-earthquake machizukuri.

Kesennuma city 191

In addition to this author, who is an architect, an urban design team, consisting of a landscape architect, a civil engineer, a lighting planner and a commercial planner, participated in the Council to provide technical support.[3]

The author would like to present the details of three projects, which were subsequently brought to fruition.

Projects realized by post-earthquake machizukuri

The waterfront as a place for creation of a port city culture (Figure 16.1e, f)

The current location of the ferry jetty in the Naiwan District, where the fish market was located until its relocation in 1956, was the place where the "port city culture" was created. It was decided to build the seawall in this symbolic place. In order to carry on the "port city culture" after the earthquake, the place needed to be restored so as to create culture in the modern sense.

Accordingly, members of the Council proposed a plan to build behind the seawall a tourism facility for tourists, and a public service facility for local citizens. To bring this plan to fruition, Council members, government experts and engineers held repeated discussions through design workshops, as shown in Figure 16.2, and designed a waterfront that seamlessly connects the sea and the town.

The resident-initiated machizukuri company established by the chairperson of the Council then rented the public land behind the seawall to develop a tourism facility with "a restaurant featuring slow food" and "a travellers' café in collaboration with a tourism DMO [Destination Management Organization]." In addition, in 2019, Kesennuma City restored the functions of the jetty for the ferry to Oshima Island and the welfare center for working youth, and built public facilities with new functions for citizens, such as the citizens' college; Miyagi Prefecture constructed the seawall and a seaside park on the sea side of the seawall, with a green slope, stepped garden and event plaza.

The above-mentioned tourism facility by the machizukuri company, the facility complex by Kesennuma City and the seaside park by Miyagi Prefecture create a space that integrates the sea with the town through the adoption of a seamless design for the boundary between each, and the whole area is managed by the machizukuri company.

Main street of the town created by combining unused land (Figure 16.1d)

In addition to developing the tourism facility, the machizukuri company also operated a number of other commercial small-scale machizukuri projects.

192   *Toshihiko Abe*

As was the case in other affected areas, there was concern in the Naiwan District that after the completion of the urban infrastructure development, plots of unused land might remain on which nothing was built. It was proposed at the Council that unused land be combined to build a commercial facility.

In response to this proposal, the government combined plots of land for which there was no designated use, and the machizukuri company rented the land from the landowners. The machizukuri company built the commercial facility on the ocean view road connecting the waterfront to the existing shopping street at the foot of the mountain, thus forming the main street of the town that would support the daily life of residents.

Regional community bases and post-earthquake public housing built in spearhead blocks (Figure 16.1a, b, c)

Local residents were concerned that reconstruction of the shopping street would be delayed if construction did not begin until after infrastructure development was completed. Thus, leaders of the neighborhood associations and shopping streets in each district requested the city government to develop blocks where housing and stores could be rebuilt ahead of other blocks by combining the land of landowners who were considering early restoration. The intention was to aggregate in these blocks functions that support daily life and to build regional community bases there.

The city government developed a spearhead block in each district. In each spearhead block, the machizukuri company established by the leaders of the residents of each district planned the construction of a building incorporating a commercial facility and community facility on the lower levels and residential units on the higher levels.

Kesennuma City on the other hand was required to expedite the development of post-disaster public housing. The basic policy of the government was to build the post-disaster public housing on public land outside the inundated area. However, such land could not be secured in the Naiwan District. Accordingly, the Council requested that Kesennuma City buy the residential units on the higher levels of the building to be constructed by the machizukuri company.

In the Council, the machizukuri company of each district presented building plans for the redevelopment of the cityscape and restoration of functions in the area. In June 2017, building complexes were completed in four districts and a community base was developed in each district. Kesennuma City bought 147 residential units as post-disaster public housing, which were made available to victims of the earthquake.

As described above, under the initiative of local residents, post-disaster public housing and regional community bases were constructed that were of unique design.

Conclusion

In most of the areas affected by the Great East Japan Earthquake, the local economy had been in decline before the earthquake. Therefore, reconstruction in the affected areas generally relied on urban infrastructure development, such as the construction of seawalls and development of residential land, and restoration projects initiated by the national government, such as public housing. However, such government-led restoration projects alone could not bring about the regeneration of Kesennuma as a fisheries city, which was what the citizens wanted.

As shown in Figure 16.2, in the Naiwan District of Kesennuma, post-earthquake machizukuri was implemented through a collaboration, that is, joint governance by a number of project-implementing bodies, finding points of interaction with each other by using as a platform the Council participated in by fisheries industry entrepreneurs. This resulted in the following achievements. First, an attractive physical environment was created through the implementation of small-scale projects, such as the waterfront tourism facility, the main street of the town ("Ocean View Road") and regional community bases. Second, the creation of this kind of physical environment led to the restoration of landscape ensuring a view of the sea as well as ensuring safety and the development of urban infrastructure and the continuation of the fisheries-based lifestyle and culture. Third, young entrepreneurs established new businesses leading to the creation of a new culture in the regenerated town.[4]

The entrepreneur Tamako Mitarai, who started a community business based in Kesennuma after the earthquake, describes the situation in Kesennuma seven years after the earthquake as follows:

> The other day, a new commercial facility opened at an excellent location commanding a view of the sea. When I went upstairs, I found big glass windows opening toward the sea, with the sea of Naiwan stretching out before my eyes.... I was captivated by the beautiful landscape I had never seen before.... I am delighted that a special seat is now available for me to enjoy good coffee while viewing the sea of Kesennuma.... We are entering a new phase, unlike the days after the earthquake when we were clenching our teeth. As each of us try something new in our own field, the town becomes more joyful. Currently, this is where Kesennuma is at.
>
> (Mitarai, 2018)

Notes

1 In April 2013, after the earthquake, Kesennuma became the first Japanese city to be certified as a slow city by Cittaslow (headquartered in Italy).
2 The proposal submitted by the author and a team from Waseda University Institute of Urban and Regional Studies was selected as one of the three best proposals

194 *Toshihiko Abe*

in the competition for machizukuri in the Naiwan District. The proposal consists of an integral design of the seawall and architecture, ensuring the connection between the sea and the town. In addition, we also suggested a scenario for post-earthquake reconstruction involving the establishment of a council by means of which local residents would take the initiative, with the council studying the overall district plan and commercializing projects to enable the plan to be achieved by a reconstruction company established by volunteers from the council. The reconstruction projects were subsequently implemented on the basis of this scenario.

3 This author was fortunate enough to be involved in the design of the facilities and buildings described as part of the post-earthquake machizukuri of the Naiwan District, in addition to acting as coordinator for the overall process of post-earthquake machizukuri. More specifically, the author was in charge of the design of the waterfront landscape, the design of the commercial facilities built behind the seawall and the design of one of the community bases containing four post-disaster public housing units.

4 Mitarai, 2018 cites as typical examples of new businesses in Kesennuma: a lunch-box delivery service offered by a local taxi company; a fish-processing company with permanent outlets in Tokyo department stores; and a hand-knitted knitwear business started up by herself, employing local women.

References

Abe, T. (2017a). Consensus building process of the seawall plan in the inner port area in Kesennuma. *Journal of Japan Society of Civil Engineers, Ser. D1. Japan Society of Civil Engineers*, 73(1), 37–51.

Abe, T. (2017b). Case study of action research of machizukuri. In Shigeru Satoh (ed.) *Machizukuri Kyosyo (Textbook of Machizukuri)* (pp. 269–276). Tokyo: Kashima Shuppankai.

Abe, T. (2017c). 6.1 Case study of Inner port area of Kesennuma City. In Shigeru Satoh (ed.) *Machizukuri Zukai (Illustration of Machizukuri)*. Tokyo: Kashima Shuppankai.

Abe, T., Fujioka, R. and Satoh, S. (2017). Establishment of community development corporations in local disaster reconstruction. *Journal of Architecture and Planning, The Architectural Institute of Japan*, 82(735), 1221–1230.

Kawashima, S. (ed.) (2012). *Living in the Tsunami Town*. Fuzambo International.

Mitarai, T. (2018, November 30). Kesennuma, becoming an interesting city. *Mainichi Shimbun*.

17 Community empowerment recovery after the Chichi Earthquake

The case of Taomi Ecovillage, Puli

Liang-Chun Chen, Chia-Chan Liao and Jie-Ying Wu

Preface: the reason for introducing community empowerment in Taiwan and for using Taomi Ecovillage, Puli as the example

Taiwan's community empowerment and Japan's machizukuri

As described in the previous chapters, machizukuri has been developing in Japan for many years. Japan's neighbor, Taiwan, put forward the policy of Community Comprehensive Empowerment in 1999 and has, to date, accumulated substantial experience. Although, due to the proximity of Japan to Taiwan and much academic and practical exchange between the two regions, some people think that Taiwan community empowerment is just a copy of machizukuri. However, the promotion process is different due to social and cultural differences, so while the ideas may be similar in terms of method and practice, machizukuri is very different from Taiwan's community empowerment.

The 1999 Chi Chi Earthquake was a watershed for community empowerment in Taiwan

The reasons for choosing post-Chichi Earthquake community-empowerment recovery as an example are as follows. First, the Chichi Earthquake that struck in September 21, 1999 was the most serious natural disaster in terms of dead/injured and loss/damage of facilities and property in the process of urban and rural modernization in Taiwan during the post-World War II period. Second, the earthquake brought about quite a few changes to the community empowerment that was underway in Taiwan at the time, such as expanding the promotion area from cities to farming villages (in disaster areas); after the earthquake, development themes also included ones that were relatively rare before, such as ecological conservation, community industry and community disaster prevention.

196 *Liang-Chun Chen* et al.

Great importance has been attached to Taomi Ecovillage

There were 70–80 community empowerment recovery cases with residents' participation promoted in post-quake recovery work. Of these cases, some ceased with the end of disaster recovery work in the community. In contrast, some community residents and organizations, through empowerment, have grown and become strong and their community empowerment continues. Of these growth cases, much importance has been attached to Taomi Ecovillage because not only has the community organization and practical operation continued, but it continues to grow, transform and expand. In the case of Taomi Ecovillage, the process of community empowerment, operating methods and the ideas the residents hold have been given much importance in Taiwan and have been the subject of observational visits by several Japanese and Mainland Chinese scholars and practitioners of community empowerment. Therefore, Taomi Ecovillage is a case worth discussing and sharing.

The background to the promotion of Taomi Ecovillage community empowerment recovery

Outline of the Chichi Earthquake

The Chichi Earthquake is commonly referred to in Taiwan as the September 21 Earthquake, as it struck at 1:47 a.m. on September 21, 1999. Its epicenter was near the township of Chichi in Nantou County, central Taiwan, at a depth of 8.0 km and it reached M7.3 on the Richter Scale. It was a shallow and very strong earthquake.

This earthquake killed 2,415 people, left 29 missing and more than 11,300 people slightly or seriously injured; 51,000 houses collapsed and 53,000 partially collapsed; many roads, bridges and other transport facilities, power equipment, water pipes and other lifelines, public buildings and facilities, industrial facilities and equipment were damaged. It also caused large-scale landslides, soil liquefaction and other major geological damage.

The disaster-affected area of this earthquake had the following three characteristics:

1   The impact area was wide, spanning more than 20 cities and townships; while some of the affected places had relatively large populations (such as Puli with almost 90,000), most were townships of 100–2,000 people or small mountain farming villages.
2   The main industry of these mountain farming villages was mainly traditional agriculture and forestry, however, under the impact of the quake itself and the change in social and economic conditions it caused, existing agriculture and forestry was badly affected.
3   Although some of the disaster-affected areas were remote mountain farming villages or mountain areas where the environment was relatively

fragile, they had abundant natural scenery and were multicultural areas with a mixed indigenous, Hakka and Minnan population; this being the case, even before the earthquake they were popular tourist destinations.

Development trend of community empowerment in Taiwan 1994–99

As mentioned earlier, the former Council for Cultural Development launched the policy of comprehensive community empowerment in 1994, beginning related works. In the first year or two, the emphasis was on disseminating and introducing ideas and policy and some overseas community empowerment cases; only later did some experiments, promotion involving several communities, take place, to accumulate local experience and nurture local talent. Consequently, when the Chichi Earthquake struck, Taiwan already had the promotion of a number of local cases of community empowerment under its belt; however, most were in urbans areas (especially north Taiwan) and had the aim of improving or reconstructing the external space of points in cities and preservation and restoration of local traditional culture and historical spaces, seldom involving industrial development, ecological conservation or community tourism and other development issues. However, prior to the Chichi earthquake, a number of scholars and professionals, as well as nonprofit organizations, with a certain understanding of community empowerment and with operational capability had been nurtured. These people and groups became actively involved after the Chichi Earthquake in supporting post-disaster community recovery work.

Overview of Taomi Ecovillage before and after the earthquake

Taomi Ecovillage is situated five kilometers to the southwest of Taiwan's geographical center, Puli Township. It has a warm and humid subtropical climate. Its administrative area covers $17.9\,km^2$, covering hills of 420–780 meters elevation. Six rivers and creeks run through the area, forming diverse terrain and scenery. It also has an abundance of natural environments and ecological systems such as forest, farmland, rivers and wetlands. The village had around 370 households with a population of around 1,200 (in 1999); most residents lived on relatively flat land in the valley between Taomi Mountain and Zhuzi Mountain. After its establishment, the village relied on forestry and mountain produce. However, prior to the earthquake, due to a decline in forestry and agriculture, and the relocation of the bamboo shoot processing factory, quite a large amount of land was left fallow, and the problem of loss of the young adult population and aging of residents was becoming ever more serious.

In terms of community organization, apart from the administrative village office, many community affairs were handled by the management committee of Futong Temple, the traditional belief center. In 1997, the

198   *Liang-Chun Chen* et al.

village chief of Taomi and others established the Taomi Community Empowerment Association and went on to establish various clubs and organizations. However, most of these groups were based on individual interest and there was no connection between them and no joint promotion of overall community activities. The experience of forming an environmental protection association and protest in 1982 seems to have spurred residents to attach more importance to environmental protection and ecological conservation and given them the willingness and motivation to be involved.

The epicenter of the Chichi Earthquake was around 15 km from this community. The community shook violently and, of the 369 houses, 168 collapsed completely and 60 partially, accounting for 62 percent of all houses. Also, many agricultural facilities and much equipment were damaged. The earthquake hit Taomi Community's critical infrastructure hard and also caused substantial loss of property and seriously affected the lives and production of residents.

Stages in promotion of Taomi Ecovillage disaster recovery community empowerment

Recovery actions and organizations

As already stated, that a remote village characterized by industrial decline, population outflow and aging, and which also suffered severe impacts from the earthquake, become a remarkable ecovillage through residents' participation community empowerment within 20 years is the major theme of this chapter. There are four major elements:

1   Different stages of Taomi Village disaster recovery community empowerment;
2   Major actions and strategies at each stage;
3   Internal and external organizations involved in the community empowerment;
4   Discussions about the community empowerment process.

Overall, the major recovery actions in each community empowerment stage can be classified into three kinds: first, right after the earthquake until now, actions launched by the community residents or organizations within village; second, after recovery to some extent, actions launched by the PAPER DOME New Homeland Resource Center (PDNHRC); and, third, recent actions launched by the cross-boundary organization composed of the New Homeland Foundation (NHF), organizations within the village as well as NGOs (non-government organizations) in the Puli area.

Organizations involved in the recovery actions include internal and external organizations. The internal organizations are: Taomi Village Office up to now); Taomi Village Development Association (January 1996–now);

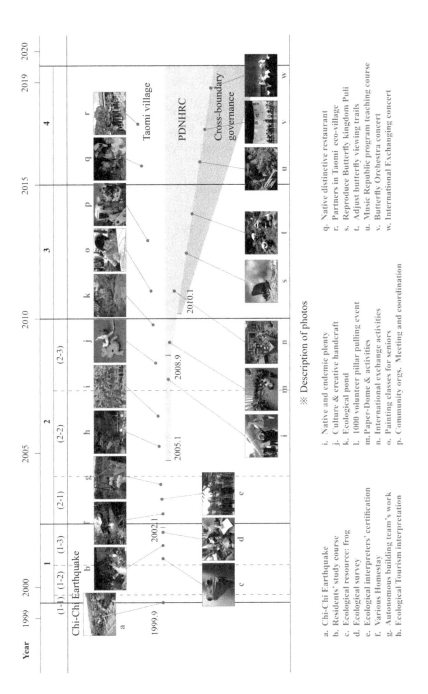

Figure 17.1 Taomi Ecovillage's post-disaster recovery promotion stages.

200 *Liang-Chun Chen* et al.

Taomi Nature Conservation and Ecotourism Association (June 2006–April 2015); the PDNHRC under the NHF (September 2008–now); Taomi Leisure Agriculture Promotion Association (April 2013–now); and Taomi Ecovillage Community Empowerment Association (January 2015–now). The external organizations are: the NHF (October 1999–now); General Education Center and Social Science Center, National Chi-Nan University (July 2007–now); Great Puli Area Tourism Development Association (January 2010–now); Endemic Species Research Institute (2000–now); Puli Management Station of Sun Moon Lake National Scenic Area (January 2015–now); and many other NGOs as well as schools.

Stages in promotion of community empowerment recovery and development of the ecovillage

Four main stages and six sub-stages can been classified as follows (see Figure 17.1) according to the suggestions of Liao (2012) and Liao *et al.* (2016).

Stage 1. Post-disaster recovery and ecotourism preparatory period (September 1999–January 2002)

The period of around two years and five months after the earthquake was the earliest stage at which Taomi Village started to look for a way to rebuild and activated reconstruction preparatory work. The main strategies or methods were still residents' participation, consultation and consensus building, searching for support from external organizations, confirming the direction of reconstruction and, through the government construction support program, promoting residents' training and study to increase overall community post-disaster recovery and industrial transformation capability.

SUB-STAGE 1-1. POST-DISASTER RECOVERY FORMATION PERIOD (SEPTEMBER 1999–OCTOBER 1999)

The month after the earthquake (October), after a period in shelter, the residents of Taomi Village began to actively seek a way to rebuild their home. The village chief at the time was introduced to the NHF by the National Jinan University, and invited the organization to establish a presence in the community to assist with post-disaster reconstruction (Chiang and Chang, 2008).

SUB-STAGE 1-2. ECOLOGICAL SURVEY AND EXPLORATORY PERIOD (NOVEMBER 1999–SEPTEMBER 2000)

When the NHF moved into Taomi village, residents were guided to form a community reconstruction committee to conscientiously ponder and discuss the vision for the reconstruction of their village. The development consensus reached was based on "environment, life, education, industry space," giving priority to the natural environment and settled life, choosing a sustainable reconstruction direction emphasizing "ecology, life, production and life" and "organizational operation" (Liao and Chang, 2009). Also, the foundation introduced external resources and set about conducting community resource surveys; for example, the deputy director of the Taiwan Endemic Species Research Institute brought a team of researchers to the community and led residents in conducting an ecological survey; it found that the community had abundant and diverse ecological resources: in the area of the community there were 19 species of frog, 35 species of dragonfly and various native plant species, a discovery that boosted the residents' confidence in and awareness of the distinctiveness of their home. Also, through the government's Training Program for Disaster Victims, the Department of Tourism of Shih Hsin University helped organize residents and carried out intensive training to nurture their capabilities required for the move towards agricultural village leisure tourism and operation of homestays and restaurants. In short, in this period, the aforementioned discussions and consultations involving residents and a series of actions in which they took part allowed Taomi Community to set its future reconstruction direction, namely developing into an ecovillage. Also, residents who had previously lacked cohesion began to form a consensus and became willing with the community as the subject to promote and operate ecotourism and emphasise the sustainable development of the community.

SUB-STAGE 1-3. ECOTOURISM PREPARATORY PERIOD (OCTOBER 2000–JANUARY 2002)

This stage saw the Taomi Community transform from a traditional agricultural village to an educational base combining organic agriculture, ecological conservation and leisure experience. The operations had seven aspects: continuing community discussion and consultation; community resources survey and utilization; holding of study courses and training certification; autonomous community ecological environment preparations; supplementation of ecotourism; establishment of a community public system; and introduction and application of external resources. In terms of concrete operations, under the government's work relief program, unemployed residents were employed to take part in the Native Nursery Program to grow native and endemic plants; residents also formed the Ecological Engineering Building Team. A series of ecological general knowledge courses and ecological interpretation training and certification exams were held to give residents an opportunity to find a new type of job; cookery training was provided to female residents and guidance provided to homestay operators; and then a visitor operations center and community provident fund system was established, with the aim of giving the community residents sufficient capability to support the ecotourism industry in the future. In summary,

202　*Liang-Chun Chen* et al.

through the active participation of residents at this stage and the strong support of the NHF, Taomi Community and its residents underwent a transformation in understanding, life and industry operation, building the capability for autonomous operation and undertaking of ecotourism; for example, in August 2000 "Taomi Community already has six homestays and nine certified ecological interpreters and the community autonomous building team had built quite a few ecological conservation facilities" (Liao, 2012). Under these conditions, some homestays opened on a trial basis.

Stage 2. Post-disaster recovery and ecovillage formation period (February 2002–September 2009)

This stage led to the start of the autonomous operation of the ecotourism industry in the community. Not only this, as ecotourism was being strengthened, the community transformed and developed in the direction of becoming an ecovillage at this stage and attempted to expand the meaning of ecotourism by building an ecological learning network. The main strategies and methods adopted for reconstruction and development at this stage included continuing the empowerment of residents, continuing to introduce and implement ecological ethics and methods, R&D and deepening of the ecological community, supplementing the ecological industrialization framework, developing and innovating community and cultural industries and cross-field and cross-area diverse cooperation. The concrete actions in the three sub-stages of this stage were as follows.

SUB-STAGE 2-1. ECOTOURISM EARLY OPERATION PERIOD
(FEBRUARY 2002–DECEMBER 2003)

With respect to operating and environmental problems found during the trial operation of ecotourism in sub-stage 1–3, correction and improvement were undertaken, in this sub-stage, with respect to systems; the visitor operations center was given operating guidance to make it a service window for room reservation, food and drink, travel, interpretation and cultural handicraft sales; a community provident fund was established and used to take care of the disadvantaged in the community and implement the spirit of the sharing of community interest (Yen and Ho, 2002). In terms of supplementing the ecological and community industry framework, a plan to close off Taomikeng River was carried out, ecological interpretation and ecotourism assessment carried out and an attempt made to control the number of visitors. In terms of residents' autonomous empowerment, cookery classes and advanced ecological interpretation training continued to be provided. In terms of community industry development and innovation, apart from the opening of various homestays and dispatch of ecological interpreters to wetlands and farmland etc. to carry out frog, dragonfly and native plant interpretation to enhance visitor understanding of the

Taomi Ecovillage, Puli   203

community environment and ecology, dishes made using local ingredients were also developed and a cultural and creative industry based on local ecological elements was developed.

In summary, Taomi Community's reputation as a place for ecotourism began to spread outwards and ecological interpreters became key players in the operation of the community's ecotourism industry. The 2002 Survey of Residents' Opinion on the Promotion of Taomi Ecovillage showed that 94 percent said they were aware that the community was promoting ecotourism and 74 percent believed it could continue to develop, with 72 percent willing to join in the effort to promote Taomi Ecovillage (Yen and Ho, 2002).

SUB-STAGE 2-2. ECOVILLAGE MOLDING AND OPERATION
ADJUSTMENT PERIOD (JANUARY 2004–AUGUST 2007)

Taomi Community launched the ecotourism industry in the previous substage and it gradually became better known; the ecotourism industry allowed the community to a certain degree move out of the shadow left by the Chichi Earthquake. Although most residents were willing to join in the effort to build the ecovillage, in actual fact there was still a big gap between the thinking of residents, their lifestyle and way of handling the environment, and the conditions required for the ecovillage. For this reason, at this stage, the community was able to move towards the vision of becoming an ecovillage through using a government grant program. At the same time, the NHF, providing support and assisting the community rebuild empowerment, followed the steps of stage 2 of its set support strategy; that is, from actively planning, matching and referring resources and promoting resident study and training on the front line, it gradually moved back to the second line, quietly accompanying residents as they grew.

In terms of concrete action, to begin with, also through government grants, various ecological actions were launched under a pioneering experimental program, such as making compost from kitchen waste, building composting toilets, building household ecological ponds, building family sewage treatment ponds, promoting community greening and creating an ecological river channel. Also, ecological education courses were held, painting classes for seniors and a series of ecological or cultural activities were held to give the community the capabilities to build a complete ecovillage. The NHF also planned and established a Learning Park on leased land for experiencing the ecological environment, green industry and arts events.

SUB-STAGE 2-3. ECOVILLAGE KNOWLEDGE LEARNING NETWORK
EXPANSION PERIOD (SEPTEMBER 2007–SEPTEMBER 2009)

This sub-stage was an important period of transformation in Taomi Community's promotion of ecotourism and moving towards being an

204   *Liang-Chun Chen* et al.

ecovillage. On one hand, the NHF handed ecotourism guidance power back to the community and the community organizations and residents had different opinions on future operation and development; on the other hand, the PDNHRC was completed, officially began operating and started to expand its learning network. In this situation, the development of Taomi Community's ecotourism and PDNHRC operation became interactive, complementary while also being in competition. The concrete actions of Taomi Community and the PDNHRC were twofold. First, in terms of community, as well as continuing the ecological actions previously begun, existing ecotourism was enhanced, such as the opening of new homestays and distinctive restaurants and development of summer night-time firefly ecology interpretation. Second, in terms of the PDNHRC, various actions were actively launched, and they can be divided into two parts: (1) to erect the relocated Paper Dome (Kobo Takatori Catholic Church) on the leased site, a 1,000-volunteer pillar pulling event was held, various Paper Dome facilities were completed and the PDNHRC officially began operating in full; and (2) a learning network was established involving black tea, organic crops, ecological restoration and other community industries of the surrounding communities and settlements, and international exchange activities were also held with disaster affected areas in Japan and China. It is also worth noting that an effort made with regard to communication about and adjustment of the relationship between the community and the PDNHRC and between community residents and the rebuilding of organizations. At the same time, local Puli National Chi Nan University academic and research units also replaced the NHF that had withdrawn to the second line, supporting the reconstruction of Taomi Community and the building of the ecovillage and serving as a platform in the new stage.

Stage 3. Internal community organization co-opetition and organizational adjustment period (January 2010–December 2014)

In this stage, the activities were much fewer than the previous stage or even halted completely. However, through this stage, there was continuing dialogue and adjustment by community organizations internally, eventually reaching consensus, breaking through the long-term unfavorable situation of co-opetition, mistrust and antagonism. In this stage, the strategy adopted by the community and the NHF was continuing communication and adjustment and cross-organization and cross-area diverse cooperation through intermediary third parties or groups and introduction of external and private resources.

The concrete actions at this stage included adjusting of internal community organizations such as the Leisure Agriculture Promotion Association and Taomi Ecovillage Community Empowerment Association, as well as the original Community Development Association. Also, through

Taomi Ecovillage, Puli 205

the framework of the Puli Tourism Development Association, the community received further financial assistance from the government which was used to launch the program to Reproduce Butterfly Kingdom Puli in order to restore Puli's former status as a butterfly capital of Taiwan. Also, in the later period of this stage, the Foundation established the Butterfly Orchestra with civil groups and music volunteers and carried out another series of remote township music talent empowerment actions.

Stage 4. Community diverse, flexible development and cross-boundary governance period (January 2015– present)

This is the most recent stage in Taomi Community's move towards becoming an ecovillage. After competition, antagonism between community organizations were overcome and community organizations and their operation were restructured, it was a new and advanced stage in community development.

In concrete terms, with regard to the community: ecological resources-based homestays, distinctive restaurants, cultural and creative products etc. had more vitality; Taomi Community's ecotourism industry had been established, providing many employment opportunities and income. Also, community organizations reformulated a community feedback mechanism for community industries and, through the setting up of the Taomi Travel Service Single Portal, the aim was to further increase the meaning and service quality of Taomi Community ecotourism. The formation of the ecological village, expansion of the peripheral community learning network that was activated in the previous stage and cross-area empowerment and governance actions continued; for example, the Butterfly Orchestra that was set up in the latter part of the previous stage was expanded and jointly promoted the Music Republic Program together with more than a dozen elementary and junior high schools in remote townships in the greater Puli area and local high schools and universities. Due to continuing efforts, the number of students from economically disadvantaged, single parent, skipped generation, aboriginal and new immigrant etc. families increased from over 100 to more than 400 a year. It is worth noting that around 90 percent of the funds for the Butterfly Orchestra's music training and results presentation concerts and overseas exchange visits etc. was donated by private individuals or civil groups.

In short, this stage in which undesirable community internal co-opetition was overcome and organization restructured, fully spurred interaction and complementarity between Taomi Community and the New Homeland Resources Center and their diverse development; at the same time, to a large degree, it expanded the cross-area cooperation and cross-area governance formed by the single Taomi Community, New Homeland Resources Center and communities, civil groups, enterprises, research units etc. in the greater Puli area, other cities and townships in Taiwan and even overseas.

206 Liang-Chun Chen et al.

Organization and discussion: the characteristics and influencing factors of the Taomi Ecovillage Case

This chapter takes the case of Taomi Ecovillage as an example, though it does not represent the full picture of Taiwan's experience. The Chichi Earthquake had significance and influence in the development of community building in Taiwan. Taomi Ecovillage was a case that attracted special attention in the post-disaster reconstruction of many communities. Below, the discussion will focus on the characteristics and several influencing factors that allowed this case to continue to be implemented.

Characteristics formed by Taomi Community's reconstruction and the ecovillage

It has been 20 years since Taomi Community suffered the effects of a severe earthquake and launched the post-disaster reconstruction effort. Although a complete ecovillage has not yet been formed, the four characteristics described below have been displayed:

1   *Reconstruction and community empowerment: community empowerment recovery has multiple functions and is worth promoting*
    Post-disaster recovery involves many things and is highly complex and not easy to implement; community building is a model for residents' participation, learning and doing things together, cooperating and sharing. Therefore, adopting this model or method for implementing post-disaster recovery not only requires that attention is paid to how to effectively carry out physical reconstruction, it also requires that, in the process of reconstruction, residents' old ways of thinking and values are changed and they obtain more related knowledge and skills and learn communication, coordination and consensus forming capabilities. A community that is empowered is not just limited to matters related to post-disaster reconstruction, residents can cooperate and deal with planning, and execution of the community's future vision or sustainable development.

2   *Ecological system and ecotourism industry: ecological resources and their use became the foundation for promoting the ecovillage*
    As described in the previous section about the course of Taomi Community's reconstruction, the four main stages involving community resources survey, understanding, learning, interpretation and ecological habitat restoration and ecological environment preparation and building were completed and then these ecological resources were used to promote ecotourism and form community industry. That is, the rediscovery of community resources spurred residents to be proud of and identify with them while, at the same time, the active use of resources

also helped reconstruct community industry, which made residents more willing to accept, take part and get involved.

3   *Diverse co-opetition (competition and cooperation), interaction and complementarity: the establishment of the PDNHRC sparked cooperation between it and the community*
    The NHF, which had initially supported Taomi Community's post-disaster reconstruction efforts, converted from an active supporting role to a passive accompanying role when a certain degree of progress had been made in reconstruction and even tried to establish cooperation and interaction and mutual feedback form with the community, and established the PDNHRC on leased land. The results, although for a time there was competition and antagonism between it and the community organizations, gradually transformed into a new relationship characterized by competition and cooperation, interaction and complementarity as a result of communication and coordination. This use of external effect to spur community internal balance of power and change organizations and their operational method is also another characteristic of Taomi Ecovillage's reconstruction course.

4   *Single community reconstruction and cross-boundary cooperation and governance: Taomi Community's post-disaster reconstruction experience linked cross-area actions and transformation in the greater Puli area*
    Local township Puli, which had previously not paid much attention to the ecological environment and ecological actions, saw some citizen and civil groups spurred into action by the sharing and stimulation of Taomi Community's community-empowerment recovery, began to pursue the vision of turning the township into an ecological museum and then went on to implement cross-boundary and cross-disciplinary cooperation and actions such as butterfly restoration and caring for disadvantaged children in the greater Puli area. In fact, some organizations in the Ecovillage (including PDNHRC) used this cross-area cooperation and action to reduce competition between the community's internal organizations and resolved opposition and conflict relating to community empowerment and even views on ecological conservation. In summary, single, closed-community reconstruction and diverse and open cross-area actions and governance were able to mutually link with and affect each other.

Factors affecting the reconstruction of Taomi Community and the building of the ecovillage

The reconstruction of Taomi Community was allowed to continue and formed the aforementioned five characteristics under the influence of the

208 *Liang-Chun Chen* et al.

factors described below, that is the various strategies and methods adopted during the process.

1 *Community consciousness:* promoting change in residents' way of thinking, consciousness and values with regard the local area, post-disaster reconstruction and ecological system and resources, willingness to take part in public affairs and identification with their own community all helped with the promotion of community reconstruction, feedback mechanism and building of the ecovillage.

2 *Learning empowerment:* Learning and training courses of different stages and content and visits continued to be held; at the same time, residents and members of community organizations were encouraged to voluntarily take part in learning courses to achieve the effect of empowerment.

3 *Reconstruction issues:* Selecting issues and objectives that were suitable and easy to identify with; for example, Taomi Community's reconstruction selected community ecological resources as the subject and used it to create a new ecotourism industry; it was an important issue that had a conceptual public benefit, but also had livelihood and production implications and was anticipated for this reason. Also, to achieve major reconstruction issues or objectives, at different stages of reconstruction, planning of different secondary issues or objectives was also necessary.

4 *Communication and coordination:* Continuing and durable communication and consultation, even carried out through a mediator, and searching for methods that would be accepted to adjust community internal organizations and their operation or the relationship between organizations, were key factors in advancing community-empowerment recovery.

5 *External support:* Community consciousness, resources and energy are, of course, important, however, the issues of community reconstruction and ecovillage building are very complex and often exceeded the existing experience and capability of the community, consequently, suitable external support or intervention was necessary and important. In the case of Taomi Ecovillage, this external support included at least:
    a Groups or organizations that provided long-term support to or accompanied the community, such as the NHF early on and National Chi Nan University's units in the later period;
    b External civil groups, professional groups, enterprises, communities and even individual volunteers who provided one-time or short-duration support or cooperation;
    c Government or public sector resources, financial assistance programs and systemic reductions and exemptions.

References

Chiang, Ta-Shu and Chang, Li-Ya. (2008). Trust Building in Community Empowerment: A Case Study of Taomi Eco-village. *Soochow Journal of Political Science*, 26(1), 87–142.

Liao, Chia-Chan. (2012). *Integration/Transformation Effect: The Experience Study of the New Homeland Foundation toward Social Enterprises*. Department of Public Policy and Administration, National Chi Nan University, Puli.

Liao, Chia-Chan and Chang, Li-Ya. (2009). The Role and Operation of Taiwan's Non-profit Organizations in Post-Earthquake Community Recovery: The Case of the New Homeland Foundation in Taomi Ecovillage. *Proceedings of the International Conference on 921 Earthquake Community Recovery*. Nantou, Taiwan.

Liao, Chia-Chan, Chiang, Ta-Shu and Chang, Li-Ya. (2016). From Community Empowerment to Communities Governance: A Case Study of the Transition Puli Eco-Township. *Taiwan Historica*, 67(3), 85–128.

Yen, Sing-Chu and Ho, Chen-Ching. (2002). Taomi Ecovillage: Starting from Community Empowerment. *Proceedings of the Workshop on Community Empowerment in an Agriculture Village*. Nantou, Taiwan.

18 "SOHO City Mitaka"[1]
Machizukuri as creative urban governance

Hiroshi Saito

Introduction

Mitaka city is one of the most advanced examples of administration reform and citizen participation based on New Public Management thought in Japan (Panao, 2005). The significant opportunity of Mitaka's innovative attempts was the accumulation of "civic entrepreneurship" (Leadbeater and Goss, 1998) culture in the local council by successive city mayors. With regard to the SOHO City concept as a substantial project, the Mitaka City Council office and Machizukuri Corporation Mitaka (MCM) supported the promotion of a new style of work in SOHO (Small Office Home Office), which was appropriated to foster micro-scale autonomy in local residents. Furthermore, they were able to organise various autonomous projects in local society via information and communication technology. This urban regeneration policy of Mitaka city had a limited relationship with the central government policy of revitalising city centres.

Machizukuri from the Western point of view

Basically, the Japanese planning system is still quite centralised in terms of "hard infrastructure" (Healey, 1997); however, the machizukuri movement, as "soft infrastructure" (ibid.), has increased in the last few decades, especially after the crash of the bubble economy and the great Hanshin Awaji earthquake in the first half of the 1990s. Currently, the discussion of autonomy in local government has developed further, and although it is not enough to realise practical decentralisation, the legitimised administration system of governance is changing, mainly through abolition of the system of deregulated function and mergers of municipalities empowering local authorities. In practical local activities such as the revitalisation of city centres, it could be identified that greater autonomy of local society was applied to substantial projects.

In Japan, there has been a unique tradition concerning the methods of improving local society in terms of both the social and physical environments,

"SOHO City Mitaka" 211

called machizukuri. Although it is difficult to translate "machizukuri" (Sorensen, 2007; Sorensen and Funck, 2007a, 2007b) into English, according to Sorensen and Funck's (2007a) definition it means "attempts to achieve more bottom-up input into local place management in which local citizens play an active role in environmental improvement and management processes" (p. 1) for "urban liveability and environment sustainability" (Sorensen and Funck, 2007b, p. 278). Another definition of machizukuri as compared to *toshikeikaku* was defined by Hein (2001) as follows:

> The particularities of Japanese cities are reflected in two different planning approaches: toshikeikaku (urban planning), administration initiatives that focus on overall physical structure and layout, and machizukuri (community-building), which is small-scale urban design that arises out of citizen participation and community organization.
>
> (p. 221)

This concept, machizukuri, could be recognised as an achievement of the transformation of the Japanese conventional rational comprehensive planning system, mainly based on the top-down system which was imported from the Western world from the late nineteenth century.

Some Western scholars such as Andre Sorensen (2002, 2007) have paid attention to machizukuri. Many Western scholars could not follow the process and dynamics of machizukuri. Therefore, in some literature written by Western scholars, machizukuri was translated as "community development" or "urban design" and so on. Recently, in some Western articles written by scholars who are familiar with machizukuri, there was an acceptable perception of it, as follows:

> [M]achizukuri processes have been established, in an enormous outpouring of local energy into attempts to achieve more bottom-up input into local place management in which local citizens play an active role for urban liveability and environment sustainability.
>
> (Sorensen and Funck, 2007b, p. 1)

This description calls attention to the unique dynamics and driving force in terms of the indigenousness of machizukuri. Furthermore, the concept of institutional capacity could be useful for understanding the indigenousness of machizukuri more deeply. Institutional capacity was defined by Healey (2002) as follows:

> Our conception of institutional capacity emphasises the way external forces and local traditions mesh together in the flow of knowledge development and circulation, social networks and bonding values and manner in which they are translated into pro-active efforts to organise

212   *Hiroshi Saito*

strategically to shape and change dynamics in which people and firms in place find themselves.

(Healey, 2002, p. 16)

In this definition, the method of meshing together the external forces and local tradition (internal forces) is emphasised. Although the way of machizukuri would be transformed and diversified, there are principles (Satoh, 2004) connected at a fundamental level of it. One of them is "regional vitality" (Miyanishi, 1986) supporting "endogenous improvement of regional environment" (Satoh, 2004). This "regional vitality" is the foundation for the implementation of machizukuri which is not worked only by government policy or private company businesses for local society.

The basic goal of machizukuri is transforming an undesirable current condition to a desirable future one through various practices with regional vitality. In terms of transforming place, its "fluidity" presented by Healey (2010) is the basic recognition for machizukuri. In reality, machizukuri practices have been trying to improve residential environments in a gradual and community-based way. However, compared to City Planning based on huge financial resources and legal authority, the feasibility of transforming current undesirable conditions through machizukuri is not enough. Thus, in order to gain the power of third-generation machizukuri (Satoh, 2004) which is oriented to managing the local society holistically, there is a need "to find ways to open up awareness of diverse conceptions of 'good life' and work out what is broadly shared and where deep conflicts lie" (Healey, 2010) through building institutional capacity. The case study of this research, urban regeneration based on the SOHO City concept, could be recognised as the third generation of machizukuri which aimed at the management of local society for implementing "endogenous improvement of regional environment" (ibid.).

Outline of Mitaka city

Mitaka city is located next to the 23 central special wards of the Tokyo metropolitan government (the distance from the centre of Tokyo to Mitaka city is about 18 km). The population of Mitaka city was 178,944 in 2008 and the total area is around 16.5 km² (Mitaka City, 2008; Budiarjo, 2005). Most of the population commute to work in the centre of Tokyo, and Mitaka is regarded as a favoured "city for living", with plenty of green and public facilities. Besides its good reputation as a residential area, Mitaka city has succeeded in inviting universities and a research centre for the mechanical and engineering industries to establish themselves there.

Mitaka city was also recognised as one of the most advanced local authorities in terms of administrative reform and resident participation in Japan (*Nihon Keizai Shimbun*, 2006). The driving force for implementing its novel method of local governance was "civic entrepreneurship", which

"SOHO City Mitaka" 213

was rooted in the history of the Mitaka city administration, starting from the post-war period. After World War II, many urban areas of Japan had been damaged by the bombing of the Allied forces; thus, most Japanese local authorities spent their major financial resources on reconstructing public facilities, especially roads. The mayor of Mitaka city at the time, Heizaburo Suzuki, on the other hand, promoted the establishment of an independent sewerage system for the whole Mitaka area (Mitaka City, 2004). Consequently, Mitaka city was the first municipality to establish a city-wide sewerage system, in 1973 (ibid.). At the time, there were many criticisms of Suzuki's reconstruction policy, but he accomplished his intentions according to his beliefs as a public health professional (he was a doctor) through the introduction of the beneficiary payment principle and application of New Public Management thought into local government administration (Panao, 2005). Alongside the establishment of the sewerage system, he dealt with neighborhood community affairs. In order to revitalise social capital at the neighborhood level, he planned to set up community centres through the citizen participation strategy both in the building process and the management of the facility. This was also the first community centre in Japan (Mitaka City, 2002). Mitaka City Council divided its municipality area into seven blocks to establish and support the community centre and residents' council, not only for participation in substantial activities to maintain the neighborhood community, but also to encourage social solidarity among the long-time residents and the relatively new residents from elsewhere (ibid.).

In Mitaka city, there was another level of citizen participation and collaboration between various actors in local governance, which was the Mitaka Machizukuri Institute, created by the local residents, researchers in local universities and local council officers. This institute was started from a study group in a project which was entrusted to the International Christian University by Mitaka City Council in 1988. In 1996, in order to involve more of the various actors in the city, as a part of the Mitaka Public Corporation of Machizukuri, the institute was legitimised by the local council (MCM, 2000, 2003). This institute had three subcommittees, and one of these specialised on the theme of the "information-based city". This subcommittee involved various members such as IT specialists, the chamber of commerce, a cable television company and the related broad division of the city council, and had a discussion leading to the SOHO City Mitaka project.

"SOHO City Mitaka" Project

In 1996, Mitaka City Council launched a unique policy supporting SOHO (Small Office Home Office) business under the banner of "SOHO City Mitaka". The concept of SOHO was introduced from the US. At the time, in Silicon Valley, San Francisco, many small enterprises had arisen and

214 *Hiroshi Saito*

succeeded in their business based on IT concerns. The object of SOHO City Mitaka was not exactly the same as that of Silicon Valley, but the application of IT and flourishing of small-sized businesses inspired Mitaka City Council and some Mitaka citizens to promote economic development through the SOHO strategy (Andaya, 2005).

This style of working, SOHO, is appropriate to the existing character of Mitaka city as a good place to live. Furthermore, Mitaka city faced a problem with an ageing society, the decline of commercial functions and large companies moving outside the city. Therefore, it was easy to anticipate that the tax revenue of the city (60 percent of the total revenue of Mitaka City Council was from municipal tax, and half of the municipal tax was paid by individual residents) would decrease, as would the vitality of Mitaka's local society (Seki, 2005). In order to tackle these problems, Mitaka City Council launched a policy to promote small enterprises, applying a community-based strategy. The expected effects of SOHO City Mitaka were: (1) promotion of an environmentally friendly city and a high level of welfare municipality; (2) encouragement to establish citizens' identity, public participation, community cohesion and a city-wide machizukuri movement; (3) contribution to the vitality of the city and stability of municipal finances through invitations to information and industrial companies to establish themselves in the city and the development of local industry (ibid.).

Then, the city council created a strategic plan to promote the SOHO City concept, as well as establishing the SOHO City Mitaka Promotion Committee, which aimed to form a private sector-based support system to implement substantial activities of the concept. Based on the strategic plan, in 1998 the city council launched a time-limited pilot project of a SOHO office facility, named the SOHO Pilot Office, in cooperation with the committee. This facility was located on only one floor ($248.1\,m^2$) and included nine office units for small businesses in a private rented building. This pilot office also provided basic office facilities such as internet access, photocopying machine, meeting room and reception desk. The standard size of each office was between 5 and $12\,m^2$, in line with research on the demands of small-sized enterprises (Seki, 2005). In this research, it was calculated that there were several appropriate size offices for small businesses managed by only a few workers. As a result, 57 enterprises applied for nine tenancies (ibid.).

After establishment of the SOHO Pilot Office, six other SOHO buildings were established up until 2003. Each building applied different project schemes, particularly financial resources. The Sanritsu SOHO Centre was created in a building which was donated by a local resident. The Hikohdo SOHO Office and Home Office Mitaka were managed as private properties by the local shop owner with support from Machizukuri Corporation Mitaka. The Mitaka Industrial Plaza Annex was established by a joint venture between Machizukuri Corporation Mitaka and a few private companies. The central facility of the SOHO City project, Mitaka Industrial Plaza, was legitimised by the Mitaka City Centre Revitalisation Plan based on the City Centre Revitalisation Law of 1998 and acquired a subsidy from a quango, the Japan Regional Development Corporation (Kamikawa, 2005). In the process of building Mitaka Industrial Plaza, it was useful to create a plan of the facility, so that the council officers could accumulate strategies for managing SOHO buildings and coordinating small companies, obtained from the experiences of the SOHO Pilot Office (MCM, 2000, 2003; Seki, 2005). To date, more than 100 businesses, mainly in the IT field, have had a connection to these facilities.

Besides the development of facilities to improve the physical environment around SOHO City Mitaka, the development of the social environment was also emphasised by Mitaka Machizukuri Institute and the city council. One of the major projects was the creation of Machizukuri Corporation Mitaka (MCM) as a driving force of SOHO City activities with TMO (Town Management Organisation) status, and the existing public corporation of Mitaka City Council, Mitaka Public Corporation of Machizukuri, was integrated into it (MCM, 2000, 2003).

Machizukuri Corporation Mitaka (MCM)

Machizukuri Corporation Mitaka (MCM) was created as a TMO and legitimised by the City Centre Revitalisation Law of 1998. MCM was legitimised within the *Local Information Technology Adoption Plan of Mitaka City* and the *Mitaka Industrial Development Plan* as the core body for the promotion of the SOHO City Mitaka project. The legal status of the corporation was as a private firm whose stocks were shared by the local council (96 percent of total equity) and some local private companies and organisations such as a bank, a chamber of commerce, an agricultural cooperative and so on (MCM, 2000, 2003). As stated above, MCM provided plenty of services promoting local businesses, as well as itself running businesses. The main income of the company was from the management of public facilities such as a public car park which used to be owned by the Mitaka Public Corporation of Machizukuri (ibid.). In terms of the financial autonomy of MCM, this actually depended on the local authority; however, this strong relationship with the local authority made MCM's activities credible. Furthermore, this relationship contributed to increase the credibility of small businesses connected with MCM. In other words, a major advantage of setting up business in SOHO facilities managed by MCM such as Mitaka Industrial Plaza was to acquire credibility for one's business (Seki, 2005).

Another significant role of MCM in the SOHO project was the promotion of collaboration among various local actors through the implementation of tangible projects. The important point in creating an effective relationship among local actors was that MCM was a separate organisation from the Mitaka City Council office (Shibata, 2005). This was because the public sector could support private activities, but could not be their business

216 *Hiroshi Saito*

partner (ibid.). Since, in the framework of SOHO City Mitaka, the local council recognised that it was impossible that SOHO could grow without collaboration from various types of businesses, organisations and people (Seki, 2005), MCM was established strategically by the local council.

Case studies of local social enterprises: *kosodate conbini* (childcare drop-in centre)

In the creative urban regeneration starting from the SOHO City Mitaka policy, Mitaka Industrial Plaza and five other SOHO complex buildings were established. However, the creative milieu in Mitaka city has been formed not only by substantial facilities but also by social institutions. Therefore, in the following section, the relationship between hard and soft constituent elements of the regeneration will be analysed through a social enterprise named *kosodate conbini* (translated as "childcare drop-in centre") and the Senior SOHO Salon.

This NPO provides information about childcare through the internet for young mothers in cooperation with the city office. The *kosodate conbini* was started as a voluntary group for housewives through recruitment by Mitaka City Office in accordance with the national policy "Development Project of the Internet Portal Site for Parenting Information" in 2001. This recruitment was a series of collaborative activities with Mitaka

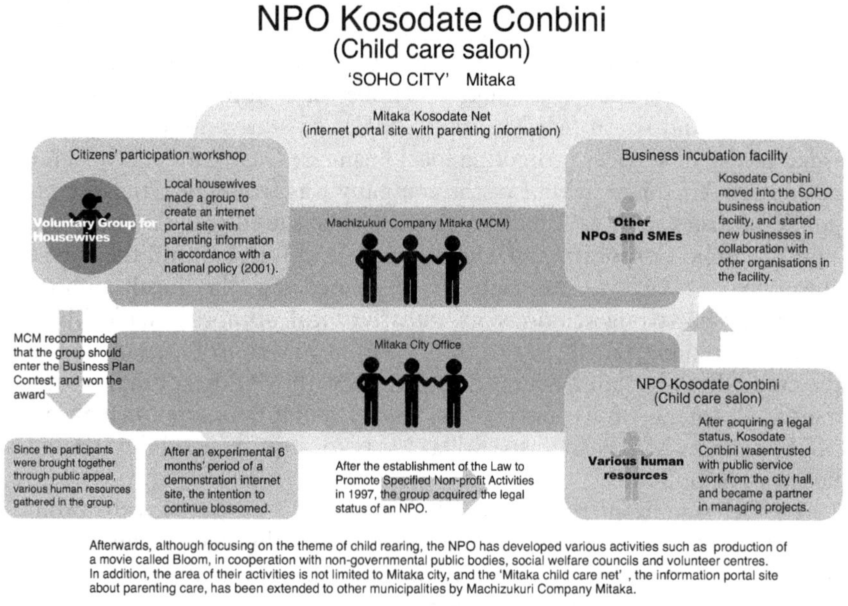

Figure 18.1 Development process of the *kosodate conbini*.

City Office, and various types of people applied. After an experimental six-month period of a demonstration internet portal site for parenting information, MCM recommended that the group should enter the Mitaka Business Plan Contest, and they won a merit award.

This event made them wish to continue this activity on a firmer basis. At the time, the Law to Promote Specified Non-profit Activities 1997 had been passed, and they acquired the legal personality of an NPO. By acquiring legal status, the *kosodate conbini* could make a contract with Mitaka City Office, which meant that they became a crucial partner in implementing the SOHO City Mitaka regeneration policy. As a consequence, the activities of *kosodate conbini* were expanded by collaborating with other SOHO companies and NPOs. Although, in the first place, *kosodate conbini* was nothing but a simple voluntary group for housewives, they were now managing a business, which placed a major responsibility on them.

Conclusions: machizukuri as creative urban governance

In the implementation process of the SOHO City Mitaka regeneration, there were many key persons that were partners of Mitaka City Office. Many of those individuals already possessed the foundations of their livelihood. One person was the owner of a SOHO company, another was a pensioner and another was a housewife. People such as these do not need to work for a living in activities concerning the regeneration project. However, they tend to be conscious of being a member of a specific local society through spending most of their time in their local places. Furthermore, some of these people finally conceive their mission in that place. In other words, maintaining their economic base, people make efficient use of their financial, temporal and practical surpluses to improve local society.

The concept of civic entrepreneurship was presented by Leadbeater and Goss as

> the renegotiation of the mandate and sense of purpose of a public organisation, which allows it to find new ways of combining resources and people, both public and private, to deliver better social outcomes, higher social value and more social capital.
>
> (Leadbeater and Goss, 1998, p. 18)

This concept is the key to the analysis of the creative processes of Mitaka city, because the city office played a crucial role in this regeneration with local people. The concept of SOHO City Mitaka caused a transformation not only in citizens' minds, but also in the attitudes of various departments of the city council.

Although in Japan in the 1990s, the concept of SOHO City was unusual, Mitaka City Office was able to develop the concept through collaborative strategies according to the recognition of their limited

218 *Hiroshi Saito*

regulatory capacity. In fact, by establishing MCM as a key agency, Mitaka City Office managed risk through innovative regeneration methods. In addition, substantial regeneration projects could be flexible and mobile in their implementation process by utilising formal and informal partnerships. The above-mentioned regeneration process was driven by creativity in individuals. In order to apply it for the SOHO City Mitaka regeneration, various resources were mobilised, mainly by Mitaka City Office and MCM.

In the context of "from government to governance", how various resources are mobilised in collaborative activities through various networks is important. Such resources include financial resources for the implementation of substantial projects, human resources for the acquisition of specific knowledge and information and social resources to establish places where various people are able to have peer-to-peer discussions to build a consensus. In order to institute this "creative milieu" in society, it is crucial to apply not only tangible formal partnerships but also potential informal networks.

Note

1 This chapter is a revised edition of part of *The Significance of Creativity in Urban Governance and Regeneration Practice through the Lens of an Institutional Capacity Framework* (Saito, 2017).

References

Andaya, A.S. (2005). Private Approach to Public Governance: A Case Study on Mitaka City, in *Report of Mitaka Community Studies, Mitaka City: A New Look At Local Governance*, College of Liberal Arts, International Christian University, pp. 22–29.

Budiarjo. (2005). Mitaka City: Citizens' Participation, in *Report of Mitaka Community Studies, Mitaka City: A New Look At Local Governance*, College of Liberal Arts, International Christian University, pp. 49–57.

Healey, P. (1997). *Collaborative Planning: Shaping Places in Fragmented Society*, Vancouver: UBC Press.

Healey, P. (2002). *Shaping City Centre Future: Conservation, Regeneration and Institutional Capacity*, Newcastle upon Tyne: University of Newcastle upon Tyne.

Healey, P. (2010). *Making Better Places: The Planning Project in the Twenty-First Century*, Hampshire: MacMillan.

Hein, C. (2001). Toshikeikaku and Machizukuri in Japanese Urban Planning: The Reconstruction of Inner City Neighborhoods in Kobe, *Jahrbuch des DIJ (Deutsches Institut für Japanstudien)*, no. 13, pp. 221–252.

Kamikawa, Y. (2005). Machizukuri mitaka, in Kobayashi, J. (eds.) *Eria manejimento – chiku soshiki ni yoru keikaku to kanri unei (Area management – Planning and Management by the District Organisation)*, Tokyo: Gakugei Shuppan-sha, pp. 169–174.

Leadbeater, C. and Goss, S. (1998). *Civic Entrepreneurship*, London: Demos.

"SOHO City Mitaka" 219

MCM (Machizukuri Corporation Mitaka). (2000). *Jyoho-toshi Mitaka o mezashite – Mitaka yume mirai (Aiming for an Information-Based City – Mitaka, Dream, Future)*, Machizukuri Corporation Mitaka.

MCM (Machizukuri Corporation Mitaka). (2003). *Mitaka-ism – Mitaka kara no hasso (Mitaka-ism – Conception from Mitaka)*, Machizukuri Corporation Mitaka.

Mitaka City Office. (2002). *Mitaka no comyuniti (Community of Mitaka)*, Mitaka City.

Mitaka City Office. (2004). *Mitaka o kangaeru kiso yogo jiten – Shisei gaiyo (Mitaka Data File 2004)*, Mitaka City.

Mitaka City Office. (2008). Mitaka-shi koshiki homu peji (Mitaka City Official Home Page) [accessed November 20, 2008]. Available from www.city.mitaka.tokyo.jp.

Miyanishi, Y. (1986). Chiiki Ryoku wo Takamerukoto ga Machizukuri – Jyumin no Chikara to Shigaichi Seibi (Establishment of Regional Vitality is *Machizukuri* – Power of Residents and Improvement of Urban Environment), *Journal of the City Planning Institute of Japan*, vol. 143, pp. 25–33.

Nihon Keizai Shimbun. (2006). *Dai go kai gyosei sabisu tyosa (Fifth Administrative Reform Survey)*, Tokyo: Nihon Keizai Shimbun and Nikkei Research Institute of Industry.

Panao, R.A.L. (2005). Mitaka City's Knowledge-Based Governance System as a Model of New Public Management, in *Report of Mitaka Community Studies, Mitaka City: A New Look At Local Governance*, College of Liberal Arts, Tokyo: International Christian University, pp. 1–11.

Saito, H. (2017). *The Significance of Creativity in Urban Governance and Regeneration Practice through the Lens of an Institutional Capacity Framework*, PhD thesis, Newcastle University.

Satoh, S. (2004). To the Third Generation of Machizukuri, in Satoh S. and Architectural Institute of Japan (eds.) *Machizukuri no Houhou (Method of Machizukuri)*, Tokyo: Maruzen.

Seki, S. (2005). SOHO CITY Mitaka kono roku nen no kiseki (The Six Years' Trajectory of SOHO City Mitaka Framework), in Seki, M. and Seki, S. (eds.) *Inkyubeta to SOHO – tiiki to shimin no atarasii jigyo sozo (Incubator and SOHO – New Business Creation by Local Society and Citizens)*, Tokyo: Shinpyo-sya.

Shibata, I. (2005). *SOHO de machi o genki ni suru hoho – jichitai to no kyodo gaido (The Method of Revitalising Towns with SOHO – Guide for Collaboration with Local Government)*, Tokyo: Gyosei.

Sorensen, A. (2002). *The Making Urban Japan: Cities and Planning from Edo to Twenty-first Century*, London: Routledge.

Sorensen, A. (2007). Changing Governance of Shared Spaces: Machizukuri as Institutional Innovation, in Sorensen, A. and Funck, C., *Living Cities in Japan*, London: Routledge.

Sorensen, A. and Funck, C. (2007a). Living Cities in Japan, in Sorensen, A. and Funck, C., *Living Cities in Japan*, London: Routledge.

Sorensen, A. and Funck, C. (2007b). Conclusions: A Delivery of Machizukuri Processes and Outcomes, in Sorensen, A. and Funck, C., *Living Cities in Japan*, London: Routledge.

19 Machizukuri as glocalization

Progress in highly dense "shitamachi" lower-town areas in collaboration with Tsukishima community school, Tokyo

Hideaki Shimura

Introduction

In highly dense lower-town areas, where traditional wooden row-houses (Nagaya) and alleys still remain, community associations based on the close local community used to solve town problems. But it has become difficult for them to do so with limited local perspectives, since the old-fashioned local community has been weakening and community association officials are aging. They are now trying to solve town problems both by collaboration with people and organizations outside the town and by promoting new residents who live in condominiums to be members of the local community.

Foreign residents and visitors such as tourists are increasing rapidly in Tokyo, and machizukuri is also shifting to a global perspective and collaborative activities beyond the town, region and borders. The interaction between local and global orientations is called "glocalization."[1] The machizukuri school which is based on a historical row-house in the lower town, Tsukishima, Chuo ward, Tokyo, is developing glocal activities involving foreigners such as foreign students through collaboration with local residents and the university.

Highly dense lower town, Tsukishima, Chuo ward, Tokyo (Figure 19.1)

Tsukishima is a town built on reclaimed land in the 1890s after modernization in Japan had started, but its town layout is the same as the early modern Edo period; row-houses stand tidily along alleys, and row-house residents have fostered close local communities and an alley culture. The historical townscape and local community which did not suffer from air raids in World War II still remain throughout the area, despite high-rise condos constructed by recent redevelopments. But they are being lost, because the town is not designated as a historical preservation district, residents are not aware of the historical, cultural and social values of the town, and the pressure of redevelopment is strong. It also means that the

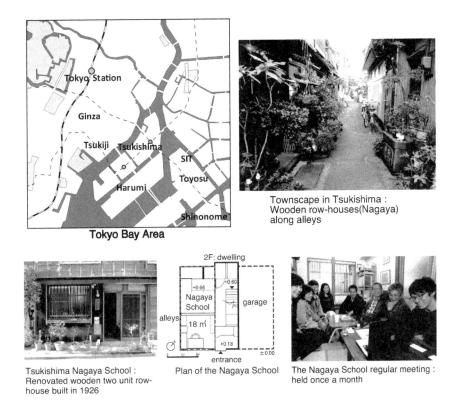

Figure 19.1 Tsukishima and Nagaya School in Tokyo Bay area.

town is losing its own identity, sustainable updating system and the chances of creative use through the renovation of row-houses.

Tsukishima has a famous local food called Monja-yaki that attracts many visitors from overseas as well as from Japan.[2] Also, as the 2020 Tokyo Olympic and Paralympic Games draw near, the athletes' village and 14 competition venues will be located in the Tokyo Bay area, including Tsukishima. As foreign visitors to Tsukishima will be increasing even more as 2020 approaches, the new method of machizukuri in a global perspective is imminently to be sought after.

I was born in Tsukishima and have been witnessing the continually changing townscape and community. As a researcher of machizukuri , it has been my constant concern to help in solving the problems of our town, while hoping to take advantage of the opportunity to be expected over the next few years in order to improve our Machizukiru project. It is good news for this purpose that Tshukishima Nagaya School established in 2013 has found enthusiastic helpmates among residents and students.

Tsukishima Nagaya School (Figure 19.1)

Tsukishima Nagaya School was opened in October 2013 as a satellite laboratory of the Regional Design Laboratory in Shibaura Institute of Technology (SIT). Since the beginning, the school has been a place where the university students and local residents meet regularly to learn and practice machizukuri . Nagaya School is on the first floor (18 m²) of the renovated building of the two-unit row-house built in 1926. The building is a shared house, and a young family of which the husband is a graduate from the Regional Design Laboratory at SIT lives on the second floor.

The SIT campus is located in Toyosu, Koto ward, which is a newly developed urban area since 2000 with big office buildings, high-rise condos, shopping centers on the old factory site, and is not suited to learning about machizukuri. The distance from the SIT campus to Tsukishima is about 20 minutes on foot, which offers great opportunities for students to study machizukuri on the spot, and this was the primary reason for opening Nagaya School. Undergraduate and graduate school courses and student seminars have been held at the school since the opening.

The school's regular meetings were held once a month with local residents who attended the Chuo ward civic college held at Nagaya School in the spring of 2014. Among 17 Nagaya School members who join the regular meetings, only one resident is native to and lives in Tsukishima, the rest are newcomers who live in condos. The main reason members started gathering for regular meetings was the relaxed feeling in a Nagaya house. Initially the main activities of the school were mostly chatting among members, then the school gradually began to develop activities both in variety and frequency, due to the increase in exchanges between residents and students. It further developed to collaborative machizukuri activities between residents and students, most of which proved to be glocal activities.

Now, our specific glocal activities will be described below, and the major points of glocal machizukuri in a lower town of Tokyo will be analyzed.

Glocal activities (Figure 19.2, upper images)

Tsukishima Alley Map

The number of foreign students is increasing rapidly in SIT, since the university was designated as a Super Global University from 2014 by the Ministry of Education, Culture, Sports, Science and Technology. The number of foreign residents and tourists is also increasing in Tsukishima. This prompted us to produce an English version of "Tsukishima Alley Map" that we had already created in Japanese to bring opinions and ideas from foreigners into machizukuri. The English version was produced by collaboration between students and a resident member of Nagaya School

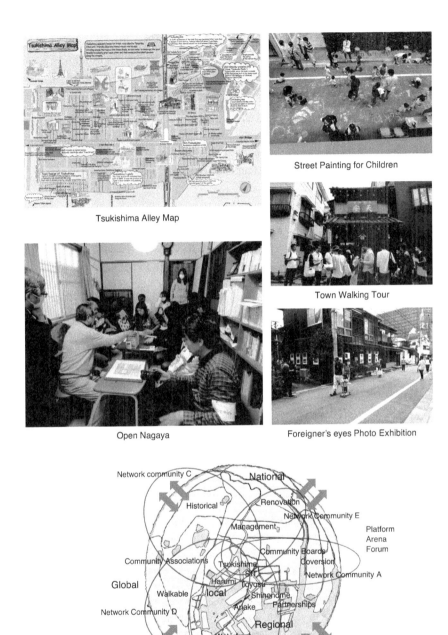

Figure 19.2 Glocal activities and interaction.

224 Hideaki Shimura

who is a translator, and highlighted alleys and historical and cultural spots in Tsukishima. This map won a prize in the Advocacy Campaigning and Social Projects category of the contest of International Conference Walk21 in 2015.[3] The human-scale and walkable town structure of many alleys and fewer cars and our town walking activities with the map were recognized. The particular local town structure and activities of ours were also appreciated by the global initiative. The school has also held a machizukuri event "Street Painting for Children" from 2017, supported by our community association on the street that operates Sunday promenade.

Tsukishima Walking Guide Book and town walking tours

We were receiving requests for visits from abroad since we started posting the Tsukishima Alley Map (English version) on the internet from 2015. First, 15 faculty and students of the Japanese Studies research institution of Michigan University visited Tsukishima, who were accompanied by six SIT students as guides around Tsukishima. After the walking tour, they came back to Nagaya School and had a Q&A and discussion time. In 2015 alone, teachers and students from the Universities of California and Utah visited Tsukishima, and SIT students performed guided walks for foreign visitors. Through this experience, students understood the need to prepare for the walking tour and created the Tsukishima Walking Guide Book in collaboration with members of the school in 2016. This guidebook in English introduces features in Tsukishima in ten concepts.[4] After the completion of the Guide Book, faculty members and students of Washington University visit Tsukishima every year, and SIT students and Nagaya School members use this booklet for guided walks in English.

Open Nagaya

While Nagaya School boasted various achievements, the student who felt the necessity of raising social recognition of Nagaya School organized the "Open Nagaya" event, in which everyone can see inside the Nagaya house and can talk with Nagaya School members. We had 75 participants in a total of 12 occasions from February to June 2017 at the event held as a collaboration between students and Nagaya School members. The planner of the event was a Chinese student who speaks Chinese, Japanese and English, which made it convenient for foreigners to participate. We had questionnaire surveys for participants, all of whom expressed satisfaction about the event. Some of them answered, "I was able to see the history and culture in Tsukishima" and "I understood the historical Tsukishima community."

Events such as Open Nagaya are able to enhance social recognition of Nagaya School and increase people's awareness of the value of their town. Nagaya School members are going to hold the Open Nagaya event every year.

Machizukuri events for foreigners

It is better that programs of the machizukuri event for foreigners are interesting enough to attract participants, even though they know little about Japanese history or culture. The foreign students of SIT planned through their own experience a series of machizukuri events consisting of three steps: games, contests and exhibitions, held from February to June 2018.

Step 1 is a "Sense of Places Game." This is a kind of treasure hunting game, where participants can find answers to the quiz by spotting seven places in the booklet, so that foreigners can understand the historical and cultural locales in Tsukishima, and with fun.

Step 2 is a "Photo Contest," in which participants take photos during the Sense of Places Game, for instance, and post them on Facebook. Participants and SIT students then vote for the posted photos. Finding photogenic scenes and taking photos are an act of sensibility, which makes it easy for everyone to participate.

Step 3 is "Foreigner's Eyes Photo Exhibition," where selected photos from Step 2 are displayed on the wall of Nagaya School, and the final votes of passers-by are invited. The foreign winners come to Nagaya School and talk with passers-by who voted.

Thirty foreigners participated in the Sense of Places Game, and 23 in the Photo Contest, posting 64 of their photos, 18 of which were selected and exhibited at the Foreigner's Eyes Photo Exhibition. According to our questionnaire surveys, most participants were satisfied with the machizukuri events consisting of three steps. We were able to develop machizukuri events in which foreigners can participate easily, and collect foreign views from the titles and comments attached to photos that can be used for machizukuri as reference.

In 2018, a "Town Features Workshop" for foreign students is being held, in which some 30 foreign students joined, and during the visit to Tsukishima and Nagaya School made posters to introduce their findings in English, Japanese and their own mother tongue (the number of languages increased to six) for posting on the internet. Globalization of our university thus is partly supported by the local community, and at the same time, our local community is enhanced by globalization of the university.

Expanding to Tokyo Bay area, and beyond (Figure 19.2 lower map)

From Tsukishima to Tokyo Bay area

Reclamation of Tokyo Bay started from Tsukishima, which was the first of such projects after urban modernization in Tokyo had begun, and expanded to Harumi, Toyosu, Shinonome, then to Ariake. These projects had been based on the context of building Tokyo Port, but these early reclaimed lands, where once factories and warehouses were located,

226 Hideaki Shimura

moved their location into the area of high-rise buildings as the original port functions moved out further offshore. This sort of shift in land use from port to residential, commercial and business aims is commonly observed in large cities of the world these days. Many phenomena that appear local are in fact global. The zeitgeist of the world presents itself regardless of locality, and urban transfiguration and challenges involved in the change are basically a common phenomenon, despite a cultural difference or a few decades' time lag between advanced countries and under-developing countries. In today's world, local challenges for problem solving are shared through various media, including the internet, and inspire synergy in global work.

Let's take the instance of community building. Young families in high-rise condos generally do not care much about joining local community activities and don't know each other due to the lack of communication. They don't even exchange greetings sometimes. Most newcomers do not seem to have a love for their own town, and their emotional attachment to the area seems very weak. In response to this situation, our project of building community in the Tokyo Bay area was to use a historical house of Tsukishima Nagaya School as a base for machizukuri and let it function as the regional "navel" (core) for building a new community, with the help of a historical townscape that attracts both new comers and foreigners.

On the other hand, in the redeveloped areas with rows of high-rise condos, the use of the waterfront is in progress, and people can enjoy cruises, waterside cafés and restaurants which have become the core of human communication. For example, in Toyosu, Koto ward, students who have learned practical machizukuri methods in Tsukishima and the local community joined forces, proceeding with the extensive use of canals, rivers and waterfronts. The Machizukuri Council, established by local residents, the university, corporations and NPOs, challenges for building an attractive community connected with the waterfront in cooperation with other councils, NPOs, private companies and local governments in the waterfront wards of Chuo, Koto, Minato and Shinagawa. One of the Machizukuri Council members, an NPO that promotes marine sports and diversity, operates with overseas networks.

Also, a few factories and warehouses left in the area have been converted into stylish cafés, shops and restaurants that attract many people, including the youth, to be a centre for leisure activities.

The above-mentioned effort of community building by utilizing a historical building as the machizukuri base, the use of historical townscape and waterfront and the conversion of old buildings is, as a matter of fact, practiced all over the world – the Thames riverside and Docklands in London, IJburg in Amsterdam, Brooklyn in New York, Lakeside in Chicago and Marina Bay in Singapore to name a few. Local and global phenomena inspire each other, and in today's globalized world, human interaction has grown huge and a global network community is being created.

The urban design of Tsukishima with alleys and dense houses is common in lower towns of the Koto ward and the Bay area, thus its machizukuri projects can inspire others across regions. Machizukuri on a human scale and to establish a walkable town is a global trend, as being typically represented in the international conference of Walk21. As is seen by our challenge in Tsukushima being presented and awarded at Walk21, global and local activities inspire each other. In other words, local challenges support global activities.

The same thing can be applied to the Community Garden initiated by voluntary residents in Tsukishima. This project is now spreading outwardly from Tsukishima and the Koto ward areas. It is well-known this started in the US, aiming for community building, greening promotion and improvement of townscape and is widely accepted in the world. The community garden movement is a typical challenge of local, regional and global activities inspiring one another.

Connecting to the global community through the internet

Nagaya School has been publishing activities on its website[5] soon after its establishment. The website introduces Tsukishima town and Nagaya school both in Japanese and English, and a pdf file of the Tsukishima Alley Map both in Japanese and English can be downloaded. The number of downloads of the English version is about 4,700 as of December 2018 since the establishment in 2015, which is greater than the number of downloads of the Japanese version (about 3,500). Interest in this town is growing globally beyond regions and borders.

The population of the Tokyo Bay area is rapidly increasing due to the construction boom in high-rise condos, and especially the growth of the numbers of families with young children is phenomenal. In response to this trend, voluntary members of such families in the Tsukishima and Toyosu areas started a life-support SNS (Social Networking Services) company to serve young newcomers. This kind of information and intercommunication is popular in the world, and our area is no exception where local activities and global trends inspire each other.

Conclusion

Tsukishima Nagaya School started as a place where university students and local residents studied machizukuri, and has gradually developed to glocal activities. Our methods for glocal machizukuri are as follows.

- The historical townscape of the lower town and the activity center of the renovated Nagaya house have become a "regional navel" that attracts local residents, students and even foreigners. The regional navel is the "stage," a setting that draws in various people, evokes activities

228 *Hideaki Shimura*

and constantly fuels regional inspirations. And while working in cooperation with local community and town associations, it generates a "new community" with a wide range of networks that connects to the world.

- Japanese cities have been characteristic of the chaotic townscape that appears as though both "the rich and the poor are living side-by-side."[6] In such cities, various people with different lifestyles live and intermingle each other, and share common views through daily communication and special events such as festivals. This characteristic itself generated energy for renewed machizukuri and created towns and regions. This diversity is now rapidly shifting to "glocal" awareness.
- Collaboration between local residents and students creates various machizukuri activities which will develop into global activities due to the increase of foreign students at the university.
- Global-oriented activities open to foreigners bring foreigners' opinions and ideas to machizukuri, and that will enhance the local community by making local residents aware of the value of their own town.
- The creation of walkable cities which is a global trend is based on the urban spaces and life culture in lower towns. Local communities around the university support part of the global exchange of universities. In other words, global activities are supported by the accumulation of local activities.

Notes

1 "Glocal" is a portmanteau word composed of "global" and "local," reflecting or characterized by both local and global considerations (Oxford Dictionary).
2 Monja is thin batter with various ingredients self-cooked on a table-top grill, which attracts tourists, young and old, not only from all over Japan but also from abroad. There are more than 70 monja shops in Tsukishima.
3 Walk21 is an international conference organized by the Walk21 International Committee, aiming for environmentally friendly and sound cities.
4 The Guidebook introduces ten concepts in both spatial and social categories to give clues for understanding machizukuri in Tsukishima.
5 Tsukishima Nagaya School website is www.tsukishima.arc.shibaura-it.ac.jp.
6 See Chapter 1 of *Japanese Homes and their Surroundings* (Edward S. Morse, 1886).

Reference

Morse, E.S. (1886). *Japanese Homes and their Surroundings*. Boston: Tichnor.

20 Machizukuri in the future

Shigeru Satoh

This last chapter presents the five main discussion points concerning the future of machizukuri.

In the first place, the main future challenge for machizukuri is to elevate its practice from the level of local residents and stakeholders, to a broader territorial scale, involving the whole citizenship. This means to glocalize machizukuri and to open it to the world. In this chapter, based on such progress, I would like to conclude by presenting the five questions that remain unanswered concerning the future of machizukuri.

First, it is clear that machizukuri activities have developed with a strong connection to the specific regional context. Nevertheless, beyond the characteristics of the different cultural backgrounds, machizukuri-like activities exist in various forms outside Japan. From community-based approaches to social enterprises, in recent years, community-based initiatives that aim at improving physical and social environments based on the resources that exist in an area have experienced great success in different countries around the world (Borzaga and Defourny, 2011). All of them are evolving independently in response to the particular institutional systems and cultural backgrounds of each country or region. However, all of them do also share the background of a common era. From the second half of the twentieth century to the beginning of the twenty-first, starting with Jane Jacobs' criticism of modern city planning, new initiatives were born.

Considering these community-based activities from a global point of view, the first discussion point would be the role they play in solving generalized issues. In the recent confrontation between Globalization and Localism, such solutions have been rooted in the activities of local residents in various parts of the world to address urgent topics, such as finding solutions to global environmental problems and achieving the SDGs (Sustainable Development Goals). The sense of value in modern society can be explained with reference to two main axes: first, the opposition of "global" and "local" approaches, and second, "ecology-oriented" and "market economy-oriented" visions. The reality is that even the set of values of a single human being is not fixed; it changes throughout a lifetime, from a young age, through the active work life period to old age. And yet, when

230 *Shigeru Satoh*

working on surrounding environments, people aim at creating a certain virtue, goodness, appropriateness, or justice. To do so, it seems impossible not to take specific criteria as a reference. "Ecology-oriented" approaches, for example, give value to all the resources that exist in a region, from the economy to the environment, and the processes that take place in it, including the circulation of such resources and their sustainability. This gives value to the existence of all living things and the relationships between them. This approach, if also oriented towards the "local" scale, corresponds with the posture adopted by machizukuri-like community projects, which are based on the value of local resources to create shared good places and communities. On the other side of the axis are approaches based on the "free market economy." This, united with a "global" scale, reflects a sets of values oriented toward the global market economy, which is maximized under neoliberal principles. These values are reflected, for example, in massive urban development, which aims at increasing economic profit and overcoming competition. Large-scale urban development strategies usually collide with machizukuri, leading to fierce confrontation and discord. The latter is eroded by the former, which brings in gentrification

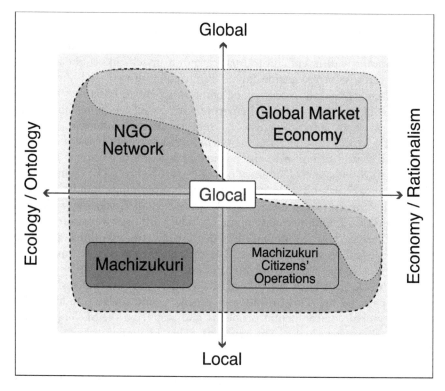

Figure 20.1 Identification and expansion of machizukuri in sense of value structure.

Machizukuri in the future 231

and speculation. In the case of urban space projects in central areas of Tokyo, it might look like machizukuri activities coexist close to large-scale global urban contexts in great contradiction, resulting in the discontinuity of built environments. Nevertheless, looking at this situation from a different angle, both approaches, and their products, do not present great conflicts, but rather complement each other.

Linked to this, in recent years, movements that promote regional economic activities stand out. Their work links to global corporations and financial institutions, based on the rationality of the market economy, but jumps into the local world, based on the ecological value of the place. This is notable in developing countries, which are working on the coexistence of on-site machizukuri activities with the regional market economy. Alternatively, local entrepreneurs may also participate in machizukuri activities, incorporating market mechanisms, and expanding the scope of machizukuri; examples of this are machizukuri companies or machizukuri citizens' activities. Also, it does not need saying that ecology-oriented and market-oriented economics are well known for exploring common points and paths for coexistence, such as the SDGs and other international agreements. Thus, values have become mixed and this now requires changes in the market economy. Furthermore, among the leaders of the global economy, there is a tendency to reaffirm the regional value and to work on social businesses.

Until the end of the twentieth century, conflicting views of the world used to clash violently, resulting in a disconnected and irrelevant world. Nevertheless, when both postures unite, diverse coexisting values in which actions and organizations supported by diverse standpoints can be built. On the other hand, local community-based initiatives, which tended to have been confined to narrow local scales before, have expanded either to connect to global scales, or to join cooperation platforms to work together with global groups. With this, what could be called a "global network" has been formed, and a new potential has been created. Based on this, the world has the potential to change significantly by expanding the range of community-based initiatives, but still focusing on solving problems in an ecological way, always with a strong commitment to their local regions, territories or work areas.

The second point leads us to consider machizukuri as a way to rebuild democracy. During its first consolidation period, in the 1960s and 1970s, the implicit goal of machizukuri was to establish what was called a "school of democracy" or "experiment in democracy," practiced by groups of individuals in their neighboring living areas. Keeping this utopia in the back of their minds, machizukuri stakeholders have attempted different practices and methods to overcome the existing fragmented identities, to gather and integrate them, and to finally reach a form of democracy that takes place in the public sphere, with machizukuri at its base. As democracy has been described as "thinking about the problems in our society by ourselves and

232 Shigeru Satoh

solving them through our own power" (Uno, 2013, p. 12, l.15) it can be said that a local democracy has in fact emerged through the practice of machizukuri. Community-based initiatives unite to solve local problems in more autonomous ways. Through them, the community is educated, grows up and opens up, and these projects become the basis for assembling a form of local democracy. On a bigger scale, similar activities in various parts of the world can cooperate to learn from each other's ideas and methods, having as main premises the continuity and a gradual integration of knowledge and experiences.

In this way, transcending the Rousseauan classic democracy, this new form of democracy is based on the local community and starts from the accumulation of experiences through personal endeavours. In each area different results emerge, but if these small sprouts were assembled together a super-democracy could be realized.

In order to overcome existing problems, democracy normally discusses a variety of options and visions depending on the basic idiosyncrasies of each region or country. From a deep belief in democracy, a stable society can be dynamically maintained, including diversity, while at the same time emphasizing individual independence, and strengthening the mechanisms directly related to decision-making and policy implementation. This represents somehow the generalized idea on what modern democracies should be. For example, E-democracy trusts in technological advances and the information society as ways to facilitate public voting and participation. On the other hand, Ecological democracy is based on the coexistence of ecological systems through which various subjects coexist. Super-democracy is based on an altruistic and reciprocal spirit to overcome confusion and conflict. Compared to these global tendencies, machizukuri democracy is also based on experiences of sharing and the knowledge acquired through collaboration. However, the key question is to understand if individual efforts in each different location can constitute an effective holistic system. Machizukuri does not only express its results through the built environment, but also shares similar concerns, interactive editing methods and results with these new forms of democracy.

In this context, based on past achievements, there is evidence to support the notion that community-based activities could achieve full-scale development extending to every field, and become the base for this new society.

The third point of discussion is the cultural value and whole systems that machizukuri can produce. This needs to be considered in relation to the climate and culture links (*fudo*[1]) present in a region or action area, and the relation with the spiritual culture nurtured there. If "true good beauty" exists as a universal absolute value, machizukuri is also moving in the direction of the pursuit of truth and goodness, even if it is still only halfway there. However, on the other hand, it can be argued whether such beautiful shared places and communities have been achieved, or whether the results do truly orient toward them. Machizukuri has surely produced something that can be

Machizukuri in the future 233

called a "culture of machizukuri," but is it also able to produce aesthetic values that correspond with such culture? This does not refer to a simple beauty, but of the worth that is rediscovered through exploring our living areas, that is shared and that unites locals' actions, becoming the development path for machizukuri. As a result, what such machizukuri produces is a cultural landscape. It creates not only tangible things, but also an imagery of living landscapes. In them things are not unified by beauty, but they do share values that link them together even in diversity and discontinuity; these intangible relations can be somehow comparable to beauty. Thus, even through a discontinuous process, machizukuri does gradually bring together a complete image of the "machi," physical and intangible elements included.

Fourth, from the shared place and community that are nurtured through machizukuri practice, the special character that is co-created could be expressed as follows.

The principle of Discontinuous-continuity explains how different things can coexist in contradiction. When this is applied to living space, public and private domains, for example, are not clearly divided, and share somewhat vague boundaries and grey spaces. Under such circumstances, opposites mutually support each other, and throughout this interaction process discoveries take place repeatedly, weaving intangible bonds opposites unite in a coherent manner. Diverse merits and sets of values coexist while also influencing each other; and with this a new entity takes shape.

Again, the question is if the accumulation of machizukuri practice, which grows independently through bottom-up actions, can consistently and comprehensively manage the territory. This refers to understanding specific whole districts, regions, or even the whole earth as a full picture. In modern times that require global environmental control, European-style planning makes use of traditional systems controlled by master plans, regional planning methods or spatial planning. On the other hand, in the Japanese planning system the control exerted by upper spheres is confined to public works such as roads or river embankments. However, master plans regarding the control of residential environments exist independently for each municipality but there are no mechanisms to control wider areas beyond fixed administrative borders.

In this book, Chapter 6 discussed the future direction of machizukuri, and described the mutual editing of a discontinuous reality, and Chapter 5 addressed area management and territorial management. These two present alternative methods to address the management of dynamic areas beyond these rigid systems. The crux of the matter here is how to make this management work effectively. If the work areas could be perceived as close to us as our immediate vicinity, the formation of a multi-subject collaboration model, or in other words, the mutual editing of projects and ideas based on human connections would be possible. However, for wider areas, could human links alone, through mutual editing, lead to a consistent whole image?

234 *Shigeru Satoh*

Finally, fifth, as mentioned in Chapter 5, *fudo* and spiritual culture are also closely related to the individual spatial image that machizukuri should aim for. The question is whether, even if both things are not unified, a value could still be recognized in their diversity and coexistence.

With regard to this, the cases of Mishima in Chapter 5 and Tsuruoka in Chapter 9, show that the ecological skeletal component of the territory can be the base of the whole editing process for a future image of the areas. These cases present an image typical of East Asia monsoon climates, in which due to high temperatures, humidity and rainfall, many typhoons and other natural disasters occur. In these areas wind, water and mountains are the main structural elements of the territory, and urban and rural areas integrate. The design of such cities are based on common empirical methods such as *fengshui* (wind and water) and *sanshui* (mountains and water). Above all, the flow of river water is essential, and water catchment areas supported by clear surrounding ecological systems are often drawn on regional pictures and maps as intrinsic to the territory. Running from the surrounding mountains, water streams simulate a kind of skeleton or blood vessel that flows through the human body, and the wind flows as a kind of skin creating unique regions. In this context, territorial management should awake such an image and inter-edit it locally through machizukuri, layering diverse scales and topics, and connecting it to the rest of the world.

On top of that, these are far from being unified centripetal territories as many diverse gods are said to inhabit different places inside these sacred micro-cosmoses. Inside the regional ecological system, every place is important individually and as part of the whole, as they connect and support each other. Each of these relations represents a world in which different integrating parts mutually edit each other, but which also exist autonomously presenting discontinuities and contradictions.

In big cities, such ecosystems are fading. Notwithstanding, aiming at the accumulation of autonomous individual machizukuri initiatives for the recovery of such an ecosystem can work in a similar way to regional area management strategies. The autonomous machizukuri movements that emerge for a specific area dynamically configure the entire ecosystem, and at the same time contribute to the ecological management of the specific action area. Even for master plans, through which it is possible to fix and superordinate whole areas in advance, it is important to count on an ecological and dynamic mechanism in which both machizukuri and wide ecosystems mutually edit.

Again, here, these machizukuri activities become assembled as a mosaic. Besides, as parts of this whole, each one of them does open up and connect to others, which lets them resonate with the eco-system. This also leads to connecting with machizukuri in surrounding rural areas. Physical space is not limited in scale; parts are wholes and the whole is a part. Recognizing an area in a holistic way means connecting it boundlessly to a farther outer world. Graphic expressions of this vision of the world can be found, for

Machizukuri in the future 235

example, in maps of Japanese historical villages and castle towns, or in fish-eye maps, as Takamasa Yoshizaka proposed (see Figures 9.2 and 19.2). In them, the space represented is not divided by boundaries, but presents an out-of-scale context, vague and continuous. These visions are not centripetal either; various realities coexist, creating flexible bonds between them, and letting them change continuously. Through them, zooming out and looking at a landscape far below, it is possible to feel a connection to this world, reaching to understand its regional and local connections simultaneously, and perceive the constantly weaving intangible bonds, nomadic and circulating.

Methods based on the recognition of such a reality must enable the continuity of a dynamic diversity, but at the same time embrace the great weakness that it entails from the point of view of territorial stability as an ecological system. Overcoming this, machizukuri should study how to gently integrate these diverse realities and how to combine them into a harmonious holistic regional image beyond its limits.

The spread of machizukuri

Thus, since the 1990s, when machizukuri is clearly established as a community-based bottom-up method, it will be generally treated as a part of urban planning. However, machizukuri is no longer confined to be a part of it. What is more, urban planning is also transformed by incorporating machizukuri practice.

On the other hand, machizukuri will be considered a wider method. For example, the terms "welfare-machizukuri," "health-machizukuri" and "art-machizukuri" are also used.

Besides, as urban redevelopment became more normal and widespread, the word "machizukuri" extended to the realm of "urban renewal" or "urban development"; in some cases, "machizukuri" has even been used in an ambiguous way to refer to these projects. For example, in the case of the extensive high-rise business areas developed around Tokyo station by big companies, the "Otemachi, Marunouchi, Yurakucho District Machizukuri Council" was established.[2] In these cases, even when the main goal of the project is large-scale new development, the integration of machizukuri-like discussion groups responds to the intention of corporate leaders to contribute to the quality of urban space and work environments.

Responding to the council's intention to co-exist with the surrounding community, machizukuri can be thus considered an activity that facilitates the integration of diverse actors, including corporations and citizens, to work in common to make the most of the town as a community. In this way, there is no need to avoid the use of the word "machizukuri." Rather, the principles and methods that machizukuri has cultivated should be welcomed and incorporated in large enterprise-led private urban development.

236 Shigeru Satoh

However, the term "machizukuri" should not be utilized with a soft nuance (referring just to people's kindness and humanity). As long as "machizukuri" is used it should not deviate from the basic principles of the narrow definition presented in Chapter 1.

The term "machizukuri" has reflected the negative legacy of high economic growth and started to target a very large number of troublesome built environments. In this context, through residents' own thinking, action and autonomous problem-solving, various machizukuri initiatives with practical power have taken shape through history; This machizukuri started as a "school of democracy" or "experimental democracy," so we discovered a different type of democracy which is very different from post-war democracy. Besides, the machizukuri that was once proposed as the antithesis of city planning and administrative planning led by the government, gradually became an important part of them and grew into a broader concept that encompasses them.

Thus, the most important thing here is the "spirit of machizukuri," which is cultivated through the development of machizukuri practice. Building on that spirit, in response to the demands of different times, changes in community development and the expansion of objectives, machizukuri continues to tackle new challenges and explore new visions.

In the near future Japan will have to confront the increasing aging and decline of its population, and may probably face frequent severe earthquake disasters. All over the world, numerous problems have risen, intensified by the latest development trends and the pace of modern consumer society. It is imperative now to find solutions for common problems such as the widening of social disparities or global warming. This situation has highlighted the gaps in impersonal top-down governance models, and the urgent need for the creation of well-prepared resilient societies.

Trying to solve these problems, Japanese "machizukuri" has evolved to become an exceptional example of adaptive action design process, which involves bottom-up creative approaches based on collective action and the conscious use of the available local resources and human skills.

Nowadays, machizukuri represents a change of paradigm to a new kind of bottom-up democracy and encompasses the search for adaptive methods to guide this change. This volume constitutes, thus, an essential piece of literature that not only helps develop a more complex understanding of Japanese urban planning, but also inspires the creation of much needed comprehensive specific models for sustainable community and regional development worldwide.

Notes

1 The term "*fudo*" (translated into English as "climate and culture"), which is composed of the Japanese characters for "wind" and "earth," was coined by Watsuji Tetsuro (1889–1960) to refer to the natural environment of a certain

land. *Fudo* refers to the role of climate and spatiality in shaping a particular culture. For more, see: https://plato.stanford.edu/entries/watsuji-tetsuro.

2 According to a description provided by the organization, the objective of this council was to increase the added value of the area and contribute to the sustainable development of downtown Tokyo in the Otemachi, Marunouchi, Yurakucho District. The project is based on "machizukuri guidelines" for the appropriate and efficient development of urban space. They were established through a round-table conference, which served to plan the collaboration strategies between the main actors involved in the machizukuri project, such as companies, groups and the administration.

References

Borzaga, C. and Defourny, J. (2001). *The Emergence of Social Enterprise*. London: Routledge.

Uno, S. (2013). *Minshu-shugi no Tsukurikata* (*Method for Making Democracy*). Tokyo: Chikuma-shobou (in Japanese).

Wastuji, T. (1931). *Fudo* (*Climate*), Tokyo: Iwanami-shoten (in Japanese).

Glossary of technical terms particular to Japanese

Chounai-kai and *jichi-kai* are the traditional neighborhood associations and neighborhood self-governing bodies in Japan. Traditional and conventional *chounai-kai* and *jichi-kai* are just neighborhood associations, but some of them have developed and become the base of machizukuri practice. They could be generally referred to as "community associations" in English. In this book, both "neighborhood association" and "community association" are used according to each particular situation. These groups support everyday life in the neighborhood, for example they are in charge of the management of garbage collection, delivering notices from the local administration and information related to the neighborhood. It is common that these groups expand to constitute machizukuri councils or platforms together with other actors in parallel with their original activity.

District Plan refers to the legally binding regulations based on agreements reached by the different groups operating in a district. The plan is based on the District Planning system incorporated into the City Planning Act in 1980.

Land readjustment The land readjustment method for urban areas is unique to Japan. It was applied to the recovery projects in the areas affected by the Great Kanto Earthquake. All the different landowners and leaseholders of a group of urban lots are involved in establishing a new land division and housing sites, and with it, develop the required urban infrastructures, such as water, sewage and electricity. Through this method the land is redistributed among the local landowners. The procedure for the transfer of horizontal surface property rights is regulated by law, and entails incentives like public investment on local urban infrastructure and facilities, or tax benefits. Thus, agreement and cooperation of all the different rights-holders, and sharing a common vision for the future of the targeted area, are the focal points of these land readjustment projects.

Machi is a community and its shared place (see Chapter 1).

Machiya (*machi*-house) is a traditional type of Japanese merchant townhouse composed of a shop, living spaces, warehouse and workplace. It is usual that districts where groups of *machiya* have survived until modern times, accumulating a historical value, are designated as Conservation Districts for Groups of Traditional Buildings and receive financial support for their rehabilitation and maintenance.

Machizukuri Council   Machizukuri Councils were formed with representatives of community groups in an area (e.g., the *jichi-kai* (community association) among others). This council represents the residents and takes the responsibility for promoting and managing machizukuri activities.

Machizukuri citizens' operations   is a collection of machizukuri activities implemented by a cooperative organization of citizens through the use of the local potential resources and responding to demands in the community.

Machizukuri ordinance   For promoting particular machizukuri, each municipality sets up a particular regulation. There are two types, one is an anonymous ordinance independent of state law, including a comprehensive contract, the other one is delegated by District City Planning Law.

Machizukuri plan   expresses a general framework for the future through several discussions at the machizukuri council, but which has no legal binding force.

Model project   A method for implementing public works financed by the government as a trial experiment through which it is possible to verify the effects, establish a method and generalize it later. With regard to the improvement of the housing environment, it is often adopted to support local efforts and proposals by easing the requirements for project adoption and implementation by law. It involves, for example, the improvement of defective housing areas and the construction of public housing (e.g., Model project for improvement of living environment or Model project for improvement of community living environment).

Rolling method   refers to the connection of small urban redevelopment projects developed over a long period of time according to the availability of vacant land within a targeted area and the particular circumstances of the place. This means that to achieve a final development goal, once the project starts in one particular spot, it has to wait until land empties again in the same district to continue developing the same strategy (see Chapter 2).

Urban Redevelopment Project   Under the 1968 amendment of the current "Urban Redevelopment Law" built floor areas were given the same rights as land based on the land readjustment method. This means that land areas and building floors, three-dimensionally, can be exchanged and rearranged under similar conditions according to the "Property Rights Exchange Method."

Index

Page numbers in *italics* denote figures.

Abe, T. 189–90
"Absolute Height Limit" (until 1969) 38
accumulation 7, 49, 57, 61, 76, 96, 145, 181, 210, 228, 232–4; of autonomous individual machizukuri initiatives 234; of generations of wisdom 145; of machizukuri practice 233; personal 75; of small local actions in Ichitera-Kototoi 49
action plans 20, 66, 122–3, 128, 130–1
activities 3–5, 19–20, 22–3, 26, 28, 39, 41–2, 50–1, 56–8, 60–3, 68–9, 85–7, 181–2, 217; citizen 50; collaborative 216, 218, 220; community-based 229, 232; creative 126; cultural 103, 105–6, 108, 128, 179, 203; environmental 182; global 227–8; local 51, 140, 210, 227–8; post-earthquake 182
administration 19–21, 23, 25–7, 30–1, 33, 35–6, 38, 42–3, 51, 53–4, 128, 131, 133, 146; and citizens 96, 128; and experts 36, 42; local 9, 18, 26, 29, 60, 144, 165; local government 138, 213; public 17, 23, 27, 81; reform 210, 212
advocacy planning 91–2, 94
aging population 56, 120, 141, 160
agricultural areas 163
Aiba, S. 83
alleys 51, 62, 126, 138, 220, 227; decorative 137; highlighted 224; intermediate 74; narrow labyrinthine 29; and streets 78
Allied forces 213; *see also* World War II
Anti-Disaster Machizukuri People's Conference, Sumida 1990 57
apartment buildings 56, 81

approach and effect of self-reconstruction housing support by the regional style housing *147*
approach of revitalization by the community management committee in Nabari area *125*
architects 17, 36, 51, 138–40, 148, 150, 191
architecture 32, 76
architecture schools 41
area management 61, 64, 66, 83, 174
area residents 124, 131; *see also* residents
Asia 12, 16
autonomous organizations 15
autonomous projects in local society 210

Bakuro-machi Machikado Salon Initiatives 108
Bakuro Neighborhood Plan 108
bases 27–9, 39, 41–2, 51, 69, 74, 108–9, 145–6, 150, 175–7, 179, 181–2, 231–2, 234; community 192; local 109; of operations 176–7; for reconstruction support activities 179
blocks 38, 40, 117, 119, 133–4, 136, 138–40, 181, 192, 213; apartment 25; community housing 43; cooperative housing 35; high-rise 39; mixed-use 133; new housing 81; public housing 181
budgets 43, 80, 125, 169, 175; allocation for urban development 28; city resource 128
builders 148, 150
Building Standards Act 1976 81
buildings 102, 105, 107–9, 129–30, 133–4, 137–40, 175, 177, 179, 192,

202, 206–8, 214, 226; apartment 56, 81; construction 38, 150, 188; damaged 176–7, 189; high-rise 4, 19, 33, 38, 226; historic 101, 129; historical 105, 110, 134, 226; old 81, 133, 155, 226; reconstruction of 190; redeveloped 164; regulations 38; renovated 110, 136, 139, 222; residential 95, 97, 126, 129–30, 149, 153

businesses 19, 105, 110, 118, 120, 133–4, 140, 167, 171, 177, 179, 182–3, 186, 213–17; citizen-based 171; construction 148, 150; development 163, 165, 171; establishment of 110; owners 107, 138, 177, 179; private company 212; small 154, 214–15; social 82, 179, 231

Butterfly Orchestra 205

campaigns 13, 15, 19, 38; anti-pollution 18; machizukuri 5; resistance 19

canals 39, 96, 226

capital 57, 164–6, 171, 205; cultural 105; increase 166; investments 179; personal 148; projects 167; social 213, 217; total 165–6

Capital Region Comprehensive Planning Institute 6

carpenters 148

cars 4, 134, 224

case studies 99, 133–4, 156, 160, 174, 186, 212, 216; of local social enterprises 216; of post-earthquake machizukuri 186

castle towns 64, 103, 112–13, 116–17, 123, 235

catastrophes 62; *see also* earthquakes; *see also* tsunamis

Central City Area Revitalization Plans 63

central urban areas 62, 106, 122–3, 128, 130–1, 136, 169, 174–7, 179, 181; of Echizen city 136; of Ishinomaki City 174–5, 182; of Nabari City 123

Chamber of Commerce and Industry 106, 166

Chichi Earthquake 15, 195–8, 203, 206

China 16, 153–4, 156, 158, 204

Chinese land owners 156

chou-chou-moku (zones) 30, 32

choukai (district councils) 15

chronological table of Japanese machizukuri 8, 122

chu ying tsao (citizen participation) 12–16

Chuetsu Earthquake 144

cities 6, 8, 29–30, 60–1, 63, 101, 105–6, 120, 122, 153–4, 160–1, 195–7, 228, 234; Chinese 154, 161; historical 101, 109; Japanese 29, 92, 101, 141, 211, 228; preservation and restoration of 197; small 96, 122

citizens 12–14, 16, 66, 68, 80, 83–4, 93, 95–7, 116–17, 128, 139–41, 169, 171–2, 191; local 5, 31, 64, 73, 102, 167, 191, 211; organizations 95, 97; participation 12, 14, 16, 68, 91, 96, 116–17, 210–11, 213; and private sector organizations 106; senior 28; volunteer 167

city administration 122, 129, 131

city area 63, 66, 156, 163, 175; historic 103, 136, 141; revitalization 63

City Center Revitalization Act 84

city centers 9, 38, 40, 96, 140, 163–4, 169, 171, 186

city councils 137, 213–15, 217

city government 22, 125, 164, 187, 192

city owned land 164, 167

city planning 36, 54, 87, 165–6, 212, 236

City Planning Law 1980 15–16, 23, 43

City Planning Master Plan 16, 18, 91, 95–7, 116–17

CMP *see* City Planning Master Plan

coalitions, project-oriented 158, 160–1

coastal areas 175–6

coexistence 31, 57, 83, 85–6, 231, 234; and autonomy of diverse entities 87; of ecological systems 232; of on-site machizukuri activities with the regional market economy 231; of urban spatial patterns 156

"Coexistence of Public Housing with Cooperative Redevelopment of *Nagaya* areas" (program) 25, 34–5, 133, 220

collaboration 48–50, 83, 95, 97, 154–6, 182, 185–6, 190–1, 193, 213, 215–16, 220, 222, 224; and co-creation in designing local urban spaces 7; in design projects 112, 120; of government 155; of inhabitants 50; of local residents 25; in machizukuri

242 *Index*

collaboration *continued*
 by multiple project-implementing
 bodies 185; multi-business 163; of
 multiple stakeholders 82–3, 120, 154;
 in planning methods 91
collaborative framework for post-
 earthquake machizukuri *190*
COMICHI Ishinomaki project 179
commerce 81, 106, 127, 134, 140,
 164, 166, 176, 188; chamber of 165,
 213, 215; fisheries-related 185;
 revitalizing 127
commercial facilities 192
committees 116, 146, 165–6, 171, 214;
 Community management 126; and
 investment decisions 166; and
 regional housing 146
community 57, 81–2, 198; associations
 19, 22, 84, 108, 158, 220, 224;
 based *machizukuri* 123, 128; centres
 133, 213; councils 19, 30, 117;
 development 3, 5, 19–20, 62, 174,
 181, 205, 211, 236; groups 38, 41,
 43, 48, 83, 181; housing 35–6, 50;
 industries 195, 204–5, 207;
 initiatives 7, 19, 23; management
 committees 126; organizations 60,
 73, 80, 196–7, 204–5, 207–8, 211;
 principles 153, 155–6; protection
 areas 158, 160; reconstruction 208;
 residents 54, 56, 196, 198, 201,
 204; roads 62, 79, 124
"community building" (translation for
 machizukuri 3, 206, 226–7
"community consciousness" 208
"community design" 3, 5
"Community Development Committee
 for Good Living" 123, 126
Community Development Policy
 13, 15
community empowerment 195–7, 203,
 206–7; comprehensive 197; process
 196, 198; recovery 195–6, 208;
 stages 198; in Taiwan 195, 197
companies 6, 19, 73, 103, 107, 110,
 163–4, 166–7, 169, 171, 215, 227;
 cable television 213; fishing 176;
 industrial 214; joint venture 181;
 local 68, 81, 117, 119, 166, 188;
 multiple local private-sector 109; and
 organizations 171; private 80, 84,
 212, 214–15, 226; railway 103;
 small-scale 82, 215; town
 development 107, 165

competition 107, 188, 204–5, 207;
 community empowerment 207; and
 governance 207; for machizukuri by
 Kesennuma City 187; overcoming
 of 230
condos, high-rise 220, 222, 226–7
consensus 42, 53, 56, 78, 81, 140–1,
 201, 204, 206, 218; buildings 34, 49,
 57, 81, 175, 188, 200; on
 machizukuri 53
conservation 38–40, 69, 85, 101, 103;
 and community development
 methods 101; ecological 195, 197–8,
 201–2, 207; of historic buildings 101;
 movements 101, 105; residential
 environments 21; of traditional
 culture 39
construction 34–5, 38–9, 43, 62, 64,
 119, 123, 148, 176, 179, 181, 185,
 189, 192; businesses 148, 150;
 community-based 150; market 143;
 new 32, 139, 143; plans 38–9;
 projects 39; of public housing 239; of
 seawalls 193
cooperation 9–10, 18, 22, 27–8, 61, 66,
 68–9, 80–1, 106–7, 207, 214, 216,
 226, 228; and collaboration 9; cross-
 area 205, 207; cross-boundary 207;
 cross-disciplinary 207; diverse 202,
 204; of experts and local
 administration 9; of residents 40, 49;
 strategies 69
cooperative redevelopment 25, 36, 48, 80
councils 23, 25–6, 28, 32, 34, 42, 54,
 61, 138–9, 164–7, 188–93, 213, 226;
 local 210, 213, 215–16; social
 welfare 84; *see also* city councils; *see
 also* community councils; *see also*
 district councils
countries 12, 16, 26, 41, 44, 58, 64, 68,
 82, 154, 229, 232; advanced 226;
 Asian 16; developing 231; under-
 developed 226
CRCPI *see* Capital Region
 Comprehensive Planning Institute

damage 25, 144–5, 149, 175, 186; air
 raid 105; of buildings 176–7, 189;
 degrees of 146, 149; earthquake 150,
 174; economic 18; escaping 145–6;
 flood 131; geological 196
Davidoff, Paul 91
democracy 231–2, 236; ecological 232;
 experimental 231, 236; grassroots

Index 243

20; local 232; machizukuri 232; new forms of 232; post-war 236
Democratic Progressive Party 15
democratization 6, 12–14, 16
demolition sites 177
design game in Tsuruoka *94*
design methods 137–8; new urban 112; participatory 49, 53
design simulation game workshop using landscape simulation system *79*
design strategies 158
design support organizations 148
design workshops 191
development 20–3, 31–3, 35, 49, 63–4, 94–7, 145–6, 153–4, 156–8, 163, 175–6, 192–3, 204, 214–15; community industry 202; economic 214; human resource 110; industrial 197; institutional 63; large-scale 153, 156, 235; projects 95, 216; regional 102, 236; of residential land 193; sustainable 66, 101, 201, 206
development process of the *kosodate conbini* 216
disabled people 48
disaster-affected areas 185, 192–3, 196, 204
disaster prevention 28, 32–3, 36, 38, 50–1; actions 30; activities 49; centers 49; measures 30–1, 108; performance 30
Disaster Prevention Living Areas 50
Disaster Victim Livelihood Recovery Funding 148
disasters 25, 29, 33–5, 51, 61–2, 74, 144, 146, 151, 176–7, 179, 181–3, 204; *see also* earthquakes; *see also* tsunamis
district councils 15
District Plans 15, 23, 42, 54, 57, 61, 97, 159–60, 188, 238
diversified methods of district renewal *159*
diversity 85–6, 109, 160, 181, 226, 228, 232–4; dynamic 235; human 4; of individuals and organizations 181

earthquakes 34, 49, 56, 61–2, 144–5, 148–51, 174–7, 179, 181–3, 185–7, 191–3, 195–8, 200, 206; Chichi Earthquake 15, 195–8, 203, 206; Chuetsu Earthquake 144; disasters 9, 236; Great East Japan Earthquake 9, 174–5, 182, 185–6, 193; Great

Hanshin-Awaji Earthquake 28, 36, 56, 58, 60–2; Great Kanto Earthquake 30; Great Kobe Earthquake 16, 60; Hanshin-Awaji Earthquake 25–6, 210; insurance 148; Kanto earthquake 34; Kobe City earthquakes 16, 60; proof reinforcement 108, 182; strong 61–2, 196; Tokyo 34
East Asia 12, 153, 234
East District Autonomy Promotion Organization 137
Echizen City 133, 136–7, 140
ecological 60, 201–3, 205, 234; conservation 195, 197–8, 201–2, 207; environment preparation 206; ethics and methods 202; interpreters 202–3; management 234; principles 66, 113, 116, 119–20; resources 206, 208; surveys 200–1; systems 39, 66, 68, 197, 206, 208, 232, 234–5
Ecological Engineering Building Team 201
ecology 63, 201, 203
economic activities 101, 231
economic growth 5, 12–14, 17–18, 40, 101–2, 105, 236
ecosystems 68
ecotourism industry 82, 200–3, 206, 208
ecovillages 198, 200–8; building of 208; complete 203, 206; formation period 202
education 4, 28, 69, 82, 103, 177, 201, 222; ecological courses 203; environmental 130; vocational 182
embankment roads 122, 124
empowerment 5, 196, 198, 202, 208; actions 205; autonomous 202; community 195–7, 203, 206–7; cross-area 205; learning 208; recovery community 196, 198; stage and cross-area 205
engineers 95, 191
English versions and translations 3, 211, 222, 224–5, 227
enterprises 177, 205, 214; community-based 229; fishery 119; machizukuri 116–18; private 165; small-sized 213–14; social 63, 82, 216, 229
entrepreneurs 101, 187–8
environment 26, 28, 30, 66, 69, 101–3, 113, 116, 119, 177, 179, 201, 203, 230–2; design 87; ecological 60, 203,

244 *Index*

environment *continued*
207; educational 105; global 66;
historical 38, 119; natural 68, 85, 101,
113, 197, 201; physical 4, 13, 23, 28,
56, 76, 78, 88, 102, 186, 193, 210,
215; problems 69, 202; regional 212;
residential 212, 233; restoration and
conservation 69; sustainability 211
ethnicity 91–2; *see also* religion
exchanges 16, 77, 84–5, 195, 222;
between diverse stakeholders 18;
between experts and neighbours 77;
diverse interactive 7; global 228;
international 69; of property rights
81; of property rights of residents
and landowners 80
experiments 96, 157–8, 181, 197; great
democratization 16; real on-site 5;
and themes 122
experts 5, 9, 17, 20, 22, 26–7, 29–30,
32–3, 36, 38–43, 56–8, 60–1, 77,
139; and academics 17, 29; and city
officials 20; and local governments
33, 53; and residents 87; support of
38–9

Facebook 225
facilities 6, 51, 64, 80, 108, 117, 128,
167, 181, 187, 191, 195–6, 213–15;
agricultural 198; central 119, 214;
child-care 167; industrial 196;
medical 167; office 214; public
service 191; shipbuilding 175; tourist
187; transport 196
factories 19, 35, 38, 225–6; abandoned
51; cheese 169; metalworking 105;
small-scale 19
families 3, 6–7, 63, 123, 205, 227
farm guest-houses 149–50
farmlands 32, 163, 197, 202
features and systems of COMICHII
Ishinomaki *180*
feedback 73, 78, 112; mechanism of
205, 208; use in improving the
machizukuri process 77
first generation 7, 17–18, 26, 40, 43,
50, 56, 60, 78; and local
communities 51; of machizukuri 17,
26, 62; and the role of the local
community in disaster prevention 51
fish markets 176, 186, 191
fisheries 176, 185, 187, 193
flood damage 131; *see also* disasters
foreigners 154, 220–2, 224–8

forestry 119, 196–7
framework 23, 101, 108, 113, 116,
205; community industry 202; for
new urban design 113; of sustainable
development 101; of urban
development 116
fudo 143, 232, 234
Fukui Prefecture 133, 136
Funck, C. 211
funding 80–1, 109
"Furano Brand" 163, 169
Furano City 163–5, 169, 171; hospitals
in 165; organizations in 66, 163–4,
169, 171; redevelopment of 171;
urban core revitalization in 163
Furano City Tourist Association 171
Furano Machizukuri Company 163,
167, 172
Fureai Machizukuri Projects 28

galleries 51, 118, 128, 130, 133–4, 138
Genbei-gawa River projects and trail
map 67, 68
generalization period 13, 15–16
Ginza (shopping street) 118–19
global trends 82, 227–8
globalization 225, 229
glocal activities 220, 222, 223, 227
"glocalization" 220
goals 49, 57, 62–3, 69, 77, 83–5, 95–7,
116, 118–19, 127, 235; common
development 49, 80; diverse 62; fixed
182; of regional management 119; set
by machizukuri practice 81
Goss, S. 210, 217
governance 69, 155, 207, 210; joint
193; local 63, 84, 212–13; regional
83; social 160
government 13–14, 17, 33, 35, 53, 91,
95–7, 117–18, 153, 155, 157, 185,
187–9, 192; funding 81; grants 203;
municipal 165; national 43, 113,
117, 193; new 15; officials 17, 27;
policies 210, 212; regional 119
Great East Japan Earthquake 9, 174–5,
182, 185–6, 193
Great Hanshin-Awaji Earthquake 28,
36, 56, 58, 60–2
Great Kanto Earthquake 30
Great Kobe Earthquake 16, 60
Green Flag Project 171
Gregory, J. 49
Groundworks Mishima organization
68–9

groups 12, 14, 20, 22, 31–2, 34–5, 39–40, 48–9, 61, 63–4, 84, 148–9, 188–9, 197–8; action 26, 181; citizen 68, 108; civil 28, 205, 207; community 38, 41, 43, 48, 83, 181; local 26, 53, 66, 117, 139; opposition 33, 38–9, 185, 187; self-governing 83; study 20, 213; volunteer 28, 216–17
"Gulliver Map" (method of workshop to collect information) 85, 93

"Handmade Regional Prize" 130
Hanshin-Awaji Earthquake 25–6, 210
Hase Highway 123–4, 129–30
Healey, P. 210–12
high-density residential districts 153, 158, 160
high-rise condos 220, 222, 226–7
high schools 205; *see also* schools
historic cities 101–2
"historic landscapes" 120, 143–5, 148, 150
historic protection areas 57, 112–13, 116, 133, 156, 159–60
historic townscapes 13, 40–1, 57, 124, 220, 226–7
historic urban areas 41, 101, 103, 112–13, 117–19, 133–4
historic warehouses 58, 118
Hitokoto Society (disaster prevention) 50, 53
Hokuriku region 102, 136
Hokuriku Shinkansen (public transport system) 106
homes 35, 126, 144–6, 149–50, 179, 200–1; family 146; new 149–50; rebuilding 145; single-family detached 32; *see also* households
homestays 201–2, 204–5
Horai-chou Area Regeneration Project Promotion Council 138–9
horizontally expanded collective housing model. Source: courtesy of Ting LU 157
Hosokawa Residence 122–4, 129–30
hospitals 117, 164–5, 167
households 49, 76, 108, 146, 149, 197
houses 34, 57, 76, 81, 117, 119, 124, 134, 145–6, 148, 150, 186, 196, 198; abandoned 118; decaying 133; merchant 57, 129; old 29, 109, 150; private 76, 145; shared 106, 222;

tenement 133; terraced 19; vacant 108–9, 143, 146
housing 63, 81, 101, 110, 118, 145–6, 148–9, 159–60, 165, 179, 181–2, 186, 188, 192; cooperative 50; low-rent 106; municipal 164; new 148; production 144; reconstruction 188; redevelopments 41; regional style disaster restoration 145–6, 149–50; rental 81

Ichitera-Kototoi district 36, 49–51
Ichitera-Kototoi Machizukuri Center 51
Ichitera-Kototoi machizukuri projects 52
identification and expansion of machizukuri in sense of value structure 230
implementation 25, 27, 31, 36, 43, 57–8, 78–82, 84, 156, 189, 193, 212, 215, 218; local project 35; of machizukuri 212; procedures 155, 217–18; and research 156; stage 84, 160
industry 68, 81, 106, 119, 145, 149–50, 166, 186, 196, 205; ecotourism 82, 200–3, 206, 208; engineering 212; financial 103; fisheries 175, 185–7, 190; green 203; local construction 146; textile 105; tourism 41
infrastructure 130, 149, 153, 175, 185; industrial 150; redevelopment projects 185; urban 185, 190, 193; water-related 69
initiatives 16, 20, 30, 32, 35, 48, 51, 82, 86, 109–10, 145, 165–6, 185, 187; administrative 116; autonomous 36, 60; community-based 7, 19, 23, 229, 231; experimental 177; global 224; local 82, 174–6; machizukuri 50, 53, 60, 234, 236; private-sector 36, 166
'institutional capacity' 211–12
"interactive editing" 73, 83, 85–7, 232
internet 216, 224–7
investments 81, 165–6
investors 165–6
Ishinomaki City 174–7, 179, 182

Japan 12, 14–19, 40, 63–4, 66, 68–9, 91–3, 133–4, 138, 144–5, 153, 155–6, 210, 212–13; architecture 76; collaboration 155, 220; communities 30; historical villages 235; land owners 156; legal system 43; and

246　*Index*

Japan *continued*
　Limited Liability Companies 63;
　northeastern 112; planning method
　91; planning systems 210, 233;
　post-disaster machizukuri 145;
　traditional towns 74; urban planning
　236; urban spaces 76
Japan Regional Development
　Corporation 215
"Japanese Association for Historical
　Townscape Conservation" 41
Japanese Communist Party 14
jichi-kai (community associations) 22,
　25, 238–9

Kanaya-machi (residential area for
　foundry workers) 103, 107
Kanazawa City 102, 105
Kankeimaru Shoten 182
Kanto earthquake 34
Kawagoe City 58
Kawana, Kichiemon 6, 22
Kesennuma City 185–8, 190–3
Kitazawa District 32–3, 53
"Kitazawa Machizukuri Council" 33
Kobe City 15, 18–23, 25, 28, 32, 42,
　44, 58, 60–1, 103
Kochi City 22, 58
kosodate conbini (childcare drop-in
　centre) 216–17
Koto Disaster Prevention Plan 30
Koto ward areas 222, 226–7
kougai (public nuisance and
　environmental pollution) 18–19, 38
Kubo, K. 165, 169
kura (historical warehouses) 58, 133–4,
　136–8, 140–1
Kyojima district 34–6, 38, 43, 50
Kyojima machizukuri plan and
　projects 37
Kyojima Machizukuri Public
　Corporation 36
Kyoto City 3, 30, 39–40, 76, 105, 136

lacquerware 102–3
land 33, 35, 80–1, 124, 130, 137–41,
　143, 149, 155, 177, 179, 185, 192,
　197; acquisition plans 140; leased
　203, 207; parcels 157; public 191–2;
　reclaimed 220; unused 191–2; vacant
　118, 185
land readjustment projects 29–30,
　61, 164
land redevelopment projects 188

land transfer system 161
landowners 25, 36, 77, 80–1, 112, 117,
　123, 133, 138–41, 174, 179, 181,
　192; and citizens 123; individual
　small 138; local 128, 141; private 35,
　138; and residents 36, 77, 80–1, 141;
　small-scale 138
Landscape Design Guide Plan 113,
　116–17, 120
law 16, 23, 39–40, 54, 216; constraints
　of 158, 160; existing 158; martial 13;
　new 43
leaders 19–20, 27, 35, 51, 63, 82, 140,
　192, 231; community group 22; local
　27, 61–2; of machizukuri 63;
　resident 6
legal systems 6, 12–13, 41, 63–4
legislature 93, 95
Liao, Chia-Chan 200–2
lifestyles 14, 17, 39, 42, 57, 78, 102,
　118–19, 146, 160, 190, 203, 228;
　diverse 113, 118–19; fisheries-based
　193; local 53, 59, 74; modern 102
Limited Liability Partnership 2005
　63, 84
living environments 4–5, 18–21, 23, 25,
　28–30, 32–4, 38–41, 43–4, 48, 53,
　57, 66, 69, 79–81; destruction of 19;
　improvement of 5, 23, 25, 34, 44, 62,
　80, 126; Japanese traditional 76;
　official 26; protection of 38
local communities 4–5, 9–10, 30, 42,
　51, 53, 69, 80, 82, 91–3, 171, 220,
　225–6, 228; environment 31;
　initiatives 231; leaders 17
local governance 63, 84, 212–13; *see
　also* governance
local governments 5, 13–16, 18–19, 23,
　25, 33, 56, 64, 81, 83, 112, 119,
　134, 136; administrators 138; and
　machizukuri council 25; planning
　117, 119
local housing production system
　143–50
local initiatives 82, 174–6
local people 26, 74, 92, 217; activities
　of 78; activities of the 78; of the Edo
　period 51; importance in the Mano
　area 27; integration of 92; preserving
　"canals and stone warehouses as
　cultural assets" 39
low-rent housing 106
lower-town areas (highly dense)
　220, 222

Index   247

Ma blurred boundaries and intermediate shared areas 75
"machi units" (concept) 3–5, 10, 21, 26, 33, 39, 41, 57, 74, 76–8, 85–6, 88, 233, 238
machikado hiroba (street corner plazas) 54
machinami (historical townscape) 57–8
machiya town houses 39–40, 51, 64, 76, 82, 133–4
machizukuri 3–7, 9–10, 14–23, 25–36, 38–44, 48–51, 53–4, 56–66, 77–88, 91–3, 116–20, 185–93, 210–15, 224–36; autonomous 31, 49; and citizen participation 91; community-led 29; comprehensive 23, 58; concept 22, 53; contemporary 7; creative 19, 40; culture of 233; democracy 232; design and practice 54, 85; development 27, 29, 36, 41, 63–4; disaster prevention 36; discovery of 7; enterprises 116–18; events for foreigners 224–5; first generation 17, 25, 27, 41, 43, 49; generation 10, 29, 36, 48–9, 56, 58, 61, 64, 78, 82; glocalizing 222, 227, 229; goal of 231; history of 7, 12, 53, 62, 119; implementing 79, 82; "improvement type" 36, 62; indigenousness of 211; initiatives 50, 53, 60, 234, 236; Japanese 8, 122; methodology 73; model projects 15, 117; planning 20, 22–3, 41–3, 48, 50, 53, 77, 79, 93; post-earthquake 176, 186–7, 190–1, 193; power of 29; pre-reconstruction 62; private-citizen directed 112; processes 6–7, 18, 22, 26–7, 29, 33, 74, 77–8, 83, 85, 87–8, 93, 131, 133; projects 23, 25, 40, 42–3, 48, 50, 62–4, 66, 69, 73, 78, 80, 82, 116–19; resident-oriented 122, 131; restoration 58
machizukuri actions 27, 64; anti-disaster 57; dedicated 32; discontinuous 88; first 18
machizukuri activities 9–10, 25–6, 28–9, 50–1, 58, 60, 63, 66, 78, 80, 88, 131, 228–9, 231; collaborative 222; conducted 36; linking 56; managing 9, 25, 38; on-site 231; open 61
Machizukuri Citizens Operations 79–80, 82
Machizukuri Company 64, 66, 81, 163, 165, 171, 189–92, 210, 213–16, 218,

231; and agricultural producers 169; resident-initiated 191
Machizukuri Council 23, 25–6, 28–30, 32–3, 36, 41–2, 48, 50, 53–4, 61, 84–5, 149, 187, 226
"Machizukuri Design Game" (method of workshop) 51, 77–8, 93, 117–18
Machizukuri District Plan 54
"Machizukuri Hub" 93
Machizukuri Notebook 93, 96
"Machizukuri Ordinance" 23, 26, 28, 41–3, 53, 79
machizukuri practice 5, 7, 9, 18, 26–7, 36, 38–43, 48–50, 53, 60, 62, 80–3, 85, 232–3; contemporary 9, 88; development of 236; evolution of 53; goals set by 81; new methods for 41; process of discovery in 77; touchstone for 18, 26
maeul mandeulgi (town development) 12–16
management 4, 48, 60, 69, 78, 87, 120, 130, 163, 172, 174, 181, 212–13, 215; of public spaces 48; territorial 82, 233–4; urban 5
Mano 18–30, 32, 43, 101–2, 106–8, 110, 174–6, 179, 182; machizukuri experience 26; machizukuri plan and projects 23, *24*; machizukuri process 18, 25–7, 29
Mano District Machizukuri Council 28
Mano Machizukuri Promotion Council 20, 22–3, 26, 29
master plans 20, 95–7, 165, 233–4
mayors 14, 20–1, 23, 31, 50, 213
MCM *see* Machizukuri Corporation Mitaka
mechanisms 63, 69, 83, 92, 148, 154–5, 232–3; developing 82; dynamic 234; market 231; renewal 153; self-governance 53
Meiji Period 103
merchant houses 57, 129
merchants 3, 35, 75, 102, 105, 175
methodology 56, 153–4; Community Renewal Program 21; of *machizukuri* 154; new 41
"methods of machizukuri" 5, 61, 226
Metropolitan Government 31, 34, 36
micro-initiatives 82, 107, 177
Mie Prefecture 122–3
Mie University 122, 124, 129, 131
Ministry of Construction 23, 34, 41, 43, 123–4

248 *Index*

Mitaka City 210, 212–17; administration 213; milieu in 216; population of 212; urban regeneration policy of 210
Mitaka City Centre Revitalisation Plan 214
Mitaka City Council 210, 213–15
Mitaka City Office 216–18
Mitaka Industrial Plaza 214–16
Mitaka Machizukuri Institute 213, 215
Miyagi Prefecture 174, 185–8, 191
Miyanishi, Yuji 22
MOC *see* Ministry of Construction
model cities 113, 117
model formation period 13–16
"Model Projects for the improvement of living environments" (Mano district) 25, 34–5, 43, 50, 68, 118
models 13–15, 78, 88, 119, 131, 145, 149, 158, 190, 206, 236; autonomous decision-making 62; experimental 79; multi-subject collaboration 233; profit-oriented 161; special administrative 18; sustainable development 76; top-down governance 236
motivation 48–9, 77–8, 198; changing people's 22; for machizukuri 77
movements 12, 14, 17, 19–20, 23, 38–41, 50–1, 53, 102, 137, 141, 165, 171, 176; "democratic movement" 14; enhanced 138; "peasant movement" 14; Saemaul Undong (New Community Movement) 14; "urban poor movement" 14
multi-stakeholders 155–6

Nabari City 122–4, 126, *127*, 129–31; community management committee 126, 128; machizukuri started by the residents from several districts spread throughout 130
Nabari City Revitalization Plan 1986 123
Nabari River embankment 123–4, 128–30
Nagahama City 64
Nagaoka City 144–6, 148
Nagata Ward 18, 22, 61–2
nagaya houses (wooden-row houses) 25, 34–5, 133, 220, 222, 224, 227
Nagaya School 222, 224–5, 227
Naiwan District Machizukuri Council for Reconstruction 187–8, 190–2

Nara Community Research Society 57
Nara Machizukuri Center 57
neighborhoods 25, 32–6, 50, 62, 77–8, 80, 82, 84, 108–9, 153, 160, 188, 192; anti-disaster bases 50; community affairs 213; day-care centers 63; environment 109; high-quality 154; maintenance 25; protest movements 14; renewed 160; revitalized 158, 160; traditional 76, 154–5
New City Center Basic Revitalization Plan 165–7
New Homeland Foundation 198, 200, 202–4, 207–8
NHF *see* New Homeland Foundation
Niigata Prefecture 144–6, 148
Noda-hokubu Machizukuri Council 61–2
non-profit organizations 16, 63–4, 82, 84, 129, 140, 174, 182, 216–17, 226
NPOs *see* non-profit organizations

offices 106, 120, 181–2, 214, 222; administrative village 197; pilot 214; public 117
operations 64, 79–80, 109, 127, 174, 176–7, 196, 201, 203–5, 208; autonomous 202; cooperative redevelopment 80; organizational 201; trial 109, 202
opposition groups and movements 33, 38–9, 185, 187
organizational 7, 22, 26, 56, 64, 84–5, 117, 120, 156, 158, 201, 204; adjustment periods 204; forms 64; structures 22, 26, 84; systems 7, 56, 117, 120
organizations 61, 63–4, 82–5, 95, 97, 122–5, 137–8, 140–1, 150, 165–7, 171–2, 181–2, 198, 204–8; affiliate 165; autonomous 15; citizen 95, 97; civic 68, 110; community 60, 73, 80, 196–7, 204–5, 207–8, 211; cooperative 80; design support 148; external 198, 200; internal 198, 207–8; local 28, 62, 66, 122; machizukuri 81, 141; non-government 198; nonprofit 117–18, 197; rebuilding of 204
owners 106, 108, 138, 148–9, 217; absentee 105; business 107, 138, 177, 179; Chinese land 156; factory 22; Japanese land 156; private 124; shop 22, 49, 80, 97, 164–6

Index 249

Panao, R.A.L. 210, 213
PAPER DOME New Homeland
  Resource Center 198, 200, 204, 207
partnerships 83–5, 88, 97, 107,
  109–10; arena-type 84; business 174;
  formal 218; informal 218; local
  governance 85; multi-sector 102;
  multi-stakeholder 60; network-type
  83–4; platform-type 84; and projects
  82, 84, 88; regional 109
PDNHRC *see* PAPER DOME New
  Homeland Resource Center
"peasant movement" 14
pedestrians 117, 127, 134, 137, 165
people 27, 29–31, 54, 91–2, 94–5,
  128–9, 138, 143–4, 174–7, 181–2,
  186–7, 195–7, 216–18, 226–8;
  disabled 48; elderly 127; local 26, 74,
  92, 217; and organizations 138, 220
physical environment 4, 13, 23, 28, 56,
  76, 78, 88, 102, 186, 193, 210, 215
Plan to Promote Development of
  Disaster-Resistant Cities 56
planning 20, 23, 91, 106, 109, 112–13,
  146, 149, 161, 166, 174–5, 203, 206,
  208; administrative 6, 236; of
  business development in Furano
  central city 168; community activity
  182; conditions 43; documents 95–6;
  and Kyojima machizukuri projects
  37; legal district 49; and Mano
  machizukuri projects 23, 24; methods
  9, 63, 91; objectives 57; processes 16,
  95, 108; top-down 155
planning organizations 138, 140
planning systems 91, 95–7;
  collaborative 97; and master plan for
  machizukuri 96; rational
  comprehensive 211; statutory 156
plans 20, 22–3, 25–6, 32–5, 42–3, 54,
  87–8, 91–2, 95–7, 116, 123–4,
  126–9, 131, 187–9; action 20, 66,
  122–3, 128, 130–1; administration's
  131; basic 123, 164; building 192;
  construction 38–9; government's 23,
  95; master 20, 95–7, 165, 233–4;
  physical 6; redevelopment 30, 123,
  128, 136; renovation project 139–40;
  strategic 214; urban 34
plazas 54, 134, 137, 140–1, 167, 169;
  public 137–8, 140; recreational 136
policies 13–15, 20, 43, 97, 108, 164,
  195, 197, 214; community 15;
  environmental 17; livable city 15;

public 5; social 43; urban planning
  18, 95
pollution 18–19, 38, 68; air 19;
  environmental 18; problems 18–19, 74
port cities 39, 174
"port city culture" 187, 191
possibility of large-scale cooperation
  linking agriculture and tourism 170
post-disaster public housing 181,
  189, 192
post-disaster reconstruction 145, 174,
  200, 202, 206, 208
post-earthquake machizukuri 176,
  186–7, 190–1, 193
private citizens 112, 116–20; *see also*
  citizens
private companies 80, 84, 212,
  214–15, 226
private partnerships 128, 130–1
programs 6, 25, 73, 97, 107, 109–10,
  161, 174, 179, 181–3, 205, 225;
  experimental 203; government
  construction support 200;
  government's work relief 201, 203;
  historic building reconstruction 109
project development 79, 108
project map of each phase
  corresponding to spiral diagram 115
project map of the revitalization plan
  for the central urban area in Nabari
  City 127
project organizations 156
project teams 106, 113, 177
projects 25–8, 33–6, 38–9, 42–3, 48–51,
  80–2, 96–7, 106–9, 116–18, 126–8,
  136–41, 167, 171–2, 188–91;
  business 169; and coalitions 158,
  160–1; cooperative 81; Genbei-gawa
  river projects and trail map 67, 68;
  individual 36, 84, 88, 112, 116–17;
  Kurokabe Machizukuri 65; land
  readjustment 29–30, 61, 164;
  machizukuri 23, 25, 40, 42–3, 48, 50,
  62–4, 66, 69, 73, 78, 80, 82, 116–19;
  nursing care service 63; and
  partnerships 82, 84, 88; of post-
  disaster reconstruction in central
  Ishinomaki 178; promotion-related
  163, 167, 169, 171; public 35–6, 50,
  64, 117, 181; realized by post-
  earthquake machizukuri 189;
  reconstruction 9, 25, 34, 61, 185,
  188–90; redevelopment 113, 136;
  renewal 155, 161; street-widening 118

250 *Index*

promotion-related projects 163, 167, 169, 171
promotion system of town planning during development and later *139*
property rights exchange 80–1, 155, 157–8
protection 9, 38, 68, 153, 158; community areas 158, 160; environmental 19, 198; historical landscapes 57, 112–13, 116, 133, 156, 159–60; of historical townscapes 40
protest movements 18, 20; anti-establishment 17; former 19; to machizukuri 18
public facilities 13, 19, 49, 53, 95, 117, 119, 188, 191, 212, 215; and design of parks 53; development of 13, 117; management of 215; reconstructing 213
public housing 25, 35, 81, 149–50, 181, 189, 192–3; low-rent 35; and regional community bases 192; for residents 35; units 25, 146
public projects 35–6, 50, 64, 117, 181
public spaces 48, 80–1, 106, 108, 116, 129, 137, 140–1, 153, 176
public squares 31, 133
public transportation 106
Puli 195–6, 198, 205, 207

questionnaire surveys 224–5

real estate 64, 106, 119–20, 177, 182
rebuilding 38, 81, 102, 109, 128, 131, 145, 148–50, 204; cooperative 179; houses 145; living environment by 81; plan for 38; process of 102–3, 145
reconstruction 15–16, 25, 61–2, 107–9, 149, 164, 174–7, 179, 181, 187–90, 192–3, 200, 202, 206–8; activated 200; of buildings and urban structure development 190; closed-community 207; integrated 61; machizukuri 61–2; processes 9, 29, 62, 176–7, 206; projects 9, 25, 34, 42, 61, 185, 188–90; of Taomi Community 204, 206–8
reconstructions, joint 48, 155
redevelopment 36, 113, 129, 136, 141, 158, 164, 169, 171, 186, 192, 220; of landscape 158; large-scale land 185; plans 30, 123, 128, 136; processes 79; projects 38, 49; of

public spaces 141; small-scale 80; urban 29–30, 153, 235
redevelopment projects 113, 136; cooperative 62, 80–1; developing cooperative 49; government-funded 136; post-earthquake 187; small-scale cooperative 35
regeneration 9, 41, 68–9, 101–2, 105, 119, 130, 176, 185, 193, 216–17; Mitaka city 210; project promotion council 136; projects 107, 217; SOHO City Mitaka 217–18
regional community bases 192–3
regional management 113, 118–20, 122, 163, 171
regional partnerships 109
regional style housing 145–6, 149–50
regions 3, 12–13, 15–16, 30, 105, 110, 113, 119, 143–6, 182, 185, 195, 220, 227–33
regulations 16, 28, 38–9, 134, 158, 160–1; establishing new 39; existing 160; superior 155; technical 161; for urban renewal of old residential districts 160
religion 91–2
religious organizations 38
renovation projects 118, 138–40
research 20–1, 32, 34, 66, 76–7, 156, 160, 179, 212, 214; and implementation of urban renewal 156; institutes 31; and pilot projects 160; units 204–5
residential buildings 95, 97, 126, 129–30, 149, 153
residential districts 19, 38, 49, 84, 102–3, 106–7, 123, 128, 160–1, 212; high-density 153, 158, 160; old 160; poorly prepared 41; traditional 156
residential land 175, 190, 193
residents 124, 131, 221–2; community 54, 56, 196, 198, 201, 204; district 123–4; foreign 220, 222; and landowners 36, 77, 80–1, 141; local 18–20, 23, 25–7, 29–36, 48–9, 53, 76, 122–4, 181, 187–9, 192, 213–14, 222, 226–9; low-income 81; unemployed 201; voluntary 227
resistance movements 18–19, 39–40; *see also* opposition movements
resources 5, 10, 39, 50, 102, 131, 133, 144, 206, 208, 217–18, 229–30; cultural 102; external 201; financial 92, 131, 155, 212–14, 218; historic

102, 119, 126, 141, 185–6; and people 217; regional 169
restaurants 124, 130, 133–4, 150, 167, 171, 176, 201, 204–5, 226
revitalization 5, 57, 62–4, 113, 122, 131, 164, 167, 171; central city 164; planning 128–9, 131, 164, 167; projects 66
river maintenance 68–9; *see also* rivers
rivers 34, 68–9, 103, 116, 125, 129–31, 175, 197, 226
roads 6, 25, 35–6, 39, 62, 95, 102, 108, 124, 127, 130, 189, 192, 196; administrative 124; coastal 186; community 62, 79, 124; construction of 190; embankment 122, 124; farm 34; structure of 74; undeveloped neighborhood 21
row-houses 220–1

Saemaul Undong (New Community Movement) 14
Sanno (shopping street) 118–19
Sanriku Coast 174, 182
Satoh, S. 10, 43, 78, 80–1, 88, 112–13, 116–17, 158, 212
schools 84, 126, 200, 222, 224
SDGs *see* Sustainable Development Goals
Sea of Japan 103
seawalls 175, 185–91, 193; concrete 124; construction plans 187; and land use plans 187–8; new 187; and tourist facilities 187
Seki, S. 214–16
self-governance mechanisms 53
Setagaya Machizukuri Center 58
Setagaya Machizukuri Ordinance 33
Setagaya Ward 15, 31–3, 38–9, 42, 53–4, 58
sewerage systems 213
Shanghai City 154, 156, 158, 160
Shanghai Historical Landscape Protection Planning 2002 156
Shinmachi District 122–4, 131
shopkeepers 22, 49, 80, 97, 164–6, 179, 181
shopping areas 49, 176, 179; central 176; old 80
shopping districts 105, 131, 137, 164, 169; downtown 126; historical 64; local 136; organizations 167
shopping streets 58, 74, 118, 120, 186, 188, 192

shops 35, 58, 64, 81, 107, 133–4, 164, 177, 183, 226; damaged 177, 179; retail specialty 105; and showrooms 107, 110; vacant 93, 127–8, 130, 134
Silicon Valley 213–14
sites 38, 48–9, 107–9, 133, 138, 164, 166–7; creation of 109; demolition 177; demonstration internet portal 216; evacuation 49; old factory 222; temporary evacuation 62
situation and development method of block area before and after project *135*
small cities 96, 122
Small Office Home Office *see* SOHO
snow 145–6
social businesses 82, 179, 231
social enterprises 63, 82, 216, 229
social environment 9, 31, 215, 229
social welfare councils 84
Socialist Party of Japan 14
SOHO 210, 212–15, 217; companies and NPOs 217; facilities 215; Mitaka City project 210, 213–17; policies 216; projects 214–15; strategies 214
Sorensen, A. 211
South Korea 12–16
specialized subcommittees 127–8, 213
spiral diagram showing the process of machizukuri in Tsuruoka City *114*
stakeholders 4, 54, 60–1, 73, 77, 83–4, 88, 112, 120, 155–6, 171, 229; and communities 59; development 155; local 59; machizukuri 231
storehouses 129–30, 133–4
strategies 35–6, 41–2, 69, 81, 83, 86–7, 179, 181, 198, 200, 202, 204, 208, 215; community-based 214; design 158; of development and protection 153; flexible area management 87; global 60; and methodologies 153; regional area management 234
streets, and alleys 78
students 41, 61, 106, 205, 221–2, 224–8; foreign 220, 222, 225, 228; local high school 182; university 17, 222, 227
subcommittees, specialized 127–8, 213
Sumida Ward, Tokyo 34, 49–50, 57
sustainability 107, 150, 154–5, 176, 230; of community heritage 154; development environment 177; operation 109; updating system 221
Sustainable Development Goals 229, 231

252 *Index*

systems 6–7, 14–16, 18, 20, 29, 34, 36, 43, 63, 83–4, 138, 144–5, 160–1, 232–3; administrative 18; area-management 62; commercial 136; democratic 43; financial 122; institutional 22; recycling 144; social 9, 63

Taipei City 14
Taishido district 33, 39, 53, 56, 58
Taishido machizukuri projects 55
Taisho Period 103
Taiwan 12–16, 151, 195–7, 205–6; Chi-Chi earthquake in 16, 151; cities and townships in 205; community empowerment 195; community empowerment in 195, 197; development of community building in 206; and South Korea 13–14, 16
Takaoka City 82, 101–4, *105*, 106–7, 109; history of 102; initiatives in 109; and local industry 106; new public image of 107; policy for disaster prevention 108
Takaoka City Board 103
Takaoka Old Town 102–3, 105
Takaoka Town Development Partnership and Initiative 109
Takefu City 133, 136, 138, 140; Horai-chou Area Regeneration Project Promotion Council 138–40
Taomi Ecovillage 195–8, 203, 206, 208; community 198, 201–7; post-disaster recovery promotion stages *199*; promotion of 196, 198, 203; reconstruction of 207
Tarumi, E. 21–2, 28
television stations 51
temples 102–3
textile industry 105
three periods, social change, and legal systems changes *13*
timber housing 148
TMO *see* Town Management Organization
Tokyo 29–32, 34, 38–40, 42, 49, 53, 57–8, 94, 149, 212, 220, 222, 225, 231; beltway 32; citizens 31; earthquakes in 34; urban space projects in central areas of 231; wards 31
Tokyo Bay 221, 225–7
Tokyo Metropolitan Government 30–2, 34, 36, 50, 56, 212

Toshi-Jutaku (magazine about urban housing) 5–6
tourism 9, 41, 58, 64, 130, 169, 171, 182, 188, 201; facilities 181, 186, 190–1; initiatives 171; and operations of homestays 201
tourists 108, 167, 171, 191, 220, 222
town development 10, 12, 129, 140
Town Management Organization 63, 84, 164, 215
town planning 143, 163
townhouses 25, 34–5, 103, 122, 124, 129, 133
towns 3–4, 15, 40–1, 76–9, 102, 106–7, 175–7, 179, 182, 185–6, 191–3, 220–1, 224, 226–8; disaster-stricken 181; fishing 186; gourmet 176; regenerated 193
townscapes 40–1, 57, 220, 226–7
townships 196, 205, 207
Tsukishima 220–2, 224–7
Tsukishima and Nagaya School *221*, 222, 226–7
tsunamis 186
Tsuruoka City 93–4, 96–7, 112–13, 116–17, 119–20, 234
Tsuruoka Machizukuri Center 119–20

Umezu, M. 53, 56
UNCED *see* United Nations Conference on Environment and Development
United Nations Conference on Environment and Development 66
units 15, 21, 160, 214; administrative 15; healthy elderly 160; housing estate 154; newly-married 160; residential 153, 192
universities 93, 107, 187, 205, 212–13, 220, 222, 224–6, 228
university students 17, 222, 227
unused land 191–2
urban areas 29–30, 34, 77, 80, 101, 106, 119, 123, 136, 140, 172, 174, 181, 183; dense 32; historic 105, 133, 138; old 156, 160; populated 80
urban design 96, 113, 211, 227; new 113; policy 96; projects 112; small-scale 211; teams 191; of Tsukishima 227
urban development 28, 43, 106, 116, 230, 235
urban planning 17–18, 38, 102, 105, 112–13, 117, 120, 122, 154–5, 165, 175, 211, 235; and building

Index   253

regulations 38; committees 95;
existing 112, 116; government-led 4;
and *machizukuri* 112, 117, 120;
partnerships 109; policies 18, 95;
regulations 38; traditional 7
Urban Planning Laboratory 122, 124,
129, 131
"urban poor movement" 14
Urban Redevelopment Project 155,
164, 167
urban regeneration 36, 210, 212, 216
urban renewal 101, 154–8, 160–1, 176,
235; based on community principle
155; based on historical landscape
protection 156; of Chinese cities 161;
discipline 153; methodology 155;
principles 160
Urban Renewal Act 155
urban spaces 35, 120, 134, 154–5, 228,
235; designing local 7; fragmented
153; modern 4; standardized 154;
traditional 156

vacant houses 108–9, 143, 146
values 29, 49, 57, 74, 76–7, 85–6, 91,
102, 107, 206, 208, 224, 228–31,
233–4; aesthetic 233; collective 40;
cultural 232; ecological 231;
historical 101; polarized 92; regional
231; social 220
village chiefs 198, 200
villages 7, 102, 197–8, 200, 221
visitor operations center 201–2
visitors 58, 93, 128, 150, 202,
220–1, 224

volunteers 57, 61, 80, 109, 167,
176–7, 179

warehouses 39, 107, 133, 136, 225–6
Watanabe, S. 3, 9, 69, 179
water 68, 234; catchment areas 234;
flows of river 234
waterfront area 191–2, 226
welfare 26, 28, 63, 69, 127; centers 28;
councils 84; municipality 214;
services 63, 81
wooden houses 29, 51, 81, 134, 138
"Working Group for Public Facilities
and Tourism" 188
workshops 49–50, 53, 56, 58, 77–9,
93, 96–7, 106, 108, 110, 117, 123–4,
129–31, 179; council design 62;
design 191; multiple 94; and research
179; self-organized 56; series of 58,
108; and stakeholders 77; and
studios 106; and surveys 93;
traditional craft 107
World War II 6, 12, 14, 32, 34, 40,
102–3, 105, 213, 220

Yamagata Prefecture 93, 96, 112
Yamakoshi area 144–6, 148–50
Yamamoto, T. 36, 50
Yoshisaka, T. 32, 83, 86
Yuyuan District 158, 160

zones 32, 35, 106; core development
106; strategic action 36
zukuri (concept) 3–4